TITO'S MAVERICK MEDIA

Dr. Tito prescribes for his patient (the ''Party''): ''With the shape you're in, you have to become more active — start moving around!''

Jez (Belgrade), May 26, 1967.

Tito's Maverick Media

The Politics of Mass Communications in Yugoslavia

GERTRUDE JOCH ROBINSON

UNIVERSITY OF ILLINOIS PRESS

Urbana Chicago London

Library of Congress Cataloging in Publication Data

Robinson, Gertrude Joch.
  Tito's maverick media.

  Bibliography: p.
  Includes index.
  1. Mass media—Yugoslavia. 2. Yugoslavia—Politics
and government—1945-   I. Title.
P92.Y8R6   301.16′1′09497   76-30606
ISBN 0-252-00597-X

To my parents

Sarah Blaisdell and Frederick W. Joch

Contents

A Note on the Spelling and Pronunciation of Serbo-Croat Words

s	s as in single
š	sh as in shell
c	ts as in hats
č	ch as in change
ć	similar to but lighter than č — as ch in march
ž	g as in mirage
z	z as in zoo
j	y as in yes
nj	ny as in canyon
g	g as in get
dž	j as in jump
dj	similar to but lighter than dž
lj	li as in billion

Acknowledgments

Material for this book was collected over more than a decade. This makes the list of those who helped with the project both lengthy and nearly impossible to recall. There are, however, certain institutions and individuals without whom the study would not have been begun or been completed. Among these are the Institut za Novinarstvo (Institute of Journalism) in Belgrade and its then director Milan Popović. This institute served as my temporary home during my initial research visit of a year to Yugoslavia in 1964. I am indebted to its personnel, among them Stevan Marjanović, for providing the important introductions to the national news agency and other media enterprises. The introductions launched me as an observer of the Yugoslav communication scene.

In addition Tanjug correspondents and editors, radio-television personnel, journalists, scholars, writers, and friends too numerous to mention and scattered throughout the country's six republics gave unstintingly of their time and expertise. They helped explain Yugoslavia's historical background, its diversified culture, and its novel political and social setup. Without their sympathetic cooperation and support no foreigner could have entered into Yugoslav life as fully as I did. In this context, special thanks must go to Jelica Ivković, linguist and translator, who taught me the fundamentals of the Serbo-Croatian language and accompanied me on my initial interviews and travels.

Working on a study of this magnitude is a costly business both in time and money. I would, therefore, like to acknowledge my indebtedness to the Institute of International Education which supervised the Yugoslav government award for doctoral research. It brought me and my three young sons to the country of the South Slavs. In addition, I would like to thank the McGill Social Science Research Fund, which contributed financial support, and the Department of Sociology, which provided a partial reduction of teaching load to support the completion of this book.

In the preparation and multiple revisions of the manuscript the critical comments of various readers proved challenging to my reasoning and mode of expression. Three mentors and colleagues, all of whom read the entire version of this study, require special thanks for the gift of their time, their special knowledge in media and Yugoslav studies, and their unflagging encouragement. They are Dean Theodore Peterson of the College of Communications, University of Illinois (Urbana); Dr. Alexander Vucinich of the Department of History, University of Texas; and Dr. Vito Ahtik of the Department of Sociology at the Université du Quebec, Montreal.

McGill sociology colleagues, Dr. Richard Hamilton, Dr. Maurice Pinard, Dr. David Solomon, and Dr. William Westley, made valuable suggestions on the handling of problems of politics, ethnicity, professionalization, and management theory. Throughout the years two intelligent women, Mrs. M. Herskovici and Mrs. W. Keogh, spent many hours transposing innumerable handwritten drafts into the finished manuscript. Another woman, Harriet Cooper, now a graduate student of anthropology, expertly checked and edited the bibliographical material. Whatever errors of fact or interpretation remain in the text are solely my own responsibility.

Final and grateful appreciation is due those individuals who loaned human encouragement during the long and lonely struggle required to write a book. Three of these supporters occupy a special place in my life. Dr. Petar Kokotović of the University of Illinois (Urbana) encouraged me in my professional ambitions and gave unstintingly of his time and energy in interpreting the often incomprehensible Yugoslav scene. His counsel was also crucial on those occasions when it seemed the project would never come to fruition. Dr. Eleanor Blum also of the University of Illinois helped me through her continued friendship and expertise in locating reference materials and new publications, without which this study would have been greatly weakened. Last, but by no means least, my son Beren W. Robinson's contributions require mention. He was my travel companion on various repeat visits to Yugoslavia in the 1970s and served as goodwill ambassador to his scholar-mother on both official and unofficial occasions.

TITO'S MAVERICK MEDIA

SOCIALIST FEDERAL
REPUBLIC OF YUGOSLAVIA

- - - Republic   ····· Autonomous
      boundary   region
  ⊛ Federal capital   ⊙ Republican capital

CHAPTER 1

Introduction

Goals and Perspectives

For well over a quarter of a century socialist Yugoslavia has attracted world attention and earned a reputation for maverick solutions to political and social issues. Soon after 1948 Yugoslavia asserted its independence from Stalin's interpretation of communism and it was leader once more in the early 1950s when it propounded the economic heresy of "different roads to socialism." The country's nonconformist behavior generated many studies of its unique Marxist ideology, its political and economic decentralization, and its factory organization based on worker participation.[1] Very little, in contrast, is known about Yugoslavia's equally startling innovations in media organization and programming. Only a handful of scholars have investigated how the press, radio, and television operate in this multinational country. Little is known about who finances and runs the media, and even less about the perspectives which help Yugoslavs understand themselves and their surrounding world.

This study is designed to remedy this paucity by portraying the Yugoslav mass media in their sociopolitical setting. It has three fundamental purposes. First, it provides a coherent description and analysis of the organization and functioning of the press, radio, and television in contemporary Yugoslavia. Second, it identifies the power interrelationships between the major groups involved in the mass communication process. Third, it investigates the way in which the mass media structure and interpret social reality for the Yugoslav citizen.

For many years mass communication research has been characterized by a multiplicity of models and conceptions which have made systematic theorizing difficult. Studies of interpersonal communication with psychological perspectives have had little relation to studies of mass communication utilizing an economic or political focus. Investigations of the eastern European mass media have, in addition, suffered from the influence of "totalitarian" theory, which viewed them primarily as political instruments. Such an outlook overstressed the organizational intermingling between the party and information hierarchies as well as the propagandistic and social control functions of the Leninist press. It also tended to downgrade the importance of geographic, social, and historical differences in explaining media structure and content. Irrespective of what ideology a politician subscribes to, if people cannot read what he says because they are illiterate, or hear what he says because there are no radio sets, communication between ruler and ruled is likely to suffer.

This study takes a broader approach. It views human communication as a form of exchange through symbolic interaction which takes place in a particular setting.[2] Such a theory posits that there is a dialectical interdependence between human beings and their natural and social environments. This interdependence is unique because the human organism selectively perceives and responds. As one writer notes: "Human action is at the same time a creative response to a subjectively meaningful environment as it is constrained by the objective nature of natural and social phenomena."[3]

In human communication individuals and groups do not respond merely to the "raw event data" of existence. They are instead guided by digested information about their world. Interactions between humans are thus "symbolic" in the sense that participants respond to the behavior of others not for some inherent quality in them, but for the significance they impute to this behavior. Actions become meaningful if they arouse the same response in others. These common meanings in turn constitute the basis for social organization. Stable social positions, roles, moral codes, customs, and laws distinguish the communication behavior of one group of people from that of another.

Three characteristics, Thayer points out, define the uniqueness of human communication, which is based on self-reflexivity, or the ability to talk to oneself.[4] Communication is, in its most general sense, taking account of something to some end. In addition, contrary to animals which are preformed to take into account only what they must, man learns through social interaction what to pay attention to. Finally, man in his interactions with his environment evolves and is continuously altered. Whatever someone says to him will affect the way in which he perceives his "reality." All of these characteristics must be included in developing a general theory of communication. They also affect the way in which such concepts as the "human environment," "social institutions," and "society" itself are defined.

A symbolic and dialectical theory of communication has a number of advantages. Contrary to other theories it encompasses and explains both interpersonal and mass communication processes as symbolic exchanges occurring in different settings with different kinds of actors. This draws attention to the fact that a communicative act or event cannot be understood without relating message form to context of use. Symbolic interactionism is unique in stressing that the actor's interpretation is one of the most significant components in explaining how the context of "who says what, to whom, when and with what effect" adds meaning.

A symbolic theory also provides a scheme for understanding the mass media as both institutional and symbolic realities, which has long confounded analysts. It does this by interrelating the subjective meanings which actors attach to their environment with the objective or social meanings which emerge from interactions in common situations.[5] Newspapers and radio stations as social institutions develop persistence, because the people who work there share similar interpretations about common goals and functions. Consequently the media content produced is influenced by what journalists perceive to be commonly accepted ways of viewing reality. Expressing, transmitting, and maintaining these constructions is then a major social function of a country's mass communication system.

In addition, such a theory encourages a view of communication channels as a network for social communication, rather than as neutral hardware. The kinds of "pictures of the world" and valuations which this network transmits will depend among other things on who owns and controls the channels. Consequently there is a marked difference in communication content between countries where the channels are privately or publicly owned. The fact that a professional group selects and evaluates mass media messages and thus creates the most persuasive "constructed reality" stresses the need to better understand journalists as professionals. We also need to know what kinds of selection and valuation take place and how these differ from country to country.

Symbolic interactionism also breaks down the monolithic concept of the audience. It points out instead that audiences are composed of a multitude of social groups, each with their own characteristic symbolic universes. The varying uses these differentiated audiences make of media programs is not merely a result of psychological differences, but of the subjective meanings particular groups attach to them. Audience studies thus become group studies in styles of leisure behavior and taste. Cultural selectivity which provides the foundation for individual membership in different audiences is best studied according to Chaney by investigating accessibility, conception, involvement, and reward.[6]

All communication behavior, the symbolic theory stresses, occurs in a historical setting. Predictions and interpretations about how groups of people will act depend not only on their world of objects, their set of meanings, but also on their existing schemes of interaction and interpretation. These can and do change since they are situationally determined. A historical perspective is therefore mandatory. Change occurs because groups are only incompletely integrated at different levels of society, because each human has multiple selves or roles in different social contexts, and because vested interests help maintain "undeserved" rewards for those in privileged positions. This may be the case for certain professional communicators by virtue of running the media or by virtue of being party members.

Why Yugoslavia?

This study was undertaken because Yugoslavia's unique mass media system has never been extensively and systematically studied by an outsider. While the fact that it is relatively unknown may be sufficient justification in itself, there are additional considerations which add increased relevance to such a study. A number of unique characteristics make Yugoslavia a particularly good example for the illumination of broader empirical and normative communication questions noted earlier. First of all, it provides an excellent example of how historical precedents color even the most determined attempts at conceptualizing and organizing a new kind of communication system. In spite of a political break between the monarchical and communist systems of government, the Tito government was left with legacies which affected the organization of information media long after 1945. Primary among these was a dearth of newspapers and radio sets in comparison to the rest of western Europe, an underdeveloped sense of professionalism among journalists, and a history of media dependence on government.

Another unique feature is the fact that Yugoslavia's media development is compressed into a short thirty years, during which the impact of sociopolitical change on newspapers, radio, and television growth and distribution can be easily traced. Throughout this interval, the country abandoned a centrally planned for a mixed market economy, developed its own brand of Marxism, revamped the functions of the communist party, instituted worker participation in media management, and decentralized its government.

Yugoslavia also constitutes an ideal setting for clarifying the interrelationships between media development and three additional factors. Among these are: levels of economic development, changes in ideology, and multi-ethnicity. National statistics show that in the 1970s, after thirty years of industrialization, Yugoslavia had achieved a per capita gross national product of $850 a year, which means that it has passed the Rostovian takeoff point from under development to middle development. These general figures, which are one-eighth of the American average, obscure large internal variations between the six republics. The northwestern parts of the country are similar to the economic levels of Italy and Austria, while the southeastern parts are on a par with under-developed Thailand. These imbalances make it possible to compare and contrast media growth in the different republics. Finally, the country's change from a Stalinist to a novel conception of Marxism after the 1948 Cominform expulsion provides an opportunity to check the adequacy of the hypothesis which claims that media growth is primarily determined by ideology.

For those unfamiliar with Yugoslavia, a humorous saying typifies this diversified country. The stranger visiting Belgrade, Zagreb, and Ljubljana is told that the Federated Socialist Republic consists of six republics, five nationalities, four languages, three religions, two scripts, but only one president, Josip Broz, called "Tito." Closer acquaintance corroborates that the "Land of the South Slavs" is indeed a complex and potentially divided nation. In 1971 it had a population of 20.5 million distributed over an area roughly the size of Wyoming.[7] This makes it eighth in population among European countries and second in eastern Europe.

Geographically straddling the Danube basin, which has been a major link between Europe and the Orient for centuries, parts of the country were under Turkish hegemony for 500 years. It was Serbia, Macedonia, and Montenegro which missed the social and cultural influences of the Middle Ages and the Renaissance, and became the cradle for national unification at the end of the nineteenth century. Yugoslavia was born twice: first in 1918 when parts of the Austro-Hungarian empire, Slovenia, Dalmatia, and Bosnia-Hercegovina, were added to the kingdom of Serbia, encompassing Montenegro and Macedonia, to constitute a new nation; then again in 1945 when Tito's resistance forces set up a Socialist People's Republic after the Soviet model.

The country is divided into six republics which roughly coincide with the ethnic divisions of its population. These are, in order of size: Serbia, Croatia, Bosnia-Hercegovina, Macedonia, Slovenia, and Montenegro. The republic of Serbia, in addition, includes the autonomous provinces of Vojvodina and Kosovo, the latter peopled by Albanians. Three of these six republics, Bosnia-Hercegovina, Montenegro, and Macedonia, are mountainous, which affects both their level of industrialization and the distribution of mass communications.

Five ethnic groups reinforce the country's cultural diversity and together account for 82 percent of the total population. Among these the Serbs are the largest with 42 percent, followed by the Croats (23.1 percent), Slovenes (8.5 percent), Macedonians (5.6 percent), and Montenegrins (2.6 percent).[8] Of the remaining 18 percent of the population, nearly 1 million are listed as "Moslems by ethnic affiliation." Most of these live in Bosnia-Hercegovina while the non-Slav minorities, approximately 11 percent of the total, are spread throughout the country. Among these are the Albanian Shiptars, Hungarians, Turks, Rumanians, and Italians. Next to the Soviet Union, Yugoslavia has the largest population of national minorities relative to total population in Europe.

In addition to being multinational, Yugoslavia is multilingual. It has four official languages. These are first of all Serbian and Croatian, which though separate[9] are relatively similar and are spoken by the majority of the population. "Serbo-Croatian" is, however, written in two different alphabets, Cyrillic being used in Serbia, Montenegro, Macedonia, and parts of Bosnia, and Latin in the rest of the country. Two other languages are Macedonian and Slovenian.

along with at least sixteen others used in Yugoslavia today. The major effect of this disparity is a regional system of communications which serves each republic in its predominant tongue, and for the press and publishing, a further fragmentation of an already small reading audience.

Three religions further diversify the population. Almost half of the people belong to the Serbian Orthodox church (including Serbs, Macedonians, and Montenegrins), 30 percent are Roman Catholics (Croats and Slovenes), and the rest are Moslems. This kaleidoscopic multiplicity of heritages, cultures, peoples, tongues, and temperaments is being molded into one federated society under the leadership of the League of Communists and utilizing a decentralized system of mass communication.

Table 1 summarizes the social characteristics of these republics for easy reference, and adds migration and urbanization trends to round out this brief introductory sketch of Yugoslavia's media setting. The level of urbanization will doubtlessly influence not only the structure of the mass communication network, but also the relative availability of information and entertainment for the Yugoslav audience.[10]

Despite rapid industrialization since World War II, and a drop in those depending on agriculture for their livelihood (less than 50 percent of the total population), Yugoslavia is still one of the least urbanized countries in Europe. At the time of the 1961 census, 28 percent of the total population lived in urban communities, with this figure rising to not more than about 34 percent ten years later. A majority of this urban population, in contrast to other countries, is concentrated in small towns of between 10,000 to 20,000, with the remainder of the nonagrarian Yugoslavs working in such towns but not living there.

Urban growth rates indicate that immigration rather than natural increase plays the most important role in accounting for the expansion of the urban sector. Today Yugoslavia has nine cities with over 100,000 inhabitants, seven of which are republican and provincial capitals, to which are added Split and Niš, which grew as a result of tourism and industry. All of these cities are well served by all three media, whereas the hinterland with its many villages often receives few newspapers and little television.

The major direction of Yugoslav migratory movement is from the mountains of the south and west to the plains and valleys of the north and east, except for central Bosnia where massive industrialization has attracted people into an otherwise under-developed region. More specific directions of movement are to a large degree determined and limited by ethnicity, with middle-developed Serbia the primary attraction for Serbs scattered all over the country and highly developed Slovenia protected by its distinctive language and culture. Dr. Ivanka Ginić, a Belgrade demographer, concludes that Yugoslavia's unique pattern of urbanization, which is based on a stratum of small towns dominated by a few large cities, can be explained by two factors: "First . . . changes in the economic structure of the population which also took place in the village, where

Table 1
Social Characteristics of Yugoslavia's Six Republics and Two Autonomous Provinces
(in thousands)

	SFRY Total	Serbia Proper	Serbia Vojvodina	Serbia Kosovo	Croatia	Slovenia	Bosnia-Hercegovina	Macedonia	Montenegro
Area (sq. km.)	255,804	55,968	21,506	10,887	56,536	20,251	51,129	25,713	13,812
Republican and prov. capitals		Belgrade	Novi Sad	Priština	Zagreb	Ljubljana	Sarajevo	Skopje	Titograd
Population (1971)	20,553	5,280	1,953	1,244	4,426	1,727	3,746	1,646	530
Level of econ. development	middle dev.	middle dev.	middle dev.	under dev.	middle dev.	dev.	under dev.	middle dev.	middle dev.
Per capita income ($) (family of 4, 1970)	2.2	2.2			2.2	3.9	1.2	2.0	1.3
Language		Serbian	Serbian	Albanian	Croatian	Slovenian	Serbo-Croatian	Macedonian	Serbian
Script		Cyrillic	Cyrillic	Latin	Latin	Latin	Latin	Cyrillic	Cyrillic
Religion		Orthodox	Orthodox		Catholic	Catholic	mixed and Moslem	Orthodox	Orthodox
Illiteracy (10 years and over, 1971)	15.2%	17.7%	9.4%	32.2%	8.9%	2.5%	22.7%	18.0%	17.2%
Persons temp. employed abroad (1971)	672	115	61	24	225	48	137	54	8
Migration trends	migration out	migration in	migration out	migration in	no migration	migration in	migration out	migration out	migration out

SOURCE: Lines 1;3;9;10: *Statistical Yearbook of Yugoslavia, 1972*, pp. 21, 22, 26-27, 30-37. Lines 2;4; 11: *Yugoslav Review*, May-Dec., 1971.

new employment possibilities are created. Second . . . decentralized urbanization, i.e., the urbanization of suburban and village settlements.''[11]

Background of the Study

The material for this study was gathered over a ten-year period, during which
the author spent varying amounts of time in different parts of Yugoslavia. It
began in 1964 with a government grant for doctoral research which took me to
Yugoslavia for a year. At this time the primary task was to study the national
news agency, Tanjug,[12] and to interview journalists and politicians who were
or had been active in the country's media development. Five subsequent
summer visits, each of about three months' duration, provided an additional
opportunity to observe and record the country's rapid economic growth and
continuing media expansion. Between 1968 and 1973, travels to all six republics brought contacts with the major social and media research institutes,
university training centers, and opportunities for participation in UNESCO and
locally sponsored congresses.[13] Papers and conversations at these meetings
clarified the role of local stations, satellite communication, and the problems of
network expansion.

Even a decade is not enough, however, to explore and comprehend all
aspects of a country's mass communication system. A single investigator is
furthermore handicapped by limited resources and a lack of expertise in all
potentially relevant subareas. It was therefore decided from the beginning to
focus on only a small number of macro variables which have been shown to be
most influential in determining media structure and functioning. These are level
of economic development and the country's political culture, ideology, and
ethnicity.

Level of economic development determines very roughly when, where, and
how the press, radio, and television are innovated and the rate at which they are
diffused. In Yugoslavia's political culture, the system of one-party rule, press
and broadcast laws, and workers' self-management affect the way in which the
media are organized, the degree of party control, and the system of media
governance. Ethnicity influences the country's network organization, the language and content of programming, and the way in which journalists are
trained. Since the author is not a specialist in history, law, literature, or
economics such material is introduced only where it is directly relevant.

The time period studied in this book encompasses the thirty years between
1945 and 1975 when Yugoslavia was reborn as a Marxist state. During this time
its media system grew spectacularly and Titoist media philosophy emerged as a
separate doctrine. Within this period three major crises substantially changed
the country's sociopolitical setting, requiring adaptation by the communication
system. Yugoslavia's 1948 Cominform expulsion, its economic rethinking in
the early 1960s, and the 1971 Croatian secession crisis thus provide natural

breaking points indicating shifts in media organization, legal codes, and filtering practices within the country's four information periods.

Previous research indicates that processes of communication may be viewed from a variety of vantage points: the intra- and interpersonal, the organizational, and the sociotechnological.[14] This study ignores the first two levels of analysis pursued by social psychologists and focuses instead on the organizational and social dimensions. Its units of analysis therefore are institutions and groups of people who are intercommunicating with each other.

The institutions sampled include the national news agency, Tanjug (Telegrafska Agencija Nova Jugoslavija), the bureaus of its international suppliers in Belgrade, such as Associated Press, Reuters, Agence France Press, Tass, and its competitor, the feature agency Pres Servis. There were also meetings with personnel from the Yugoslav Radio Television Association (Jugoslovenski Radio Televizija), members of the country's major media research institutes, and the directors of the journalism schools.

In Belgrade the Yugoslav Institute of Journalism (Jugoslovenski Institut za Novinarstvo), the Institute for Social Research (Institut za Društvene Nauke), and the Yugoslav Radio Television Association provided opinion polls, federal statistics on programming, and plans for the future. Zagreb's Institute for Social Research/and RTV Research Department (Radio-Televizija Zagreb), as well as Ljubljana's Center for Public Opinion Polls and Mass Communication (Center za raziskovanaja javnega mnenja in množičnih komunikacij pri FSPN) contributed cross-sectional data on media utilization among Yugoslavia's diversified publics. At the same time contacts with the faculties of journalism in Ljubljana, Zagreb, and Belgrade added insights into the country's training programs and professional needs.

Senders, communicators, and the audience, which constitute the three major groups engaged in the social communication process, were also sampled. The ministers of information for Yugoslavia and the Socialist Republic of Croatia and members of the Ideological Commission of the Central Committee illuminated the position of senders, the relationship between party and media personnel, and the system of media regulation in Yugoslavia. The social and professional portrait of the communicator emerged from interviews with the president of the Yugoslav Federation of Journalists and from a systematic survey of its membership. The interrelationship between regional media and the national news agency was gleaned from meetings with the directors of the six republican broadcasting studios and from talks with press personnel. Among these were editors from *Politika, Borba, Vjesnik,* and various news and humor magazines.

Literary and philosophical journal editors and publishers of books, plus filmmakers, rounded out the picture of Yugoslavia's unique communication system and the interrelationship between the various media. Data on the audience, finally, was gleaned from the research institutes in the three large republics mentioned above, and from Radio-Televizija Sarajevo and Skopje, as well as interviews with top Yugoslav Radio Television (JRT) personnel. The latter elaborated on Eurovision links and color television innovation. Throughout these travels and contacts I was greatly aided by a knowledge of Serbo-Croatian which made conversations easy and large amounts of printed material readily accessible. It also proved invaluable in analyzing Tanjug output data and preparing the press and broadcast content analyses which add flavor to the discussion.

Book Outline

Before presenting the general layout of the material to be covered, the terminology used in this book will be clarified. Many contemporary researchers use the terms "mass communications" and "mass media" synonymously, following the customs of general discourse. For our purposes it is, however, important to be able to distinguish between the institutions which are socially designated to produce and transmit messages, and a process of interaction between sender and receiver in modern society. The term "mass media" will, therefore, refer to broadcast stations, newspapers, magazines, and film studios,[15] while "mass communications" embraces that which is transmitted, that which transmits, as well as those who receive.[16]

"Communication," it should be clear from the theoretical discussion, is not used in the restricted sense attached to the term by information theorists. It is instead a generic concept referring to an interaction through messages which may convey emotional as well as other types of meanings. By using the term in this way, prejudging of whether a person's actions are rational or not in a particular circumstance is avoided. "Content," finally, refers to the symbolic representations of events produced by the mass media. These may be newscasts, articles, dramas, musical performances, stories, educational programs, and so forth, produced by radio, television, film, or the print media.

The book is divided into two major sections. The first views radio and television stations, newspaper and journal offices, as well as film studios as social institutions with persistence over time, organizational structure, and identifiable personnel. These mass media function in a unique historical setting which has undergone great changes in the thirty-year time span surveyed. Their personnel must furthermore create information and entertainment for a multinational country. The second half of the book deals with the "meaning," or the symbolic dimension, of various mass communication processes. It explores the way in which the mass media select dominant perspectives, order these, and attach value to them. An understanding of these processes clarifies both the nation's news values as well as what its audience will pay attention to and find important and good.

Unfortunately these two approaches cannot be kept strictly separated because they stand in a dialectical interrelationship with each other at all points. As a consequence the analysis will first highlight one and then the other perspective. Chapters 2 and 3 provide a historical overview of the changing social conditions which have determined the structure and functioning of the Yugoslav mass media in the past thirty years. The former traces technological, ideological, economic, and demographic changes and their effect on media growth and diffusion. The latter assesses how the legal and political environments, as well as organizational structure, mold the functioning and content of broadcasting and print in contemporary Yugoslavia.

Where the first two chapters take a long-term historical perspective, Chapter 4 focuses on the structure and functioning of one particular medium, the national news agency Tanjug. A case study of workers' self-management in action clarifies the boundaries of journalistic freedom in Yugoslavia, as well as the degree of media autonomy from government agencies and the League of Communists. It appears that the government's control over information collection and distribution is minimal and informal rather than centrally structured, as in the Soviet Union.

Chapters 5 and 6, in turn, explore the personal and social characteristics of communicators in Yugoslavia's mass communication process. They view mass communicators as a professional group with privileged access who are developing new relationships with politicians, and investigate the factors which have contributed to the growing independence of journalists in Yugoslavia. Their changing professional role emerges from the country's nonmonolithic communism and the increasing professionalism encouraged by Titoist media philosophy.

Chapter 7 explores how the Yugoslav media make sense out of and interpret international events for their people. A case study illustrates the systematic way in which Tanjug's foreign selection practices structure the "meaning" of these events. Foreign affairs perspectives, it appears, emerge not only from ideological outlooks, but also from the geographical location, the political and economic saliency of an international happening, as well as the production and distribution needs of the national news agency.

In Chapter 8 a comparative content analysis reveals the impact of social context on meaning. It identifies those elements of the international scene to which Yugoslavia pays attention, how these events are ordered, and what values or interpretations are attached to them. A comparison with United States selected and valued items explains how and why Yugoslav and United States news perspectives differ and what these differences mean for their respective audiences.

Chapter 9 investigates the question of media effects in Yugoslavia by scrutinizing which expressive performances the audience values most and why. The data suggest (1) that it is impossible to provide a general definition of the "audience" for a given country and (2) that although audiences are largely unable to be message originators, they are not indiscriminate in their use of media performances. The effects of media performances on different readers, listeners, and viewers vary according to life-styles. These in turn are affected not only by selective perception and retention, but also by varying accessibility, conceptions of "legitimate" media performances, personal involvement, and rewards accruing from media use.

Chapter 10 comes full circle and demonstrates the symbolic as well as the social control functions of the mass media in modern society. It is concerned with the way in which the Yugoslav media portray local political realities and influence the internal political process. In this decentralized country the media become republican forums for debate co-opted by the politicians of the day. In such a setup, communicators seem to be torn between acting as justifiers of the government line instead of as independent interpreters for the audience. This conflict mirrors the basic contradiction inherent in Yugoslav press theory, which tries to combine freedom of expression with Leninist requirements of social responsibility. The epilogue places this dilemma in historical perspective and traces the ebb and flow of journalistic freedom in Yugoslavia. It finds that the movements of curtailment and liberalization in the past thirty years are not mysterious but closely tied to the vagaries of diplomatic relations with the Soviet Union.

---

1 The most recent publications include George Macesich, *Yugoslavia: The Theory and Practice of Development Planning;* Wayne S. Vucinich, *Contemporary Yugoslavia, Twenty Years of Socialist Experiment;* Ichak Adizes, *Industrial Democracy Yugoslav Style;* Svetozar Pejovich, *The Market-Planned Economy of Yugoslavia;* George Zaninovich, *The Development of Socialist Yugoslavia.*

2 For a similar interpretation from which this study has benefited, see Peter Singelmann, "Exchange as Symbolic Interaction," pp. 414-424.

3 *Ibid.,* p. 415; see also Lee Thayer, *Communication and Communication Systems,* for a similar formulation.

4 Lee Thayer, "On Theory Building in Communication," pp. 217-235; see also "Some Persistent Obstacles" in J. Akin, *et al., Language Behavior,* pp. 34-42.

5 Herbert Blumer, *Symbolic Interactionism: Perspective and Method,* p. 19.

6 David Chaney, *Processes of Mass Communication,* especially Chapter 4 on "The Positive Study of Audiences."

7 Zagorka Ančič, "Population Changes in Yugoslavia," p. 1.

8 *Statistički Godišnjak SFRJ, 1969,* p. 329-330.

9 The Serbs refer to the joint language as "Serbo-Croatian" (srpskohrvatski) and the Croats call it "Croato-Serbian" (hrvatskosrpski). For a discussion of the differences between these two languages consult Dalibor Brozović, *Standardhi jesik.*

10 Since detailed 1971 population statistics are not yet available, much of this information is based on Dennison I. Rusinow, "Some Aspects of Migration and Urbanization in Yugoslavia."

11 Ivanka Ginić, *Migracije stanovništva Jugoslavije,* p. 75.

12 For further detail see Gertrude Joch Robinson, "Tanjug: Yugoslavia's Multi-Faceted National News Agency."

13 The congresses were held in Ljubljana in 1968, "Mass Media and International Understanding"; Novi Sad in 1970, "The Future of the Yugoslav Press and Broadcasting"; and Bled in 1971, "New Frontiers of Television."

14 Juergan Ruesch and Gregory Bateson, *Communication: The Social Matrix of Psychiatry,* Chapter 2.

15 Because of space limitations the discussion of film is very fragmentary. Hopefully future research will further highlight the position and importance of this medium in Yugoslavia's communication system. Film-makers, especially in the early 1960s, sparked the drive for increased creative freedom of expression.

16 See Chaney, *Processes of Mass Communication,* p. 8, for a similar formulation.

CHAPTER 2

From Leninism to Titoism, 1945-61

Although many countries are undergoing a communications' revolution, the reasons for media growth and development are as yet incompletely understood. Several studies have documented the existence of a close association between national levels of economic development and communications development,[1] but these studies fail to note that media growth, particularly newspaper growth, is not closely tied to these levels. A nation's real gross national product, literacy, and newspaper circulation predict national radio growth fairly accurately but say little about the development of press and television. Several scholars have consequently hypothesized that the political systems in which the media are embedded and the time span during which growth occurs must also be taken into account in making such predictions.[2]

Two approaches to media growth in socialist countries have consequently emerged. The first distinguishes merely between communist and capitalist societies. The second proposes that individual differences *within* communist nations must also be taken into account in predicting a country's media development. Fagan's comparative study of media growth in communist and noncommunist countries establishes that the communist media do grow more rapidly as a group than the noncommunist media. He explains this phenomenon by the more single-minded mobilization of resources in communist states. The same study, however, reveals that three of the eight communist countries, Yugoslavia, the German Democratic Republic, and Czechoslovakia, had less media growth between 1950 and 1960 than anticipated.[3] The author suggests that only a historical and "in-depth" analysis can explain this deviance.

The present chapter focuses on the internal differences between communist states in order to make sense out of their disparate media development. While it agrees that these states differ from others in their goals and strategies,[4] it documents that each communist system is unique in the sense that its goals are influenced by the particular sociopolitical "setting" in which it finds itself. Yugoslavia, Rumania, and Bulgaria, for instance, differ from many western nations by single-mindedly mobilizing their resources for a limited number of ideologically defined goals. These goals include the dictatorship of the pro-letariat, rapid industrialization, and the development of an effective media system to aid in the creation of a modern citizenry. How these goals are implemented in the three countries, however, depends on a number of sociopolitical factors. Chief among them, according to Johnson, are a nation's level of economic development, its political culture, the means by which its regime assumed power, and the problems it faces in protecting its national independence.[5]

A historical review indicates that in the past thirty years Yugoslavia has faced three major crises. These, it turns out, provided radically new sociopolitical

Table 2
Media Theory and Organization Change, 1945-75

	History			
	Administrative Media (1945-50)	Transition Media (1951-61)	Decentralized Media (1963-70)	Uncertain Present (1971-75)
Media Theory	Leninist agitation and propaganda	Leninist with questions	Titoist social responsibility	New political responsibility augmented in political actions
Financing	Government subsidies	Subscriptions and license fees	Subscriptions and license fees (80%), advertising (20%)	Same
Organization	Part of government information hierarchy	Semi-autonomous cooperatives, region-ally organized	Autonomous coopera-tives, regionally organized	Autonomous coopera-tives supervised by Socialist Alliance
Management	Director's one man rule; centralized decision-making; top personnel appointed	Modified workers' self-management with workers' council, management board, and *appointed* director	Workers' self-manage-ment with workers' council, management board, and elected director	Social management plus workers' self-management
Product	Primarily official speeches, declara-tions, little individ-ualized reporting	Switch from official, to content with audi-ence appeal. Intro-duction of entertain-ment features	Balanced mix of information and en-tertainment; individ-ualized reporting; specialization and competition	Increased politi-cization plus interest in entertainment
Media Growth	Print fastest growing; radio slow	Print declines; radio grows; T.V. experimentation	T.V. grows fastest; radio begins to level off; print innovates evening papers and special interest journals	Continued T.V. growth; print declines, radio levels off

settings to which the country's information policy had to adapt. From each of these breaking points, differences in information organization and filtering emerge. These differences, therefore, provide a clue to those intervening operative variables which constitute the logical link between the macrosocietal setting and information changes. The three crises are the country's 1948 Cominform expulsion which isolated Yugoslavia from Stalinism, the economic crisis of the early 1960s which uncovered basic contradictions in adapting a command economy to market influences, and the Croatian secession crisis of 1971 which threatened Yugoslavia's national unity. Table 2 summarizes the observable changes in the country's media ideology, organization, financing, product, and growth throughout four discernible periods and provides a temporal basis for relating differences in information filtering and distortion to these changes.

Though the typology does not intend to establish linear causal relationships, because no specific stimulus can be viewed as the cause of a particular event in a complex society,[6] it suggests that a distinction must be made between what Smelser calls "parameter" and "operative" variables. Parameters are suspected of influencing the outcome under investigation but are assumed not to vary. Operative variables are made or allowed to vary.[7]

The "givens" in our case are the universal organizational and development orientations of communist states; the "operative variables" are Johnson's four factors. These are useful in explaining the differences within and between the information systems of countries that share the same ideological outlooks. History thus provides the perspective for explaining several important points: what factors determine a country's media structure; how past experiences, political culture, economic capabilities, and changing ideology affect the rate at which the media grow; and how the media function and what kind of content they carry.

Local scholars[8] divide Yugoslavia's media growth into three distinct periods: (1) the administrative media (1945-50) immediately after the war, (2) the transition media (1951-61), during which the foundations for a new information policy were laid, and (3) the decentralized media (1962-70). To these a further period must be added, describing media policy since 1971, when President Tito's re-assertion of party control over the country's destiny signaled the need for yet another information adaptation. For the sake of clarity, this chapter covers only the first two periods, in which drastic political and social changes occurred. The next chapter will focus on contemporary media organization and functioning.

The Media in "Administrative Socialism," 1945-50

During the five years between 1945 to 1950, the Federal People's Republic of Yugoslavia was modeled on the Soviet Union. It resembled the USSR closely, not only in structure but also in operation. In sum, it was a bureaucratically centralized state under the dictatorship of the Communist party. President Tito and his associates were different, however, in that they came into the Soviet orbit by free choice, not under the pressure of conquest, as did the other eastern European states. Not only had Marshal Tito's partisans fought for over four years and finally won their country's liberation; they also were firmly in control of Yugoslav governmental machinery through wartime liberation councils.[9] The November, 1945, constitution merely extended the federated political organization laid out at the second session of the Anti-Fascist National Liberation Council of Yugoslavia (AVNOJ),[10] creating a bicameral People's Assembly which elected the governing Presidium.

Hoffman and Neal summed up the difficulties faced by the new regime: "In post-war Yugoslavia, economic chaos and extreme poverty made the task of governing especially difficult. If those who had hope for political democracy were repelled by the hard-boiled dictatorial practices of the regime, many more were embittered by hunger and privation alone. . . . The economic impact was apparent in loss of manpower, destruction of productive facilities, exploitation by the occupying powers, and disintegration of the country as an economic unit."[11] To ameliorate the disastrous situation created by the war, a bootstrap operation of unprecedented magnitude was called for. According to Yugoslav sources, 11 percent of the total population, especially the productive younger generation, had been killed in the war. Over 36 percent of Yugoslavia's industry and half of its railway stock were destroyed. Of all prewar landholdings, 40 to 60 percent lay fallow, and there was an acute shortage of gold reserves for reconstruction. Sixty million dollars lay blocked in the United States, Britain, and Brazil.

As the quickest means to industrialization of peasant Yugoslavia, the leadership chose nationalization and collectivization on the Soviet model. General "belt-tightening" was asked of the population to put the first ambitious five-year plan into operation in 1947. Soviet technicians, Soviet economic aid, and the development of joint stock companies, in addition to a treaty of friendship, were to tie Yugoslavia to the Slav motherland and to integrate it into the eastern European economic network, which supplied raw materials for the reconstruction of Soviet industry.

From the beginning, however, the Yugoslav leadership resisted economic exploitation and pushed for the development of native industrial potential. After extended negotiations, only two joint-stock companies were set up. They gave the Soviet Union a monopoly on air traffic and Danube shipping. However, such nationalistic deviations interfered with Stalin's plans for extending Soviet international power. He applied economic pressures, sent reprimands criticizing Yugoslavia's independent Trieste stand, and finally recalled all Soviet technicians. When none of these measures led to a more pliable Yugoslav policy, he shook the nation to its very foundations by arranging the young country's expulsion from the Cominform in 1948.

In the context of the time, the tasks of developing a skeleton media network and politically re-educating the 70 percent peasant population seemed almost insurmountable. Yet the Agitprop organization had functioned well during the war, and the leadership was versed in Marxist-Leninist ideology. The Agitprop chief, Milovan Djilas, was consequently instructed to develop the press and radio into an efficient mouthpiece of the ruling Communist party and to see to the dissemination of the new society's values. Chief among those were the need for a federal association of the historically differentiated republics and the eradication of religious and ethnic rivalries which had led to much of the internecine bloodshed during World War II.

A look at Table 2 indicates that the functions of the press during this period were spelled out along Marxist lines. The press was to be a collective propagandist, a collective agitator, as well as a collective organizer and two-way channel for criticism of tactics. In *What Is to Be Done,* Lenin noted: "In this respect (the press) can be compared to the scaffolding erected around a building under construction. It marks the contours of the structure and facilitates communication between the builders, permitting them to distribute the work and to view the common results achieved by their organized labour."[12] The press had two major functions: first, to mobilize activists, intellectuals, and the general population by transmitting a centrally elaborated set of programs and values, and second, to help integrate the disparate outlooks of the country's multinational groups by making viewpoints more uniform.

To enable the media to fulfill these functions effectively, the press and radio, like all other means of production, were nationalized and became part of a centralized organization based on the principle of "democratic centralism." Ministries of Information and Agitprop organizations were set up in Yugoslavia's six republics to hierarchically link local with federal levels. They controlled and supervised the reconstruction and development of the badly scarred press and radio throughout the country, coordinated branches, transmitted central directives, and acted as monitoring agencies. In similar fashion, a 1950 committee for radio diffusion acquired all power over broadcast programming, while the Tanjug news agency and the ministries supervised press content. In 1952 this committee was converted into the federally run *Jugoslovenski Radiodifuzija,* and with further decentralization it became the autonomous *Jugoslovenski Radio-Televizija* organization of today.[13]

Management and financing of publishing houses and radio stations were also affected by the political and ideological changes after the war, as shown in Table 2. The new press law of 1946 prescribed that publications were to be issued solely by political parties, trade unions, and other official groups. As state enterprises, these publications were subsidized by the government and run by a party-appointed director, who exercised final editorial responsibility. New equipment, newsprint, and other necessary items were bought through government channels.

While freedom of the press was nominally guaranteed, the fact is that only groups showing evidence of loyalty to the authorities received permits to publish and to broadcast. Article 6 of the 1946 press law denied the right of becoming a publisher, editor, or journalist to all those not enjoying political or civil rights and to those who had collaborated with "fascist" or ultranationalist organizations like the Četniks and Ustaše. Moša Pijade, the spiritual father of Yugoslavia's information system during the war, justified these restrictions in the following way: "[The press law] gives almost unlimited freedom of expression, excluding from this liberty only quislings. It protects the benefits of democracy against those who, by abusing civil liberties, seek to violate the constitutional order with anti-democratic aims in view. Through its just distribution of newsprint and its nationalization of the large printing works, the State has given the press real material aid and the possibility of developing itself into a really free press."[14]

As a result of the centralization of information collection and dissemination and the restricted access prescribed by the 1946 press law, all political, economic, and cultural content was strongly filtered, taking on the uniform coloration well known from other eastern European countries. Party control, following the Soviet model, took five forms. Chief editors and top staff were appointed by the Central Committee. Content was checked before publication, and chief editors were made personally responsible. Distribution and newsprint allocation depended on favorable relationships with the powerful economic planning committee. Individual newspapers and radio stations did not have their own correspondents; instead they received their information from republican ministry branches, which were part of the Tanjug national news collection net.

Distortion of all information content during the period of "administrative socialism" made not only political but also economic and cultural reporting heavy and official because political criteria dominated in all fields. Three factors contributed to this domination: the generality of the press law, Tanjug's monopoly over domestic and foreign news sources, and lack of a trained journalism corps. The press law prohibited the distribution of publications encouraging revolt, diversionary activities, sabotage, and the violent overthrow of the constitutional order; it also punished the spreading of "false information" that threatened the national interest.

Tanjug's collection of all foreign and domestic information precluded the emergence of differentiated or regional points of view, and the dearth of trained journalists additionally reinforced this trend. To ensure a press corps with the "correct" outlook, the Yugoslav Journalists' Association and a permanent school for top level personnel were founded in 1947 and 1948. However, the

Advanced School of Journalism and Diplomacy, to which top party members were assigned, operated for only three years and was then disbanded without explanation. Yugoslavia thus began to differentiate between and dismantle some aspects of its formal censorship system in 1952, five years earlier than other eastern European countries. It thus became a model for what happened in Soviet literature and the Hungarian and Polish press after Stalin's death.

How did party monopoly affect press and radio growth in Yugoslavia? Yugoslav media data indicate that this early period was characterized by a steep rise in print and a very slow development of radio. Table 3 shows that between

Table 3
Growth of Yugoslav Press, 1939-74

Year	Total News-papers	Circu-lation in Millions	Dailies	Circu-lation in Millions	Several Times Weekly	Weekly	Monthly	Other
1939	322	75	33	—	—	—	—	—
1946	146	73	15	—	—	—	—	—
1947	217	3,22	15	76	10	85	28	79
1948	306	4,31	17	1,12	14	113	49	113
1949	360	4,78	18	1,46	13	126	65	138
1950	357	5,89	18	1,58	11	123	61	144
1951	371	3,55	21	95	7	130	67	146
1952	401	3,23	18	78	6	130	75	172
1953	457	3,52	18	81	11	146	109	173
1954	453	3,14	18	72	10	134	106	185
1955	493	3,55	18	80	12	145	105	213
1956	497	4,01	18	85	10	134	114	221
1957	533	4,23	20	97	12	125	110	266
1958	745	5,85	21	1,07	13	128	222	361
1959	778	6,01	20	1,13	11	133	217	397
1960	904	7,10	19	1,34	12	140	265	468
1961	1,039	7,24	19	1,13	13	148	299	560
1962	1,039	7,67	19	1,32	12	191	405	412
1963	1,042	8,44	21	1,39	12	184	424	401
1964	1,092	10,06	22	1,71	14	190	427	439
1965	1,171	9,81	23	1,52	10	150	477	511
1966	1,218	8,49	23	1,48	13	162	466	554
1967	1,259	8,10	23	1,54	11	157	502	566
1968	1,350	8,74	23	1,55	10	156	538	623
1969	1,381	8,67	23	1,61	9	174	585	588
1970	1,466	8,61	24	1,73	11	164	524	743
1971	1,392	7,15	24	1,74	9	131	510	712
1972	1,518	8,48	25	1,85	11	129	559	794
1973	2,024	9,77	25	1,82	10	156	701	1132
1974	1,988	9,28	25	1,85	10	147	633	1352

SOURCE: *Naša štampa* XX:178 (Aug.-Sept., 1970) p. 12. *Statistički godišnjak, SFRJ* (1975), p. 343.

1945 and 1950 the number of papers and journals grew two and a half times from 146 to 357, and circulation rose by approximately 80 percent — from 3.2 million to 5.8 million copies. Radio, on the other hand, did not show equally rapid growth, as shown in Table 4. Between 1946 and 1950, the total number of sets merely increased from 198,000 to 336,398. This was an average yearly rate of 14 percent, only half as fast as the growth of newspapers.

Why such discrepancies, when both media were urgently needed to cement the young country with its 40 percent illiterate population? Since propaganda needs alone were not able to predict media growth in Yugoslavia, other factors

Table 4
Growth of Yugoslav Radio, 1939-74
(in thousands)

Year	Number of Sets	Growth in Percentage	Inhabitants per Radio Set	No. Main Stations	No. Local Stations
1939	155	14.6	100	5	
1946	198		78	8	2
1947	223	12.7	70		
1948	251	12.7	63		
1949	300	19.4	53		
1950	336	11.8	48	8	8
1951	357	6.2	46		
1952	387	8.4	43		
1953	421	8.8	40		
1954	496	17.7	35		
1955	592	19.1	30		
1956	710	20.0	25		
1957	890	25.0	20		
1958	1,088	22.2	37		
1959	1,309	20.3	14		
1960	1,561	19.3	12		
1961	1,827	17.8	10	8	14
1962	2,078	13.7	9	8	37
1963	2,277	9.6	8	8	43
1964	2,519	10.6	7		
1965	2,782	10.4	7		
1966	3,003	8.7	6	8	70
1967	3,059	1.8	6	8	75
1968	3,170	3.5	6	8	107
1969	3,310	4.4	6	8	129
1970	3,372	1.6	6	8	141
1971	3,476	3.4	6	8	158
1972	3,556	2.3	6	8	177
1973	3,685	3.6	6	8	176
1974	4,081	0.7	6	8	178

SOURCE: *Jugoslovenski radiotelevizija godišnjak*, p. 107. 1970-74: *Statistički godišnjak, SFRJ* (1975), p. 341.

must be found to explain what happened. Among these were Yugoslavia's media heritage, its level of economic development in the late 1940s, and the availability of trained journalists. All of these, it turns out, constituted preconditions for a given society's mobilization for media growth. Substantiating this point are Figures 1, 2, and 3, which plot press and radio data, starting in the late 1930s.

Growth did not occur uniformly across all of the media, these figures suggest, because the preconditions for print and broadcasting were quite different. In the administrative period print flourished but broadcasting made only slow gains, not so much because of ideological decisions, but because certain economic and social preconditions for technical development had not been fulfilled. At the end of the war Yugoslavia had lost 101 papers, as well as many of its radio stations and sets, according to statistics collected by the Institute of Military History.[15] Much of the country had to depend, therefore, on news transmitted by word of mouth, mass meetings, or reading circles.[16] The Agitprop organization quickly realized that this information vacuum needed to be filled as soon and as cheaply as possible, even though a high percentage of the population was illiterate.

Since the growth of print could be more rapidly stimulated than that of radio, and since most journalists had worked on wartime newspapers, the Yugoslav leadership made three decisions about how to begin media mobilization. These included government financing of all publishing, a press subsidy which kept newspaper prices at a low two dinars until 1951, and unequal newsprint distribution which favored federal papers. As a result, two things happened: the total number of papers increased drastically, and the party-sponsored papers boosted their circulation at the expense of those sponsored by trade unions and other citizen organizations (Table 2 graphically illustrates this point).

Between 1945 and 1950, the Communist party's daily *Borba* quadrupled its circulation to 625,000. In the same period *Politika,* sponsored by the Popular Front, reached only 280,000, and Zagreb's regional *Vjesnik,* organized by the Socialist Alliance, dropped from 90,000 to 55,000.[17] All of these trends were reversed after 1950 when the Yugoslav leadership, rethinking its media policy, substituted various economic priorities for its earlier interest in information and propaganda. Scarce foreign currency from this time onward was no longer used to import newsprint, but to stimulate growth. As a result, circulation dropped sharply, although total numbers of papers increased after 1950. This drop, in turn, reflects the high illiteracy which had not yet been appreciably reduced.

Media heritage, level of economic development, and the dearth of trained personnel, on the other hand, affected broadcast growth negatively. Figure 3 indicates that throughout the period of 1945 to 1950, radio grew by only 14 percent yearly, about half the press growth rate of 21 percent. The reason is that radio suffered even heavier losses than newspapers as a result of the Axis occupation. By 1945 most of the original five radio stations were destroyed,

Figure 1. Yugoslav Press and Journal Growth, 1946-72 (in hundreds)

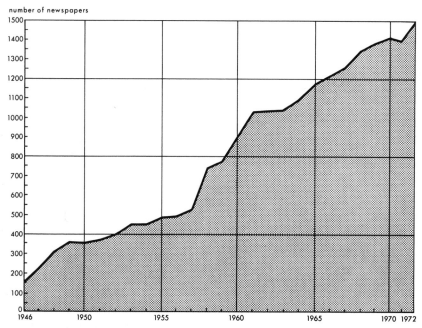

number of newspapers

Source: *Statistički godišnjak Jugoslavije* (1975), p. 343.

Figure 2. Total Yugoslav Newspaper Circulation, 1946-72 (in millions)

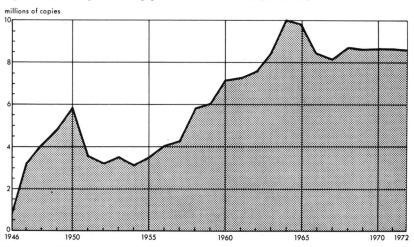

millions of copies

Source: *Statistički godišnjak Jugoslavije* (1975), p. 343.

Figure 3. Cumulative Diffusion Curve for Radio, 1930-72 (in millions of sets)

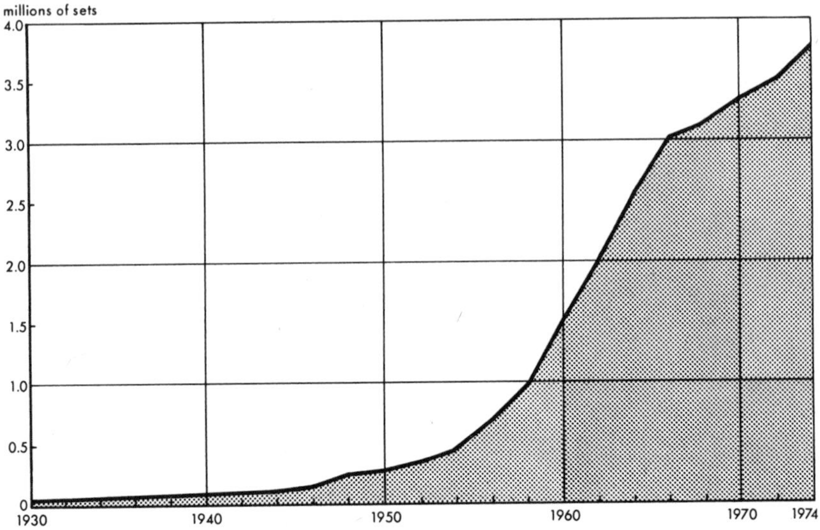

Source: *Jugoslovenski radiotelevizija-godišnjak* (1972), p. 107.

and the country had to start from scratch. One year later ten stations operated in Yugoslavia's republican capitals and major cities, and by the 1950s this number had increased to only sixteen.[18] These early transmitters were usually weak and they did not carry far beyond the city limits. Cross-country hookups were relatively primitive. The country's rugged terrain, especially in the southeastern republics, added another barrier to early radio growth.

The country's lack of an indigenous electronic industry inhibited production of radio receivers and their sale to the population outside of the city. The slow growth in numbers of sets could not be changed by ideological fiat; it had to wait for a change in the country's level of economic development, which took another ten years to achieve. Only then did Yugoslavia have adequate factories for cheaply producing radio sets, which were followed very shortly by television receivers as well. Still another hindrance, the dearth of trained radio personnel, was a matter of time and resources. Not until the late 1950s and early 1960s did special training courses begin to produce increasing numbers of broadcast professionals. Bjelica notes that even in 1963 there were only 744 radio journalists out of 2,625, an indication that ten years earlier this number must have been woefully small.[19]

The regime ameliorated the dearth of radio facilities, which provided eleven families with one radio set, by installing wired public loudspeakers in community buildings and factories. These systems accounted for most of the meager set growth of 150,000 in the decade from 1939 to 1949. Like the press, radio at the time was more oriented toward hard news than entertainment and stressed the general theme of "building socialism." It carried reports on government decisions, campaigns to entice peasants into collectives, programs combating illiteracy, and talks encouraging youth brigades in their reconstruction of the country. Music and dramas were aimed to acquaint the public with its diversified cultural heritage. Popular or light music programs were generally shunned as decadent western imports.

From the vantage point of hindsight and a drastically revised media policy, Yugoslav communicators today criticize the administrative period for "the uniformity of the press, a unilateral orientation with regard to sources of information, and a lack of professional skill in editing and technical layout."[20] One writer notes that the autocratic state-bureaucratic media were a hermetically closed communications network, in which foreign ideas were "administratively" eliminated. In such a system "communication flow is circular, serving . . . the diffusion of conservative agitprop ideology . . . and permitting only a pseudo-feedback of [what has emanated from the top]. The entire communication system has only one function: the maintenance of political equilibrium and the stifling of deviant values. The communication system is used to strengthen the political state, the planned and centralized economy, and contribute to ideological homogenization."[21]

The Transition Media, 1951-61

The crisis of the 1948 Cominform expulsion provided the first occasion for Yugoslavia's leadership to focus on local conditions and to rethink their position. Political survival, economic necessity, and the need to symbolically differentiate themselves from Stalinism and develop a new political culture became the touchstones for drastic social and political changes during the second period of media development. National economic survival required mobilization of the population to increase production, while ideological differentiation necessitated a reinterpretation of Stalinist Marxism. The former altered the structure and organization of Yugoslav media enterprises, while the latter spawned a new media philosophy. In the period between 1951 and 1961, centralization slowly gave way to decentralization, media financing switched from state subsidy to market demand, and press and broadcasting were converted from governmental institutions into autonomous cooperatives, all of which Table 2 indicates. These changes will be reviewed to find an explanation for the alterations in Yugoslavia's media policies.

Although it was not obvious at the time, the seeds for Yugoslavia's independent course had been sown much earlier, during World War II, when President Tito and his comrades came to power by their own exertions in the fight against the Axis. Consequently the regime enjoyed a relatively broad-based popularity that was its most valuable asset in 1948 when the country's Cominform expulsion caught the world by surprise. A majority of Central Committee members agreed to stand firm against Soviet demands, and they were confident that most of the population could be weaned away from Stalinism.[22] All of them furthermore agreed that Yugoslavia's existence as an independent nation-state and the country's economic development were more important than ideological fidelity to the Soviet line. The leadership justified this heresy by evolving a novel transfer culture, which came to be known to the world as "Titoism." This culture was designed in response to three immediate needs: the stimulation of its stagnating economy, the protection of Yugoslavia's sovereignty, and the safeguarding of its unique political heritage. The strategies adopted ultimately led to a reluctant abandonment of totalitarian methods in many spheres of life.

At the time of the Cominform expulsion, Yugoslavia was firmly integrated into the Soviet economic and political system. Its factories had begun to be rebuilt with Soviet machinery, for which no spare parts were available after the break. All of the country's exports went to the USSR, and no gold was available for purchases from the West. The population was furthermore suspicious of the allied nations, especially Great Britain and its Mideast interests. To make matters even worse, two disastrous droughts drastically reduced food production, and since imports from other East-bloc countries were no longer available, scarce resources needed to be deflected from industry to feed the population.[23] To stand alone politically and develop economic self-sufficiency under these circumstances seemed an almost impossible task to the Yugoslav leadership, yet only through the mobilization of local resources, both human and material, could industrialization be continued. Discouraging growth rates and overly ambitious planning convinced the Central Committee that the "command economy" needed modification and that the autocratic features in the state bureaucracy must be eliminated to hasten economic development in Yugoslavia.

To achieve this goal, economic needs were codified in a new political doctrine of self-government for the working people. This doctrine was not only acceptable for being an updated version of the classical Marxist dogma of the "withering away of the state," as one scholar notes,[24] but also had the advantage of publicly affirming that important regional differences, which had historically plagued the country, would not be overlooked. The idea of social self-management also dealt a resounding blow to the Stalinist dogma that state power must initially increase before it could wither away in the far distant future.[25] It affirmed that "participation" would overcome "alienation" and that the worker's right to participate in government originated in the profit which his work contributed to the social reproduction of life.

How did this new doctrine affect Yugoslavia's political and social organization? Within the next decade it broke down the monolithic structure of state power and made the "commune," or county, the most important administrative unit with control over its own factories. In addition, central ministries were abolished, among them the Ministry of Information and state enterprises. The Workers' Council Act of 1950 turned factories into collectively owned and operated bodies, with productivity judged by market considerations. In line with the requirements of decentralization, the party, too, shifted emphasis and changed its name in 1956. As the League of Communists of Yugoslavia, it was reorganized and made more sensitive to republican needs. From an autocratic vanguard, communists were in the future to become "social animators," functioning through persuasion.

Although this is not the place to go into a detailed analysis of the administrative forms of social self-management in Yugoslavia, some of the system's unique features need mentioning because they bear directly on the organization and functioning of the press, radio, television, and film during the country's second developmental phase. In blending the principles of free enterprise and collective ownership, Titoism has accomplished a previously unknown amalgam. The country is socialist in that there is no private ownership of industry or commerce, except in small service establishments like restaurants and some retail stores.

Yet there is no state ownership, either. All enterprises, hotels, newspapers, and broadcasting stations are collectively managed and thus become the "social property" of those who work in them. Enterprises are legally independent and compete with each other in a relatively free market. Each workers' council decides independently what and how much to produce, at what price to sell their products, and to whom. The main requirement is that they operate profitably. There is a general plan promulgated by the federal government, but it differs from the Soviet model in that it merely provides an orientation for future development. The government, making money available through development and investment funds as well as the central bank, instead relies on indirect financial control to encourage production in desired directions. The efficacy of market liberalization is borne out by the fact that between 1956 and 1961 Yugoslavia's national income grew by an average annual rate of about 10 percent, while the standard of living increased dramatically.[26]

In tracing the impact of partial decentralization and ideological reformulation on media growth and development throughout the transition period, three changes stand out most vividly. All of them are summarized in Table 2 and reflect the way in which filtering relates to media organization. First of all, there was a change in the organizational structure and financing of all the Yugoslav mass media. In addition, Leninist media philosophy began to be challenged and the foundation laid for a redefinition of the balance between journalistic freedom and social responsibility. Moreover, broadcasting grew faster than print, and content variety increased. For clarity's sake, each of these interlinked changes will be individually described and assessed.

A number of writers have described Yugoslavia's emerging decentralized media organization as "communism with a difference."[27] What are some of the differences? The most drastic change cut the mass media off from government financing, encouraging rationalization of staff and production procedures similar to factories in industry. In addition, the Newspaper Publishing Act of 1956 gave publishing enterprises, radio stations, and film studios the right to organize and to control their own affairs. For the first time a democratically elected workers' council and a managing board, not a group of party representatives, decided selection, layout, and content.

In the Yugoslav cooperative system, the workers' council, consisting of about thirty-five members, addresses itself to broad questions of planning. This rather large body meets twelve times a year. It determines economic policy, such as salary and investment, and lays down productivity norms and makes disciplinary rules. It also decides on working conditions, lengths of shifts, safety, and canteens. Initially, during the 1950s, factories disposed of a very limited amount of funds since federal law determined most investment decisions. Later, however, economic autonomy was strengthened and local decision-making increased. Presently, therefore, the only limitation on the financial autonomy of the workers' council is tax requirements, just as in the United States. The managing board, on the other hand, makes daily editorial and production decisions. It consists of ten to fifteen journalists, administrators, and support personnel. Both bodies work under the auspices of a director, who during this transition period is still appointed by the government, party, or Socialist Alliance, and is a party member of long standing. Like a gyroscope calibrated by official needs, he helps keep the enterprise on an even keel.

A second change, a lessening of state authority over reporting, also began in this period. Both Milovan Djilas in the Central Committee and a group of "modernist" writers were advocating greater freedom of expression in the cultural and information spheres. The purpose was to ideologically differentiate Yugoslavia from the Soviet Union. Such a switch, however, was not accomplished overnight. History shows that it took six years to decentralize and apply self-management legislation to the press and broadcasting, and that this application worked only by fits and starts.

The tortuous path toward freer reporting is well exemplified by occurrences during the Hungarian Revolution. Here enthusiastic accounts supporting the revolutionaries offended the Soviet Union. To dampen divergent reporting, the government decided to return to some form of supervision which was, however, to be short of overt censorship. The Publishing Council Act of 1957 consequently created a supervisory body with the following circumscribed functions: "The Publishing Council is entitled to examine the general policy of the enterprise from a social standpoint, to approve plans, or general policy. But it may not interfere with the direct affairs of the enterprise or general director. Being merely an advisory body, it does not exercise direct influence on the every-day work of the enterprise or perform censorship."[28]

Publishing councils for each newspaper, radio, or television station are today made up of groups of fewer than ten persons, including the editor-in-chief and director, as well as representatives from other media and notable personalities in public life. *Politika*'s 1957 council included a foreign affairs' secretary, an army general, and a woman author.[29] The council thus performs much like a board of trustees in the American system; it spells out general policy but keeps out of day-to-day management.

A third change during the transition period altered media growth and diffusion patterns. These are clearly indicated in Figures 1 and 3. As previously noted, print suffered most severely from having to adjust to the new economic realities, while radio was helped by economic liberalization after 1954. Various factors explain these changing fortunes of the media during the transition period.

Although total numbers of journals tripled between 1950 and 1960, according to Table 3, total journal circulation increased merely by 1.4 million copies, after taking a nose dive to immediate postwar levels. Among journals, dailies were most sharply affected. Three newspapers, including *Republika,* went out of business, and the rest suffered circulation cuts of one-half. In the three years between 1951 and 1954, Figure 2 indicates, 1.5 million dailies shrank to half that number and finally stabilized at around 900,000 by the end of the period. This meant about two newspapers for each 100 population rather than the previous four, a figure well below the UNESCO-suggested minimum of ten. Weeklies and monthlies, on the other hand, grew both in number and in circulation, perhaps because they could adjust their content to reader interests more rapidly than could newspapers.

The remarkable decrease in print circulation is a vivid example of how changed mobilization decisions affect the growth and decline of a medium. As previously noted, however, that is not all of the story. Other decisions, such as doubling the price of dailies from five to ten old dinars and producing an inadequate supply of paper, also depressed circulation. A Yugoslav economic study put total paper production in 1960 at only 10,000 tons more than the average ten years earlier.[30] Large shipments from the Soviet Union stopped with the Cominform break, and scarce foreign currency under the changed political circumstances was used for more important capital goods imports. Thrown on its own resources, Yugoslavia therefore had to slowly build up its indigenous paper industry, helped by Germany, Austria, and Sweden which provided some newsprint during the transition years. By 1959, paper problems seem to have been solved, and a UNESCO report lists Yugoslavia's total at 35.2 thousand metric tons, or 1.9 kilograms per inhabitant,[31] which compares favorably with the consumption rates of such socialist countries as Czechoslovakia and Hungary.

In contrast, the diffusion curve for radio throughout the transition period shows none of the sharp drops experienced by the press. From an initial 7 percent increase in the first two years, radio tripled to an average growth rate of 21 percent annually during the last part of the decade. This advance is due mostly to the increased production of receivers and the very low saturation level of this medium. As Table 4 indicates, between 1951 and 1961 radio sets increased five-fold, to provide an average of one set for every five families in Yugoslavia. Since distribution is generally determined by economic standards, the richer republics have more radios than the poorer ones, even at this early stage, a lead which continued when personal income grew steadily in the 1960s.

The belated television diffusion in Yugoslavia also questions the accuracy of those researchers who believe that communist mobilization alone explains media growth. However much the Yugoslav leadership might have wanted or needed television to get its message to the people, television could not be introduced until there was an adequate electronics industry with the capability for cheaply producing receivers. Since this industry did not become a reality until the 1960s, television remained "experimental" up to that time.

During the transition period, starting in 1955, television innovation was spearheaded by republican radio centers, research institutes, and the electronics industry. Much of the early history of this medium is peripheral to this study. It is enough to point out that the medium was not uncritically imported from a foreign country, as is so often the case in Africa, but that the leadership decided to develop local expertise before starting its own programming. Consequently, Yugoslavia's limited television resources were initially used to build equipment and to pick up programs from neighboring Austria and Italy. Shortly afterward, with the help of French technicians, Zagreb built the first Yugoslav sender which aired a locally produced film. Programs of filmed material remained in use throughout the first year because staffs for live shows and transmission facilities were not yet available.[32]

It took another two years, as a matter of fact, to prepare skeleton crews for the opening of the Belgrade and Ljubljana studios. By the end of 1958, the more industrialized parts of Yugoslavia, with about a quarter of the country's population, were interconnected by television relay stations. However, the 6,000 available receivers, mostly in public places, did not yet give many individuals a chance to view programs. Television at the time was not a mass medium. Receivers cost more than the average citizen could afford, and factories were not tooled up to mass production. A rising standard of living, coupled with great strides in the electronics industry, made this the fastest growing medium in the 1960s.

Filtering the News Streams

Decentralization of media organization and relative financial self-sufficiency introduced a new kind of information-filtering process during the transition period. Distortions in cultural and economic information were substantially reduced, while centrally organized political reporting remained firmly under the control of party leadership through appointed media directors. Why this easing of control in cultural and economic reporting?

The slow easing of content distortion in the cultural field had its roots in the constitutionally guaranteed cultural independence and equality of Yugoslavia's major ethnic groups and in a party-sponsored campaign against Zhdanovism.[33] It all began in 1951 when two literary journals, *Mladost* and *Kniževne Novine,* spearheaded an attack against the repressive doctrine of "socialist realism" in Soviet art, with the blessing of Agitprop Minister Milovan Djilas. As previously noted, this attack served the regime as tangible evidence of cultural liberalization at a time when the increased economic and political freedom envisaged in the self-management system still required years to accomplish.[34]

The paradoxical situation in which Agitprop was nurturing a "struggle of ideas," however, soon spilled over into politically more sensitive areas when groups of writers joined together to demand concrete steps toward cultural and social liberalization. Such demands could not be met during the critical early years when social reorganization was being attempted. In 1952, therefore, *Mladost* and *Kniževne Novine,* as well as the newly founded *Svedočanstva,* were banned, and Djilas admonished writers "Leave politics to us politicians and we will leave aesthetics to you."[35]

By 1954, however, ferment increased once more. The Djilas case illustrates the difficulties of reversing centralist methods in the cultural and informational spheres without making political changes as well. Djilas himself, in a series of *Borba* articles, became one of the most outspoken critics of the party's snail-pace progress in political and economic liberalization. He not only denounced the League dictatorship over power, but also argued for the creation of a second party to provide a genuine clash of ideas and experience. After the first shock, two journals were ordered to cease publication — the review *Nova Misao* and the weekly *Naprijed,* organ of the Croatian League of Communists whose editor-in-chief had made common cause with Djilas.

Subsequently the entire press was admonished to avoid articles prejudicial to the nation's precarious attempt at social readjustment, and Djilas was soon after stripped of his Central Committee and governmental positions and sentenced to imprisonment, which lasted off and on until the late 1960s.[36] In spite of temporary setbacks, however, the ideas of Zhdanov disappeared from Yugoslav literary and art reviews during the 1950s, and cultural experimentation by writers fighting for greater freedom of expression became the order of the day. Joyce, Proust, and Faulkner were translated for the first time, and other forms of "bourgeois art," such as jazz and abstract painting, became part of Yugoslavia's cultural scene from then onward.

The easing of economic content restrictions had other roots. It emerged, as has been seen, from the implementation of the doctrine of social self-management which gradually transferred economic decision-making from ministries to factories. As a result, factories for the first time required accurate information about raw material sources, other producers, transportation, and markets in order to engage in efficient planning and distribution. While many of these decisions initially remained in the hands of federal bureaucrats, it was recognized that the country's new social organization required an information system sensitive to the rapid and accurate transmission of economic content. It was also needed to stimulate the public on the commune level so that people would become engaged in social affairs and increase production.

The reduced filtering and distortion in the economic information flow is easily documented by the proliferation of specialty journals and the factory press and by the increased reporting of economic news without ideological trappings in the 1950s. Table 3 details the doubling of monthly and other publications between 1950 and 1960, despite the fact that total circulation remains virtually constant. Many of these publications deal with purely economic matters, trade resources, and markets.

More accurate economic reporting, furthermore, was reinforced by the founding of a statistical institute which began publishing yearly economic and trade analyses in a *Statistički Godišnjak*. Factories finally started contracting with enterprises in other parts of the country, stimulating more sophisticated economic data collection. Since the highly bureaucratized national news agency, Tanjug, was not up to this task, it lost its mandate over economic news collection during the transition period.

The slow dismantling of the politically oriented filtering criteria determining economic and cultural reporting ultimately had an impact on the reporting of political content as well. Though it did not eliminate centralized interpretation of foreign and domestic events by a group at the top, it did provide a spur for more flexible handling of political news. For the first time it was recognized that the important integrative function of political information, which led to a homogenized "official" version of Yugoslav events, needed to be blended with some feedback from the base where economic decisions were increasingly made. Two adjustments consequently occurred in the information apparatus. The first provided broadened information sources, and the second increased content variety. Both of these ultimately affected international and domestic political reporting.

To develop diplomatic contacts with neighboring states, broadened international information sources were necessary. These were gained when Tanjug entered the Association of European News Agencies in 1952 and also made the first exchange agreements with western news associations like Reuters of Britain, Agence France Presse of France, and the Associated Press of the United States. In the same year, a semiofficial news competitor, "Jugopress," was organized by the Yugoslav Journalists' Association, whose prime function it was to balance Tanjug's strictly official reporting. Here an aggressive and relatively independent correspondent corps ferreted out interesting news stories for six years before it was reorganized into a feature agency in 1958 because it had angered the powerful Ministry of Information with a story about Trieste.

On the national political level, additional points of view entered the news stream through the newspapers' desire to make their content more timely and interesting for the paying public. They created their own correspondents' net to cover republican and regional news, and also concentrated on in-service training to improve writing style and coverage. This change ultimately led to more complete and in-depth coverage of local events, as well as to greater interpretative independence on the part of regional papers. A new division of labor between Tanjug and the print media resulted, with the national news agency specializing in foreign news and verbatim accounts of plans, government reports, and speeches of national interest, and the papers using their own reporters to interpret local news in a more individualistic manner.

Increased content variety also became a necessity when media financing was switched from government subsidy to market forces. The subsequent drop in newspaper circulation indicated that large segments of the population were unwilling to pay for a newspaper crammed with official news. Throughout the 1950s, when the press in other communist countries was still rigid and monotonous, the large circulation papers in Yugoslavia began using lively makeup, cartoon strips, detective stories, and somewhat spicy love serials to arouse audience interest and provide relaxation and entertainment. They also devoted space to such general interest items as sports, crimes, and disasters, and other topics not ordinarily covered in eastern Europe at the time.

The papers that adapted their content fastest fared better than those that did not. A drastic example can be found in the reversed fortunes of Belgrade's *Borba* and *Politika*. *Borba,* now the organ of the League of Communists and responsible for publishing official texts, dropped by two-thirds from a 1949 high of 650,000 to a 1958 low of 234,000. *Politika,* on the other hand, with its long tradition of journalistic excellence, more than doubled its circulation to 284,000 in the same decade.[37]

Additional news sources and increased content variety did not, however, materially change the regime's conception of the political role of the media in socialist Yugoslavia. According to this view, which was succinctly expressed by President Tito at the 1958 VII Congress of the League of Communists, the media had to justify the dependence of the superstructure on the base. The argument went like this:

> During our country's revolutionary period of transition, the press cannot be considered an independent and autonomous factor in society, since all actions of society as a whole must converge towards one aim: the construction of Socialism. . . . The press is responsible before society for correctly informing the public and educating public opinion in a Socialist sense, but it does not have the function of interpreting social events and the most important issues of foreign policy independently and without regard to responsible social institutions. . . . There still are journalists in our country who have the wrong idea about the freedom and independence of the press here. Freedom of the press in their opinion tends to give them the monopoly of the interpretation of events and the formation of public opinion. Such a conception derives from an erroneous idea of the role and responsibility of the Socialist press.[38]

In spite of the fact that writers and intellectuals seem to have lost the twin battles for greater ideological and cultural diversity in the 1950s, they were on the way to winning the war in the 1960s. Allied in this endeavor were a set of unanticipated developments which grew out of the economic reform and the media's financial independence. First among these social developments were demands for greater political representation of the country's diverse ethnic points of view, which are difficult for a regime to silence. Coupled with these emerged the necessity to combine the contradictory requirements of uniform political control with a growing number of voices legitimately enunciating the economic needs of communal and local bodies. How this balance was struck will constitute the substance of the next chapter, which analyzes the emergence of the new Titoist media philosophy in the 1960s and 1970s.

Theories of Media Growth

A review of Yugoslav media growth and diffusion data during the first fifteen years of the country's existence indicates that the initial sharp rise of print, coupled with the slow development of radio during the administrative period, and the reversal of these trends during the transition phase, requires a new kind of media growth theory. A previously mentioned article analyzing media growth in communist and noncommunist countries argues that such accelerated growth is primarily a result of mobilization goals. Johnson notes that such goals aim at the preservation of the party's power and the newly established social system, and at schemes to implement a Marxist-Leninist culture, including among other things a classless society, socialist construction, and the molding of new socialist men.

Doubtlessly such a conclusion has some general validity. Yugoslav data presented here indicate that this is at best a partial explanation, which fails to pinpoint strategies for accomplishing these goals in a particular historical setting. Media growth, in general, follows a pattern very similar to the S-curves familiar from population, epidemology, and innovation studies. These curves may be shallow or steep, and strung out over longer or shorter periods of time. Slow initial growth is usually followed by a rapid acceleration when a certain threshhold is reached, only to taper off again after more than half the population has accepted the innovation. All other things being equal, the data suggest socialist mobilization influences growth in three ways. First, government production subsidies in both print and broadcasting tend to reduce the time-span for reaching the distribution threshhold. Moreover, government educational and training programs can upgrade the literacy level and the competence of the journalist corps. Ideological stances, finally, may favor the development of one medium over another at a particular point in time. Yet, as has been previously argued, if economic capabilities are not adequate for producing newsprint or broadcast equipment, mobilization alone will not prove sufficient to achieve these goals.

So far, it should be clear that Yugoslavia's media development cannot be adequately explained by just making a gross distinction between communist and noncommunist countries. Four additional "operative variables" were needed to explain the country's specific strategies for achieving media growth. These were Yugoslavia's relative lack of economic development, its ethnic diversity and unique political culture, the regime's popularity and legitimacy, and the country's special international status. All, it appears, affected the mass media's institutional growth and change.

To recapitulate, the country's economic underdevelopment first encouraged the forced growth of newspapers and subsequently facilitated circulation declines when foreign currency priorities were shifted to industrial needs. It also initially retarded broadcast development, which was hampered by a dearth of indigenous electronic capacity. Yugoslavia's ethnic and religious diversity and its stormy rivalry between Croats and Serbs favored a federated political structure after World War II, which made regional media organization a virtual necessity. The rejection of Stalinist conceptions of "nationalism" in the early 1950s further accentuated this trend, because multilingual populations demanded programming in their own tongues.

The regime's popularity at home in turn provided the foundation for the country's redefinition of Marxist socialism. Without it, the governmental information hierarchy would not have given way to media cooperatives, which developed increased organizational autonomy in the transition period. Finally, Yugoslavia's need for asserting and protecting its national independence constituted the framework for assessing internal questions of journalistic freedom. Leninist press theory gave way to a modified outlook of media responsibility, which ultimately gave rise to a wholly new Titoist theory of social responsibility in the 1960s.

During the transition period this theory was ill-defined and full of contradictions, placing the media in a dilemma not of their own making. By the end of the decade they enjoyed a reasonable degree of organizational autonomy, but were given no real mandate by the party to report divergent opinions. Only economic and cultural matters, when these were considered essential or convenient, could be relatively freely reported by the media. Throughout the 1950s they continued to lack trained journalists who could "think for themselves" and thus challenge interpretations emanating from the top. Consequently the transition media had to fulfill two seemingly incompatible functions: they transmitted political information as interpreted by the top, and at the same time encouraged economic and cultural comment as seen from the bottom.

Since the party at the time was primarily interested in carrying on ideological warfare with the Soviet Union, questions of the extent to which it could and should interfere with and mold all information were never clearly enunciated and were generally left to the vagaries of international conditions and chance. Such a setup created built-in frictions between the government and the media about the amount of freedom of expression to be allowed in the cultural and political streams. Especially in crisis situations, like the Djilas affair and the Hungarian Revolution, indirect censorship was reimposed in both, sometimes through Tanjug channels handing down the official foreign policy line, sometimes by more drastic measures, such as dismissing editors of literary journals who had a too independent outlook.

At mid-century, then, the Yugoslav media were still struggling for greater autonomy. It is important to note that the possibilities for expression were nevertheless far greater than in other eastern European countries. Generally speaking, restrictions on economic and cultural information were rare, but unorthodox political comment did occasionally come under attack. On the credit side, the same period witnessed the burgeoning cultural freedom reflected in such literary journals as *Delo* in Belgrade, *Krugovi* in Zagreb, and *Beseda* in Ljubljana. The writers' struggle against the official art doctrine of "socialist realism" helped the media not only to acquire greater autonomy over their own internal affairs but also to ultimately redefine the role of the journalist. After World War II, the artist was called upon to be a Leninist "engineer of the soul."[39] By the late 1950s, he began to see himself both as a critic of established social values and as an individual who desired to express himself in whatever style he chose. The same change is mirrored in the Yugoslav journalists' search for a new identity, which is more professional than political. Changes in legal statutes and in press ideology were to make this transformation a firmer reality in the following decade, which will be the focus of the next chapter.

---

1 See Karl W. Deutsch, "Social Mobilization and Political Development," pp. 582-603; and Wilbur Schramm, *Mass Media and National Development*. Also see Richard Applebaum, *Theories of Social Change*, Chapter 6.

2 Lucian W. Pye, *Communications and Political Development*.

3 Richard Fagan, "Mass Media Growth: A Comparison of Communist and Other Countries." pp. 563-568.

4 See John Kautsky, "Communism and the Comparative Study of Development," p. 14.

5 Chalmers Johnson, *Change in Communist Systems*, Chapter 1.

6 A system outlook alerts the investigator to the complexities and roughly approximate nature of plotting change, and "political culture" refers to a combination of a country's ethnic and religious characteristics mentioned in Chapter 1 and to its political style.

7 Neil J. Smelser, "Notes on the Methodology of Comparative Analysis of Economic Activity," pp. 7-21.

8 See Mihailo Bjelica, *200 Godina jugoslovenske štampe*, pp. 201-211.

9 For further details on the partisan war consult Fitzroy MacLean, *Tito: The Man Who Defied Hitler and Stalin;* see also F. W. D. Deakin, *The Embattled Mountain;* Jorjo Tadić, "Ten Years of Yugoslav Historiography, 1945-1955."

10 There are many accounts of the AVNOJ meeting. One of the most complete, including the original documents, is Slobodan Nešović, *Prvo i drugo zasjedanje AVNOJA;* and for a detailed account of foreign press coverage of the partisan struggle, consult his *Inostranstvo i nova Jugo-*

slavija 1941-1945. This book traces world coverage, especially in the United States, Great Britain, and the Soviet Union.
11 George W. Hoffman and Fred W. Neal, *Yugoslavia and the New Communism,* p. 86.
12 Vladimir Ilich Lenin, *Collected Works,* Vol. I, pp. 389-390.
13 Ivko Pustišek, "Radio i televizija u Jugoslaviji: snažno sredstvo informisanja," pp. 10-11.
14 Moša Pijade as quoted in International Press Institute, *The Press in Authoritarian Countries,* p. 122.
15 It is difficult to find adequate and complete data on the press in monarchical Yugoslavia. Among available sources are Bjelica, *200 godina,* pp. 140, 160-165; also Vuk Dragović, *Srpska štampa izmedju dva rata.* For press beginnings there are Jovan Skerlić, *Istorijski pregled srpske štampe 1791-1911;* J. Lakatoš, *Hrvatska štampa, 1791-1911;* Dejan Pejanović, *Stampa Bosne i Hercegovine;* D. D. Vuksan, *Pregled štampe u Crnoj Gori 1834-1934;* Ivo Lapajne, *Razvojne smeri slovenskega novinarstva;* and Josip Horvat, *Povijest novinstva Hrvatske.* For greater details on the names, dates, and places where partisan papers were published throughout the war consult Vojno Istorijski Institut, *Bibliografija izdanja u Narodno Oslobodilačkom Ratu, 1941-1945.*
16 Fran Vatoveć, *The Development of the Slovene and Yugoslav Periodical Journalism,* p. 85.
17 "Grafički prikaz tiraža dnevnih listova," p. 15.
18 Radivoje Marković, "The Development of Radio and Television in Yugoslavia: From August 1904 to the Present Day," pp. 123-125.
19 Bjelica, *200 Godina,* p. 226.
20 Yugoslav Institute of Journalism, *Press, Radio, Television, Film in Yugoslavia, 1961,* p. 7.
21 France Vreg, "Open and Closed Communication Systems," p. 8.
22 For a succinct version of the reasons for the Cominform break, consult Phyllis Auty, "Yugoslavia's International Relations (1945-1965)," pp. 154-202.
23 George Macesich, "Major Trends in the Post War Economy of Yugoslavia," pp. 203-236.
24 Franz Kempers, "Freedom of Information and Criticism in Yugoslavia," p. 9.
25 For a detailed analysis of Yugoslav ideology, consult George Zaninovich, "The Yugoslav Variation on Marx," pp. 285-315.
26 Macesich, "Major Trends," p. 207.
27 Carter R. Bryan, "The Press System of Yugoslavia: Communism with a Difference," pp. 291-299.
28 Yugoslav Institute of Journalism, *Press, Radio,* p. 21.
29 International Press Institute, *The Press in Authoritarian Countries,* p. 124.
30 Milutin Bogosavljević, *The Economy of Yugoslavia,* p. 76.
31 UNESCO, *Basic Facts and Figures,* pp. 39, 138.
32 Marković, "Development of Radio and Television," pp. 106-131.
33 Zhdanov was a member of the Soviet Central Committee who in the 1940s initiated literary purges against those people in the arts and culture who did not follow the socialist realist line.
34 For a detailed discussion of writers' contributions to cultural liberalization, especially the "modernist-realist debate," consult Sveta Lukić, *Contemporary Yugoslav Literature: A Socio-Political Approach,* pp. 13-19.
35 Milovan Djilas, *Razmišljanja o raznim pitanjima,* pp. 46-47.
36 The implications of the Djilas case for freedom of expression in Yugoslavia will be more fully explored in the last chapter.
37 Jugoslovenski institut za novinarstvo, *Štampa, radio, televizija, film, u Jugoslaviji, 1964,* p. 22.
38 Tito, *Naša Štampa,* 1971, p. 15.
39 See Gertrude Joch Robinson, "The New Yugoslav Writer: A Socio-Political Portrait," pp. 185-197.

CHAPTER 3

Balkan Mavericks, 1962-75

In contrast to the first political crisis resulting from Yugoslavia's 1948 Cominform expulsion, the second great reversal affecting information organization and filtering processes was economic. It grew primarily out of the myriad of contradictions inherent in the country's conversion of its command economy. The three clearest contradictions are: the need for concerted action in abandoning economic controls; the new planning requirements of a mixed market; and the power rearrangements entailed in the ascendance of local League hierarchies. All of these sociopolitical changes, as shall be seen, provided a radically new set of challenges to which the press and broadcasting had to adapt throughout the 1960s.

From Federation to Confederation

Economic evidence indicates that by 1961 the halfway measures introduced to convert under-developed Yugoslavia from a "command economy" of the Soviet stripe to a "socialist market economy" had largely run their course. From 1952 to 1960, national income increased at an average annual rate of about 10 percent,[1] but inflation had taken on dangerous proportions. In addition, administrative tampering so distorted the half-hearted market mechanisms introduced earlier that it was difficult to assess the true value of inputs. In over-simplified terms, the post-1961 dilemma facing Yugoslav decision-makers was whether to have a market, however imperfect, or to have restrictions that would ultimately lead back to a fully planned and centralized economy.

Given the difficulties of decentralizing, it is no wonder that many economists and party members hesitated about what to do. As Grossman notes, "effective decentralization in a centrally administered economy can take place only when carried out on a very broad front all at once, which requires intervention from higher quarters and calls for big political battles. Centralization, however, can and often does proceed in little steps, virtually unnoticed but important in aggregate impact.''[2]

In the end, the Croatian and Slovenian factions of the League of Communists representing the economically developed parts of the country decided that the big plunge to greater decentralization must be taken to ensure continued economic growth and competitiveness on international markets. They opted for a far-reaching economic reform in 1965 which devalued the local currency and introduced the legal mechanisms transferring most economic decision-making to factories and enterprises. This move ultimately strengthened the principle of self-management which had been on the books for the preceding ten years. While it is beyond the scope of this discussion to detail the political battles ensuing from this course of action, it is important to point out that the freeing of well over 60 percent of the total market from restrictive legislation, and the shrinking of central investment funds, drastically liberalized the economic climate and permitted press, radio, and television stations, like other industries, to seek funds for expansion in banks all over the country.

The second great contradiction, the impossible task of running a market economy from the center, also found a partial solution at this time. It required, as Hondius notes, a re-interpretation of the legal rights and capabilities of Yugoslavia's six constituent republics.[3] Three sets of constitutional amendments in 1967, 1968, and 1971 introduced legal machinery which facilitated the decentralization of economic planning and transformed the country from a quasi-federation into a genuine confederation, in which republican or states' rights were greatly strengthened.[4] As a result, the federation's control over joint financing of economic projects, over state security, over central funds, and over relations with foreign countries was to be shared with the constituent republics. In addition, the Chamber of Nationalities, dealing with republican equality, received equal status in the Assembly. Never again was the majority of foreign currency earnings to be handed over to a central bank and foreign contacts to be concentrated in the nation's capital. Moreover, Ranković's unexpected ouster indicated that there was not again to be a centralized security service or an army which was dominated by one nationality.

For Yugoslavia's mass media these developments reinforced the local or regional organization of newspapers and broadcast stations within the confines of the six republics, an arrangement originally necessitated by the country's multinational population that speaks many different languages. As shall be seen, it also led to increased local programming which ultimately propelled the media into increasingly bitter controversies about regional autonomy and ''national identity.''

A third and final contradiction requiring solution at the time concerned the role of the country's League of Communists. One writer describes the League's dilemma in redefining its role during the 1960s in this way: ''In a sense the relationship between the Communist party and the decentralized system resembles a marriage in which neither partner can live with or without the other. Instead of remaining an infallible supreme mediator of group interests and a center of unity keeping economic and administrative decentralization within bounds, the party . . . is in the midst of a desperate attempt to save itself through radical reform.''[5] Such a reform would require pluralistic decision-making not only in party councils but in state and economic matters as well. It could ultimately lead, as Djilas predicted, to the founding of rival parties to enunciate conflicting points of view.

How did this impasse arise? In theory, the party is the vanguard and inspiration of social developments. In fact, it has used the mechanisms of self-management and decentralization to mask the continued usurpation of power by top officials. According to the latest statistics, the League of Communists had 1,146,086 members in 1968, not more than 9 percent of the eligible population aged eighteen years and over.[6] Despite this, between 80 percent and 90 percent of the most active members of the political public, except for a few dissident intellectuals, belong to the League, according to an International Study of Opinion Makers compiled by the Belgrade Institute for Social Research and Columbia's Bureau of Applied Research. League members hold top legislative, federal, administrative, mass party, communication, and economic positions.

Until the early 1960s, this party was a monolithic organization subscribing to the principle of "democratic centralism." But not longer. By the middle of the decade, under the pressures of ethnicity and economic decentralization, the League subdivided into six republican party hierarchies. These were further split into two camps advocating different economic policies. Here the northeastern republics favored productivity, while the southeastern ones wanted equalization criteria applied in future economic planning. One observer noted "the Yugoslav Communist Party has a federal structure similar to the state itself. Until the mid-sixties, all crucial decisions were made by the federal party center in Belgrade. Yet the republican leaders all along had a machine and influence of their own. In other words, within the countrywide hierarchy there were regional or republican hierarchies. . . . The dynamics of economic decentralization steadily increased the importance of the republican parties, which in turn broadened their popular support to the extent that they were standing up for the interests of their nations.''[7]

The League of Communists' subsequent trials and tribulations in adjusting to decentralization and power fragmentation are vividly illustrated by three unsuccessful reorganizations of its top leadership in six years. It all began with the 1966 ouster of the Internal Security Minister, which led the Central Committee to delegate executive authority to a thirty-five–member Presidium, assisted by a still smaller Executive Committee, to protect the organization from fractional domination.[8] This setup was temporary, because Yugoslavia's headlong rush toward a market economy raised a host of new coordination problems. By the end of the decade at the IX Congress of the League of Communists of Yugoslavia another change had to be instituted. This time the aim was to restore the balance between decentralized control and the authority of the party.[9] Consequently, in 1969 the Central Committee was abolished and replaced by a Permanent Conference of thirty-two representatives from all six regional Communist Leagues. This large body was empowered to elect a smaller Executive Bureau which originally had fifteen members and was headed by President Tito.[10] After the Croatian crisis in 1971, however, it became apparent that this group also was incapable of coordinating internecine power plays, and membership was therefore cut once again in an effort to return to a pattern of centralized decision-making.

For republican politicians intent on enlarging their local support, the mass media grew in importance as Yugoslav politics became increasingly pluralistic. However, since papers and radio stations were organizationally autonomous, as in many western countries, such influence could not be officially wielded through the party hierarchy. Instead, informal pressures and arrangements were called for. How well these succeeded in co-opting the republican media is an empirical question which is amply illustrated by the involvement of the Croatian press and television in the 1971 nationalities' crisis and the subsequent reshuffling of top media and party officials. This point will be explored in the final section of this chapter.

The Independent Media, 1952-70

Three types of adaptation to the changed sociopolitical setting are evident in media organization and processing throughout the 1960s. Table 2 in Chapter 2 summarizes these under the headings of organizational, content, and filtering adaptations. To facilitate the presentation of this complex material, each of these changes will be treated separately and will be related to three new pieces of media legislation which redefined the framework for Yugoslav media structure and function during the third, or independent, media period, 1962 to 1970.

The first new media legislation was the 1960 Law of the Press and Other Media of Information, which for the first time guaranteed freedom of the press by explicitly ruling out censorship in the form of previous notification. It also specified eight areas where information abuses would not be tolerated. For the media this new press law and the absence of official censorship provide the broad practical context in which news is selected today. Yugoslavia's prosecutor's office, in contrast to practice in the Soviet Union, does not have the right to prejudge media content. Instead it must wait until a controversial article is published or a film is premiered. Only after publication is prosecution possible. The result is that informal constraints, widely known to newsmen all over the world, take on greater importance and better explain the present relationship between the party and the media. The exact way in which such indirect control functions will be reflected in the following chapter's case study of Tanjug news agency operations.

Furthermore the new law specifically provides for rectification and grants the injured person wide possibilities of answering false charges. This is quite atypical of other socialist press laws. It also specifies that damage suits are to be tried in open court, as the Mihajlov case was in Zadar. Here his proposal to found a new political party was considered unconstitutional. Another section of the law guarantees accessibility of information sources, a very important provision, since local governmental and industrial representatives have been notoriously unwilling to submit to media scrutiny. The precise extent to which journalists are able to dig up political and economic facts in present-day Yugoslavia will be covered in a discussion on professionalization in Chapter 5.

Finally, contrary to practice in most socialist countries, importation of the foreign press is permitted without hindrance or limitation. The *New York Times, Herald Tribune, Time, Newsweek,* and other selected professional magazines are readily available in the bookstores of major cities, the only qualification being that the importer must have his name listed on the foreign trade register.[11] There are foreign information centers, and the American, British, and French libraries are well patronized.

In summary, it is important to stress that the press law guides the individual communicator negatively in decreeing which topics are taboo, but it also provides positive formats for disagreeing with official views. Such methods have largely emerged from trial and error. One informant told about the *Borba* correspondent who failed to honor the provision against speaking negatively of chiefs of state, regardless of their political shadings. Here a party man had had the audacity to describe Voroshilov, then president of the Soviet Union Presidium and a visitor in Belgrade, as a "drunkard." With a chuckle, the admission was also volunteered that this information, couched in less abusive language, could have been injected as a political commentary, which, unlike a straight news release, can differ from the government position.

The second legislative document was the 1963 Constitution, which laid the foundation for liberalizing the media's access to news sources. It not only introduced the citizens' right to know but drastically changed the role of the Yugoslav journalist. Instead of being a mere recorder of events, he is today expected to function, like his western counterpart, as an interpreter and critic. In this document many sections are in principle broader than the parallel provisions of the United States Bill of Rights. They guarantee equality before the law, the right to vote, the right to privacy of domicile, to inheritance, and to religious freedom. Beyond the United States document, Yugoslavia also includes the right to employment and to minimum personal income. Thus job security on the one hand and work incentives on the other are provided in principle. The newspapers and other information units are meeting these promises or expectations in various ways.

For the present discussion, the key sections of the 1963 Constitution are Article 34, which states the "right to be informed," and Article 40, which describes "freedom of the press and other media of information." Because they are not well known, they are given below in full:

> *Article 34:* In order to achieve social self government, the citizen shall have the right to be informed about the work of the representative bodies and their organs, the organs of social self-government, the organizations carrying on affairs of public concern, and in particular, in the working organizations in which he realizes his interest, the right to be informed about material and financial conditions, the fulfillment of plans, and business, with the obligation that he keeps business and other secrets. The right to examine the work of state organs and organs of social self-government, and the organizations that discharge affairs of public concern, and to express his opinion on their work.

The citizen is supposed to put this right to information into practice by using the mass media to inform and express himself. Article 40 states:

> Freedom of the press and other media of information, freedom of association, freedom of speech and public expression, freedom of meeting and other public assemblage shall be guaranteed.
>
> The citizens shall have the right to express and publish their opinions through the media of information, to inform themselves through the media of information, to publish newspapers and other publications, and to disseminate information by other means of communication.
>
> These freedoms and rights should not be used by anyone to overthrow the foundations of the socialist democratic order determined by the Constitution, to endanger the peace, international cooperation on terms of equality, of the independence of the country, to disseminate national, racial, or religious hatred or intolerance or to incite to crime or in any manner that offends public decency. . . .
>
> The press, radio, and television shall truthfully and objectively inform the public and publish and broadcast the opinions and information of organs, organizations, and citizens which are of interest to public information.[12]

In a political system in which the press has in the past functioned mainly as a conveyer belt of handout information from the leadership to the people, these new rights of access to information created a definite stir. That the leadership was and has continued to be serious about its democratization of governmental processes became evident in 1963, when all debates of federal bodies were opened to the press. Sincerity was still more obvious when journalists were actually encouraged to present both sides of issues discussed at such meetings. Deliberations of state and local bodies, however, especially the financial status of individual enterprises, are still largely inaccessible to Yugoslav journalists, who complain about this in many of their professional meetings.

The third law modifying Yugoslav media organization and function was promulgated in 1965. It substantially redefined the goals, responsibilities, means of financing, and management of radio and television. Article 2 of the Basic Law on Radio Broadcasting Institutions states:

Radio broadcasting institutions inform the public on the events and developments concerning all spheres of life in Yugoslavia and abroad, initiate discussions on matters of public interest and broadcast opinions of citizens, organizations and public organs. . . . make and broadcast cultural, artistic, educational, entertainment and other programmes with the view to satisfying cultural requirements and other interests of citizens.

Radio broadcasting institutions shall care for the building, development and maintenance of the radio transmitting network and for securing the material means required for advancement of radio broadcasting programmes. Radio broadcasting institutions shall autonomously draw up and broadcast their programmes. No notification or permission are required for transmission.[13]

The important points here are that as a result of the economic reform, taxation levels were dropped, and all enterprises, including the media, acquired control over 70 percent of their total profits.[14] For the first time papers, as well as radio and television stations, were able to set subscription fees based on service costs and to arrange prices for special educational or other transmissions which were commissioned by the government. In addition, under the new law, stations must finance all projects out of internal funds or through bank loans, available on a competitive basis.

To make this possible, the new law decreed that radio institutions were exempt from paying certain taxes on income as well as from interest payments on their operational funds which were levied on factories. They were also permitted to increase advertising to supplement their financial coffers. In the 1960s, therefore, broadcast institutions had three sources of income: subscriptions, advertising, and government funds for special services. In contrast to the 1950s, 1971 budgets indicated that radio and television license fees contributed 73 percent, advertising 19 percent, and the government only 8 percent of the total.[15] These figures corroborate the extensive financial independence broadcasting stations enjoy in contemporary Yugoslavia, which as shall be seen, also permits them to program quite independently.

Organizational Adaptations

The three types of adaptations arising from these pieces of legislation, as mentioned earlier, include changes in media organization, content, and filtering. To substantiate the claim that the Yugoslav mass media have indeed acquired increased autonomy during the 1960s, it is necessary to clarify what is meant by this term. For the present "autonomy" has the usual dictionary meaning and refers to the "power or right of self-government." Since such a right to "self-government" has been on the Yugoslav books for the past decade, in the form of the Workers' Self-Management Act, the present investigation will focus on changes which have transformed the right into an *actual* media power during the 1960s. These included the power to elect their own top management, to plan and finance their own production and expansion, and to organize themselves into six regional rather than one central network.

Throughout the transition period, as noted earlier, most media directorships and top editorial posts continued to be filled with party appointees. Belgrade's *Borba,* the central organ of the Socialist Alliance, had Vukašun Mičunović, an ex-general and tried and true member of the Montenegrin central committee, at the helm. Its rival, *Politika,* long under the auspices of the founding Ribnikar family, was headed by Mitja Miljković, who became ambassador to Greece in 1958.

Not until the early 1960s did the workers' councils of the mass media acquire the right to elect their own directors, a practice already followed in Yugoslavia's factories for a decade. As a consequence, newspapers and broadcast stations for the first time selected men who were professional journalists rather than politicians to guide their development. *Borba*'s director, Slobodan Glumać, and *Vjesnik*'s Božidar Novak illustrate this shift. The former studied law, spent part of the war in a concentration camp, and then either edited or worked as a foreign correspondent for various newspapers before joining *Borba.*[16] Božidar Novak, *Vjesnik*'s director and chief editor from 1958 to 1971, joined the party and the national liberation fight in 1941 on the island of Hvar. After 1945 he became editor of the major Dalmation paper before joining *Vjesnik* in Zagreb, where he was also a member of the League's Commission on the Press and the city's governing body.[17] A similar shift toward professional rather than purely political leadership has been evident in Yugoslavia's national news agency, Tanjug.

Increased organizational autonomy is documented not only by the change in top media leadership but also by increased financial independence, which led to a concern for plant modernization, cost accounting, and increased efficiency. In the 1960s publishers accomplished greater efficiency by two methods, horizontal integration and increased utilization of their printing plants. For the first time, book publishers and newspapers combined publishing, printing, and selling activities and began to do printing jobs for others. Between 1963 and 1968, eight book publishers folded and the ten largest, producing 80 percent of Yugoslavia's book output, merged and purchased sales outlets and printing presses.[18] Newspapers reduced costs by publishing more popular magazines to offset press losses or by issuing joint publications to enlarge the otherwise fragmented and relatively small reader market. Zagreb's newspaper publishing house, *Vjesnik,* for instance, in addition to its morning and evening dailies, publishes a weekly *Vjesnik U Srijedu,* with a heavy cultural emphasis, and eight popular or illustrated magazines covering television news, sports, recreation, and homemaking.

The same goes for Ljubljana's *Večer* and for Belgrade's *Politika.* The first three of its seven new publications — *Politikin Zabavnik* for children, *Illustrovana Politika* for the whole family, and *NIN,* a weekly news digest like *Newsweek* — tapped potential new audiences as early as 1952. The other four appeared after 1965 when personal incomes had tripled. They cover fashion, sports, television and film, and automobiles. The last two are jointly published, one with Radio Belgrade and the other a translation of a Slovenian magazine.

The profitability of consolidation is attested to by evidence in Table 5, as well as by a private communication from the enterprise general secretary. Table 5 shows a one-fifth cut in press circulation between 1964 and 1970 from 10 million to about 8.6 million copies. During the same period, though, magazine circulation more than doubled from 3.5 to 8.2 million, a rise that demonstrates the profitability of special interest over general political publishing. *Politika's* financial secretary in a private communication makes the same point when he notes that newspaper production provides only one-half and the printing of fifteen magazines the second half of the enterprise's 316 million dinar gross income in 1970.

In broadcasting, increased organizational autonomy led to the expansion of facilities, especially in television, rather than to station rationalization. Doubtlessly this expansion had to do with a continued demand for broadcast service. Table 5 illustrates that the purchase of radio sets almost tripled in the 1960s. The sale of television sets went up by a staggering 80 percent. When broadcast stations became organizationally autonomous and financially solvent, two trends emerged: first, there was a boom in the establishment of local radio stations in small communities; second, already established republican broadcast stations emphasized the need for technical improvements. Between 1961 and 1970 local stations grew elevenfold from fourteen to 141 (see Table 4,

Table 5
Media Growth in 1960s

	No.	1959 Circulation in Millions	No.	1964 Circulation in Millions	No.	1970 Circulation in Millions
Total newspapers	778	6.01	1,092	10.06	1,466	8.67
Daily	20	1.37	22	1.71	25	1.72
Weekly	133		190		164	
Monthly	217		427		524	
Other	408		453		754	
Total magazines	775	2.36	944	3.80	1,401	8.24
Fortnightly	26		37		88	
Monthly	338		355		401	
Quarterly	122		153		211	
Periodically	281		399		701	
Radio	1,309,158	14 persons: 1 receiver	2,519,954	7 persons: 1 receiver	3,364,837	6 persons: 1 receiver
Television	12,000	3,518 persons: 1 receiver	393,438	49 persons: 1 receiver	1,798,462	10 persons: 1 receiver

SOURCE: Newspapers and magazines: (1959) *Statistički godišnjak SFRJ* (Beograd, 1964), XI, p. 329. (1964) *Ibid.* (Beograd, 1969), XVI, p. 305. (1970) *Ibid.* (Beograd, 1970), XVIII, p. 309. Radio and television: *Jugoslovenski radiotelevizija godišnjak*, 1971/72, p. 107. *Jugoslovenski radiotelevizija godišnjak*, 1971/72, p. 112.

Chapter 2), severely crowding the country's shortwave spectrum, while the number of main stations remained the same.

As a consequence, such republican centers as Zagreb and Skopje decided to add mediumwave transmitters to ensure better reception at night. In addition, the main stations in Slovenia, Croatia, and Bosnia-Hercegovina required that their local stations affiliate into a network, and Serbia initiated a broadcast club. These moves were designed to supplement local broadcast fare and to improve program quality.[19] Between 1967 and 1974 larger and more sophisticated studios were built in the autonomous republic of Kosovo (Priština), as well as in Ljubljana and Sarajevo. The three remaining republican stations renovated existing facilities. The second television program was initiated with the 1972 Munich Olympics and is pioneering a limited number of Paal color broadcasts. Revenues for all of these improvements have come from increased license fees as well as from favorable loans from Yugoslavia's newly competitive banking institutions.

Regional organization, another adaptive result of Yugoslavia's mass media to the country's multinationalism and its shift to a market economy, is also amply demonstrated by press and broadcast statistics. While most socialist countries organize their newspapers from the center, transmitting vital information through the national press, Yugoslavia has only the two national dailies, Belgrade's *Borba,* supplying political and party points of view, and *Politika,* with a more cultural and diversified content. These papers in 1970 had a combined daily circulation of only 301,000 constituting as little as 21.6 percent of total daily circulations.[20] In Yugoslavia, in other words, the press of the national capital does not dominate the opinions of the rest of the country. Table 6 corroborates that there were nine daily papers in Serbia, seven in Croatia, three in Slovenia, and two each in Bosnia-Hercegovina and Macedonia; Montenegro had no daily. Regional papers provided 73.2 percent of the total yearly newspaper output and were thus the primary source of printed information for most Yugoslavs.

The same table also indicates that not all republics were equally well supplied with papers. The three most developed republics of Slovenia, Serbia, and Croatia have from four to six times as many papers per thousand population as the under-developed ones. These inequalities persist even if population density is taken into account. According to Table 6, Bosnia and Montenegro have approximately half the number of papers they would be entitled to if the papers were evenly distributed according to population. In the case of Bosnia the high illiteracy rate of 33 percent contributes to the scarcity of the press. In Montenegro the rugged terrain and lack of railroads hamper distribution. Since papers are shipped from republican centers to smaller localities by train or truck, communities not connected by rail or road are at a grave disadvantage.

Regional autonomy is even more evident in the organization of broadcasting with its two-tiered division and in television programming, which stresses regional, cultural, and political points of view. The author of a comparative study notes:

> Broadcast leadership, owing to a variety of distinctive cultures, nationalities and languages, has encouraged the development of regional and local systems with indigenous programming. However, administrative machinery has been set up to facilitate program exchange. The PTT provided transmission links by which the main stations share broadcasts with one another and with stations in other countries. Some stations have built their own high-quality connections for cooperative programming and improvement of reception in certain areas.[21]

Eight main regional stations in the six republics, and in the two autonomous provinces of Vojvodina and Kosovo that are part of Serbia, provide Yugoslavs with radio broadcasting from eighteen to twenty-four hours daily. Since the late 1950s they have based program content on local listener surveys.

Another mark of accelerated regionalism is the startling proliferation of local stations from forty-one in 1965 to four times that number at the beginning of the 1970s. Such a boom vividly indicates the rapid progress in radio decentraliza-

Table 6
Regional Distribution of Press in 1969

1. Newspapers	Percentage of Total Pop.	Daily	Weekly [a]	Other	Total	According to population if evenly distributed
Serbia	43.7	9	92	529	630	601
Croatia	20.4	7	34	292	333	281
Bosnia-Hercegovina	18.0	2	19	133	154	248
Slovenia	7.9	3	18	136	157	109
Macedonia	7.4	2	11	70	83	102
Montenegro	2.5	0	3	16	19	35
Total SFSR	99.9 [b]	23	177	1,176	1,376	1,376

2. Magazines	Weekly + biweekly	Monthly	Other	Total	According to population if evenly distributed
Serbia	22	183	341	546	519
Croatia	16	95	201	312	242
Bosnia-Hercegovina	1	17	49	67	214
Slovenia	12	76	110	198	94
Macedonia	2	19	31	52	38
Montenegro	0	3	9	12	30
Total SFSR	53	393	741	1,187	1,187

SOURCE: *Statistički godišnjak, SFRJ* (Beograd, 1970), XVII, p. 296.

[a] Estimated figures.
[b] Less than 100 percent due to rounding.

tion, which facilitates grass-roots democracy and regional differences on the one hand, but leads to frequency crowding and inferior programming on the other. Many of these local stations broadcast merely an hour or two a day and a bit longer on weekends. Thus they function as supplementary information sources, particularly for small communities.

In television, too, economic liberalization and increased republican autonomy have accelerated growth and regional programming. Growth is documented by three interlinked trends: rapidly increasing numbers of set owners, network extension, and increased program time. Figure 4 and Table 7 vividly illustrate the very rapid diffusion of television that Yugoslavia underwent in the 1960s. During this time, television grew from an experimental luxury providing four hours of programming for privileged set owners to a mass medium watched by over 90 percent of the total population. Table 7 indicates, additionally, that there was one set for every 2.5 households in 1972, a figure that contrasts sharply with the one set for every 154 households in 1960.

Explosive growth in numbers of television sets was accompanied by a doubling of the network. Now the three original studios in the richer and more populous parts of the country (Zagreb, Ljubljana, and Belgrade) were joined by television stations in the less-developed southeastern republics, Macedonia, Bosnia-Hercegovina, and Montenegro. The latecomers, Sarajevo and Titograd, still rely primarily on joint programming from the three original stations,

Table 7
Television Growth 1957-74
(in thousands)

Year	Number of sets	Growth in Percentage	Inhabitants per TV Set
1957	4		4,465
1958	6	50	3,003
1959	12	100	3,517
1960	29	141.1	618
1961	61	106.9	302
1962	126	104.9	149
1963	211	67.8	90
1964	393	85.8	49
1965	577	46.7	33
1966	777	34.6	25
1967	1,002	29.0	19
1968	1,298	22.8	15
1969	1,542	18.8	13
1970	1,798	16.6	11
1971	2,057	14.8	10
1972	2,353	14.2	10
1973	2,544	8.0	8
1974	2,784	9.4	7

SOURCE: *Jugoslovenski radiotelevizija godišnjak, SFRJ* (1971-72), p. 112. *Statistički godišnjak, SFJR,* (1975), p. 341.

although they originate their own daily news and some entertainment shows. These six stations, like radio, are independently organized and financed by republican licensing fees, ranging from twenty to thirty dinars ($1.50 to $2.00) monthly. According to 1971 financial statements, subscription fees cover approximately 80 percent of television costs. Advertising crammed into a half-hour slot during prime time supplies the rest of the budget.

Organizational evidence leads to the conclusion that Yugoslavia today, in contrast to other communist countries, has a broadcast system which is neither nationally organized nor nationally programmed. There is no pyramidal hierarchy centering in the state capital which dominates the decision-making and programming of the constituent networks. Instead, the six republics are equal and organizationally independent, deciding autonomously what programs their audiences want to watch and listen to. In fact, Yugoslav autonomy, growing out of deep historical rivalries and a phobia against recurring bureaucratic centralization, goes so far that the republican stations cannot even agree on the desirability of fostering a "sense of national unity" among their people. CBC's mandate in multinational Canada is unthinkable in the country of the South Slavs. All they are willing to concede is that they need an umbrella organization to coordinate practical problems of program development and scheduling.

Consequently, the Community of Yugoslav Broadcasting Stations (Jugoslovenski Radio-Televizija) operates not like a control but like a trade association in the West. It keeps its eye on members' interests in three statutory areas: (1) the development of the broadcast network so that total coverage will be assured for all citizens, (2) the facilitation of cooperation between Yugoslav stations and international broadcasting organizations, and (3) the working out of practical details involved in preparing and broadcasting joint radio and television programs.

It is extremely difficult to evaluate the pros and cons of regional broadcast autonomy for freedom of expression and national survival in Yugoslavia. Three considerations come to mind. First, it has been repeatedly noted that the Yugoslav citizen is able to hear, see, and read a much greater variety of opinions, both political and social, than any other member of a communist state. Second, it is also true that regional autonomy encourages politicians in the Yugoslav system to discuss controversial issues in televised panels or live radio hotlines in order to justify their actions to constituents. Who would have thought that a high-ranking communist leader in the 1970s would discuss without false optimism such timely questions as the crisis in youth employment, rising prices, and reorganization of the party? A third and more problematical issue is the manner in which the selective strengthening of regional versus national points of view may undermine the political stability of multinational Yugoslavia in a crisis. An answer to this complex question will have to wait until the end of the book.

Content Adaptations

The shift from central to local funding, encouraging economic rationalization, also accelerated the trend toward more entertainment programming. This trend began in the transition period, when government financing began to dry up. Financial statistics throughout this period record that government sources contributed well over one-third of the budgets of newspapers and broadcast stations until 1959. In 1965, as has been seen, the new rules for broadcast stations substantially redefined the goals, responsibilities, financing, and management of radio and television, giving each enterprise control over up to 70 percent of its funds. In order to compete for and satisfy diverse audience interests, print and broadcasting during the decentralized period, according to media statistics, innovated new genres and focused increasingly on local and regional issues familiar to their diverse readers and listeners. Chief among these wholly new landmarks were the afternoon paper, consumer magazines, as well as television, with its quizzes and audience participation shows.

Afternoon papers started their existence with the country's switch to a seven-hour working day in the early 1960s. Among the original six were *Večerne Novosti* (Belgrade) and *Večernji List* (Zagreb), both founded in 1963. Ten years later these same six papers, which began with a combined daily circulation of 3,441, had mushroomed to 775,000 copies.[22] Their great popularity is further attested to by the fact that the largest and oldest paper, *Večerni Novosti,* has a daily circulation of 386,000, one-third again as many copies as its closest morning competitor, *Politika.*

The more entertaining content and breezier style of these papers are readily apparent in a comparative content analysis of Zagreb's morning *Vjesnik* and its afternoon *Večernji List.* Such a comparison shows that three-fifths of the former is devoted to "hard news," such as national, international, and economic information, while the tabloid-sized afternoon paper devotes only one-third of its total space to such news. In general, articles are shorter, spot news treatment predominates, and major space is devoted to cultural and film events, sports, ads, and photo coverage of pretty girls. Afternoon papers, in response to popular interest, are also written more flamboyantly. Their off-hand style and sexier content raised the hackles of some of the more conservative party forums, which have periodically accused the afternoon press of degrading public taste for monetary gain.

To determine the facts, Belgrade's Institute of Journalism (Institut za Novinarstvo) was commissioned to make a study of this "sensationalism" charge. Since the concept is difficult to define, researchers concentrated on both content and style of writing. Like the author, the institute concluded that the content was indeed different from the more serious and politically oriented morning press, but it also demonstrated that the afternoon press could not be accused of undermining public taste. Articles in these papers, the institute noted, "are most frequently about sport and recreation, economics, as well as 'innovations' in technology, art, science and medicine."[23] In general, local happenings were emphasized more than foreign events. Style of presentation was as serious as that in the morning papers. Researchers described it as mostly "factual-reportorial" and noted that it contained little editorializing and few opinions. "Sensationalism," defined as "opinionated reporting" according to the report, was more prevalent in weekly illustrated magazines filled with human interest stories, snippets of information, and disasters. The Institute of Journalism therefore concluded that the glossy weeklies did merit criticism, while the afternoon press seemed to be fulfilling its social function of informing and entertaining in a "non-sensational" way.

The second genre, special interest magazines, provides the most striking example of Yugoslavia's foray into consumerism. As mentioned earlier, rising standards of living and financial need led publishers to venture into magazine production to offset press losses. Today a Zagreb or Ljubljana newsstand looks as colorful as any in the West, and the magazines vie for the browser's attention, with glossy makeup and pictures of naked girls. Table 5 corroborates the diversification during the 1960s of weekly and fortnightly magazines which cater to such newly developing audiences as sports fans, car buffs, women, and children, all of whom have extra money to spend as a result of Yugoslavia's burgeoning economy. Weeklies grew by 25 percent and fortnightlies doubled in the span of ten years. When newspapers and journals declined toward the end of the decade because of price increases and increased competition from television, the popularity of magazines continued high and their circulation tripled.

In radio, where monthly subscription fees of about 50 cents a receiver provided 70 percent of a station's budget, diversification and the introduction of more popular program formats were also inevitable. In general, the trend has been to more entertainment and advertising in both the first and second programs. The third program, introduced in the late 1960s, appeals primarily to the urban intelligentsia.[24] An interview with radio Belgrade's chief editor elicited the fact that radio content is generally divided into approximately 60 percent music and 40 percent speech. In the early 1960s, the content of spoken programs was 50 percent politically informative, 38 percent culture, education, and entertainment, and 6 percent each economic news and advertising. Ten years later political programs had shrunk to 40 percent of the total time; variety shows, comedies, and quiz programs were satisfying some of the audience's craving for entertainment. Increased advertising time attested to a more affluent society. Advertising in radio accompanies individual programs, but it is bunched into a fifteen-minute slot on television. Imaginative animation and the latest hit tunes earn audience applause. A final illustration of the growing entertainment orientation of radio is Belgrade's station 202, started in 1969, which devotes over 80 percent of its program to popular music geared to the urban young. Its programs, interspersed with advertising and disc-jockey talk, sound much like any other pop music station in a large American or Canadian city.

Television innovation and its spectacularly fast diffusion through the 1960s is amply attested to by Figure 4, which indicates that there was only one set for every 618 inhabitants in 1960, while twelve years later in 1972 there was one set for every ten. Television, which started with four hours of evening programming, now provides approximately twenty hours of viewing daily. In addition, during the experimental period, half of all programs aired were foreign films; now over 60 percent of all television content is produced in Yugoslavia.[25] From the beginning, television has been more entertainment-oriented than radio, following content patterns established by countries such as Britain and Canada, rather than the Soviet Union. Like Canada's CBC or Britain's BBC, the Yugoslavs balance information and cultural uplift with solid entertainment. Interviews with television personnel reveal that information and current affairs constitute only 28 percent of the total schedule; cultural and popular shows take up 36 percent, education, 12 percent, sports, 10 percent, and commercials, the final 14 percent.

New genres like musicals, quizzes, audience participation shows, serials, and Eurovision imports chronicling sports and pop-culture festivals diversify program content today.[26] Between 1964 and 1969, satirical shows and quiz programs quadrupled, while the number of news and information reports barely doubled. Such popular serials as "Mr. Citizen" and "Relations" concentrate heavily on the satirical spoofing of Yugoslav society. Here, the human cost of the apartment shortage and shoddy house construction, bureaucratic favoritism, and ways of "sleeping" on the job are held up for public ridicule.

Figure 4. Cumulative Diffusion Curve for Television, 1957-72 (in millions of sets)

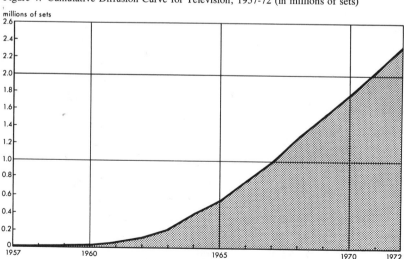

Source: *Statistički godišnjak Jugoslavije* (1973), p. 520.

Television dramas, which used to delve into the past, are now selecting contemporary themes often critical of the current scene. As a consequence, young writers flocked to television during the 1960s to earn extra income and comment on Yugoslav life with greater openness.

In conclusion it should be noted that the increasingly local and regional focus which marked Yugoslav programming from the decentralized period onward owed much of its impetus not only to the already mentioned cultural and historical differences of the population, but also to the regional power decentralization engendered by the constitutional amendments. As a result, the nationalities' issue tended to acquire renewed saliency. With decentralization of economic and political decision-making, Yugoslavs once again identified themselves primarily as Croats, Serbs, or Slovenes. This regional content focus is easily demonstrated in both print and broadcasting, but it is probably most striking in the new medium of television, where the joint television program originating from the three major studios gave way to cooperative regional broadcasting in the late 1960s. One informant noted that Zagreb today produces 65 percent of the shows going on the air in Croatia, while 27 percent originate in other Yugoslav studios and 8 percent come from abroad. In Slovenia and Macedonia this percentage is even higher, close to 90 percent of the total, because their audience speaks a language incomprehensible to the majority of Yugoslavs. However, the newer studios, such as those at Sarajevo and Titograd, which are still relatively understaffed, produce only about 30 percent of their own shows and rely on the joint program for the rest.

Filtering Adaptations

Turning now to an evaluation of changes in the filtering and distortion processes during the independent period, three points stand out most clearly. It appears, first of all, that controls over all types of filtering moved from the federal center to the republican periphery. Furthermore, these controls must now be exercised informally because the media have the right to select their own directors in addition to the top management. Moreover, there is a greater specification of the criteria to be applied to the filtering of political information.

As previously noted, the 1965 broadcasting act specified for the first time that the ''founder'' sponsoring a media enterprise would be subject to republican rather than federal laws and regulations. In the Yugoslav context such a ''founder'' is a sociopolitical organization, like the Socialist Alliance, the party, a trade union, or some other pressure group. Its job is to oversee the major policy line of a newspaper or radio station and to balance enterprise profit motives with considerations of social responsibility. With political decentralization throughout the 1960s these organizations were required to adapt to new state information laws and thus they fell under the influence of the republican rather than the federal state hierarchy. Politicians, consequently, paid increasing attention to their home media, using them as platforms for espousing divergent points of view on many issues.

The informal nature of filtering control, the second great change during the transition period, was not only specified in the 1960 Law of the Press, which abrogated overall censorship in the form of prior notification, but also reinforced by enterprise autonomy over directorial selection. It has been already noted that this led to the election of directors with greater professional abilities than when they were appointed by the League's Central Committee. In Tanjug, journalists with party affiliations took the helm in the mid-1960s, devoting, as Chapter 4 will show, the majority of their time to information processing rather than party tasks.

Greater specification of filtering criteria for political information, finally, was defined by Article 52 of the 1960 Law of the Press, which detailed eight areas where information abuses were considered intolerable. These include the:

> dissemination of printed matter containing material which (1) constitutes a criminal offense against the people, the State or against the armed forces of Yugoslavia; (2) revealing or disseminating false reports or allegations causing public alarm and menacing public peace and order; (3) revealing military secrets (4) or confidential information or documents that are an official or economic secret of special importance to the community. The law also prohibits (5) propaganda inciting to aggression, (6) acts which directly disturb the maintenance and development of friendly relations between Yugoslavia and other States or (7) cause harm to the honor and reputation of the peoples, their supreme representative bodies, the President of the Republic, and similar injuries to foreign peoples and . . . (8) printed matter which constitutes a violation of public decency.[27]

During the 1960s, most of the friction between the regime and individual communicators centered on alleged violations of points 1 and 4, which are still too broadly defined and thus subject to erratic interpretations. In addition, the sections on friendly relations with foreign countries (point 6) and respect for top officials (point 7) have been troublesome, as their interpretation has always depended on the current temper of diplomatic relations with the Soviet Union.[28]

Throughout the period the two other information streams, economic and cultural, remain relatively undistorted, though by 1969 to 1970, with the reheating of nationalist tempers and a delicate foreign situation after the Soviet invasion of Czechoslovakia, the published expressions of writers, philosophers, and students once again came under closer scrutiny. Between June, 1968, and December, 1969, there were forty cases of court interventions against offending texts, constituting more harassment, according to one observer, than in the previous eight years put together.[29]

Examples of such harassment included Zoran Gluščević's near jailing for an anti-Soviet article, "Variations on a Prague Spring," which appeared on the anniversary of the Czechoslovak invasion in 1969; attacks on and reduced publication of the plays and novels of such Belgrade writers as Bora Ćosić, Dragislav Mijailović, and others who were exploring the darker aspects of contemporary Yugoslav life; and the banning of Dušan Makevejev's film, *WR: Or the Mysteries of the Organism*. The latter, a coproduction with a German company, spoofed both the Stalinist and free-enterprise ideologies of the Soviet Union and the United States. Members of the Serbian Philosophical Society (Srpsko filozofsko društvo), which held a well-attended public debate on "socialism and culture" in Belgrade to discuss the issue of artistic freedom, also came under scathing public attack for supposedly having organized an "anti-Communist opposition gathering."[30]

Though an uneasy balance presently exists, it is clear that the League's increased sensitivity to cultural criticism was part and parcel of a larger shift in outlook during the fourth and final media period, which stresses the need for increased social control over all means of expression in Yugoslavia. A League document noted "as the area of freer activity of journalists, publicists, and other creators expands with the development of self government, so the need increases to strengthen their conscientious social responsibility for the accuracy and socialist orientation of the public word."[31]

Can the Circle Be Squared in the 1970s?

A third and final crisis in 1971, threatening the country's national survival and unity, once more transformed Yugoslavia's sociopolitical climate. It arose from deep-seated internal stresses between the various nationalities making up the country of the South Slavs. As a result of it, the nation's political survival and economic existence were threatened. Details of this crisis will be discussed in Chapter 9, but it is important to note here that the replacement of Croatia's top leadership, and the subsequent resignation of Serbia's more liberal executives, Milo Popović and Marko Nikezić, drastically changed the role and composition of major League councils. Moreover, the 1971 crisis indicates the extent to which the decentralizing constitutional amendments transferred substantial political and economic powers to the ethnic republics and thus seemed to undermine the leadership abilities of the once monolithic League of Communists. It finally illustrates one of the basic political and media contradictions inherent in Titoist ideology, namely, how to combine decentralized economic democracy with one-party rule?

In the Yugoslavia of the 1970s the top leadership decided that social integration was the most important issue to be solved. Many studies of political unrest in ethnically diverse countries have documented that this is a difficult task, particularly where fragmentation is extreme. One study, comparing 114 states, notes that Yugoslavia and Canada are highly fragmented (placing seventh on a nine-point scale), and therefore particularly in need of integration.[32] But how to accomplish this task? What kinds of integrative mechanisms are at play in ethnically segmented societies? Few researchers have analyzed this question. According to one theorist, "the ways in which the component units of a social system constitute a single entity rather than disjointed parts is not well understood."[33]

Another theorist, however, notes that four kinds of integrative mechanisms are available. They are, according to Landecker, cultural integration (the degree of consistency of the cultural standards of a society), communicative integration (the degree to which there is presence or absence of barriers to communication within a society), functional integration (the degree of interdependence or self-sufficiency of the members of a society), and normative integration (the degree to which the cultural standards of a society constitute effective norms for its members).[34] Clearly, a segmented society is one in which there is a low degree of integration in all of these spheres, with cultural, normative, communicative, and functional inconsistencies delicately balanced.

History indicates that the Yugoslav leadership opted for two of these integrative strategies, functional and communicative, to pull the country together after the Croatian crisis. Both of these have implications for future media functioning in Yugoslavia's self-management system. Functional measures included both the creation of governmental mediating committees to link the center to the periphery, as well as League recentralization. Consequently, since 1971 five interrepublican coordinating committees were established in the legal sphere to counterbalance the decentralizing constitutional amendments and to facilitate the adjudication of the diverse disputes arising from economic and other disparities among Yugoslavia's constituent republics.[35]

Furthermore, functional integration was advanced by recentralizing the League of Communists itself, which turned into a polycentric grouping of six satrapies during the 1960s. At the now famous 1972 meeting in Kožara, Bosnia-Hercegovina, both President Tito and Edvard Kardelj reaffirmed the dominant power and role of the party in Yugoslavia and called for a reinstitution of democratic centralism in decision-making to counterbalance lagging party discipline throughout the ranks.[36] To reinforce this trend, the League's top decision-making body was cut from fifteen to eight members with proven administrative competencies. They were also assigned to oversee a specific area, a technique characteristic of central committee secretariats in other eastern European countries, but new in Yugoslavia. These areas represent focal points of League policy in the 1970s. The bureau in 1972 consisted of Kiro Gligorov (54), Macedonia, foreign trade; Jure Bilić (49), Croatia, party discipline; Krsta Avramović (45), Serbia, industrial management; Stane Dolanc (46), Slovenia, foreign policy and interparty relations; Budislav Soskić (46), Montenegro, press and propaganda; Todor Kurtović (52), Bosnia, economics; Steven Doronski (52), Vojvodina, agriculture; and Fadil Hodza (55), Kosovo, nationalities.

One observer noted "the reorganization is seen . . . as a return to the concept of the party representing the vanguard, with the party leadership itself a tightly controlled responsive group."[37] The reinstitution of democratic centralism in

League decision-making was to be effected through a cleansing of the ranks of dissident leaders and intellectuals. By 1974, at the X Congress of the League of Communists in Belgrade, President Tito noted that over 50,000 factionalists, technocrats, and careerists had been dropped from membership and that the League's leading role in society was once again assured.[38] The League will provide a major counterbalance to the economic and regional decentralization marking Yugoslav social developments in the 1970s.

For Yugoslavia's mass media, this change in policy raised the crucial question of how the autonomous press and broadcasting were to be integrated into the one-party state. Throughout the 1960s, as previously mentioned, cultural, and with it media, expression increased both in scope and in critical tenor. As a result, the balancing of social control and expressive freedom in the Yugoslav self-managed information system once again caused concern. While journalists argued that more voices were needed to reflect the growing multiplicity of citizen outlooks and economic realities, certain party committees and Socialist Alliance councils began to be concerned, even before the Croatian crisis, that this criticism was getting out of hand. Four accusations, all of them implicitly denouncing the media's ways of expressing opinions, were most frequently voiced. These were the media's supposed sensationalism and "undue dramatization and alarmist presentation" of social conflicts; the tendency of editorial boards to "appropriate the right to speak on behalf of all public opinion"; "vulgar commercialism and flattering of the tastes and demands of the more backward sections of the public"; and finally, the destructive criticism of socialist development and ethnic equality which was "unsupported by arguments, unprincipled and opposed to the democratic self-governing aims of Yugoslav society."[39]

Miodrag Avramović, ex-president of the Yugoslav Journalists' Association, summarized the dilemma in this way:

> The Yugoslav system of partyless socialist democracy is irreconcilable with the idea of the press as a force over and above society. . . . (The media) are (instead) an integral part of the democratic self-governing mechanism. They are simultaneously a mediator and an independent factor in generating democratic discussions. They make possible not only public confrontation of opinions held by those who practice self-government . . . but participate independently in the crystallization of decisions. . . . As public tribunes, they do not perform the function of a "mail box" for the reception of *every* public utterance. Ideologically committed, the media fight for the victory of direct democracy.[40]

The dualist character of Titoist media terminology and press philosophy creates a climate of ambiguity which critics within and outside of the country readily note. Balancing the role of the media as "public forums" within a system of citizens' self-government, with their use as developers of a socialist society, in effect amounts to the impossible task of squaring the circle. Can the Leninist dogma of the party's leading role in fact be reconciled with the people's right to self-government and adequate information?

Whether Yugoslav journalists and public officials, who defend their system on the grounds that it guards against both bureaucratic state and economic advertising exploitation, are correct in claiming such a reconcilation is an open question. It will have to be checked against the *facts* of media functioning and professional autonomy, to be analyzed in subsequent chapters. For the present, the leadership's assessment that the deep ethnic fissures in Yugoslavia's social fabric require increased communicative integration in the 1970s will be accepted. Documents and public debates indicate that this is to be accomplished through a more thorough scrutiny of media organization and media personnel. The new integrative communication strategies have taken three forms: increased Socialist Alliance supervision over media policies and statements; renewed League concern with personnel selection and performance; and an attempt to bring the new republican press laws into line with the more conservative federal document. In summary, it appears that the Croatian crisis laid the foundation for new and more restrictive answers to two critical media questions: how to combine financial and organizational media autonomy with "responsible" management and how to balance professional autonomy with "responsible reporting."

Journalistic deliberations and public documents indicate that while the media's balancing of organizational and social requirements was left up to the management board during the 1960s, this body is now to be scrutinized more carefully by the Socialist Alliance. Such scrutiny, however, is not to be exercised through a centralized Agitprop-type censorship board, but through publishers' councils, whose duty it is to approve the appointment of a responsible editor and to sketch a medium's broad programs and aims. In the 1970s, the party suggests these publishers' councils are to take a more active interest in their newspapers or broadcast stations by formulating and evaluating personnel policy, reviewing the activities of editorial boards, defining social guidelines, and requiring that editorial policies and stands, as well as criteria of "newsworthiness" and "play," be spelled out for public scrutiny.[41]

A *Borba* article, entitled "The Press as an Integral Component of Our Self-Governing Society," summarizes the new trends by observing that "responsibility for information, particularly if political questions are involved, must not be usurped by the mass media, or the editorial office or the journalist. Other socio-political organizations and self-management organs and legislative chambers must also pay attention, so that the public receives complete and objective information." It continues further "with us the slogan of 'freedom' means something qualitatively different from what this term refers to in the West. It means working for the class interest of the working people. . . . We need to develop a journalist who knows something about the politics of the party, with a strong sense of responsibility and critical faculties, who writes about conditions without preconceptions and does not make unprincipled compromises."[42]

Future media policy, in other words, is to assure that the media place social over individual economic considerations in their organizational decision-making and make each journalist more pliant and conscious of the broader party line so that he will temper his individual perception and criticism.

Furthermore, the combination of professional autonomy with "socially responsible" reporting, which before the crisis was determined by the local party hierarchy, is now to shift back to a more monolithic League in which a more uniform outlook dominates. Greater League supervision over media personnel policy was first publicized in the now famous letter of the executive bureau of the Presidium of the League of Communists to all members on September 29, 1972, which suggested that a more homogenous outlook in the editorial boards would be achieved if: "meetings are held of all communists in the press, radio and television and of all responsible political and social bodies to discuss and undertake energetic measures to put an end to destructive writing, to remove from leading positions all those who do not accept the political course of the LCY, to make impossible writings which are contrary to the LCY and factional activity through the press."[43] Up to 1974 this directive led not only to the removal of editors who were accused of editorially supporting nationalist politics from Zagreb's major papers, *Vjesnik* and *Vjesnik u Srijedu,* but from other influential papers as well, especially Belgrade's *Politika* and *Borba,* which were supposedly preaching a Serbian variant of nationalism. It also resulted in a strong public campaign against intellectuals with differing outlooks, many of whom are no longer able to freelance for the media.[44]

The re-evaluation of republican press laws, a third strategy for tightening social control over the media in the 1970s, has, however, not achieved the desired results. New republican press laws tend to be more liberal than the federal version, and local journalists and educators are pushing for more detailed specification of governmental rights to interfere in media content. In Slovenia, informants noted discussions between the Socialist Alliance and practicing journalists led to the adoption of a press law replacing the ambiguous federal catch-all Article 52 containing the description of the eight "sensitive" discussion areas. The journalists argued that dissemination of military secrets, confidential state information, and false reports was adequately prohibited by state secret and libel laws and that information "causing public concern" needed specification to make the banning of controversial material more difficult.

Another attempt at curtailing governmental interference is to be found in the contemporary journalists' campaign for liberalized information access which is to help better trained professionals get at the "facts." The previous discussions already noted that while economic information flows freely in the Yugoslav system, political information sources tend to remain inaccessible to reporters. Local and regional party headquarters and government offices tend to co-opt the media and to use them for their own parochial purposes, making political scrutiny by journalists not only hazardous but often impossible. The profession's response, as shall be seen in Chapter 5, was to develop a code of ethics, but in Yugoslavia's power context this solved only part of the problem. It alleviated threats and intimidation of individual communicators, but it did not spell out a journalist's right to scrutinize League, governmental, and industrial deliberations. The new Serbian press law and others like it, for the first time, detailed what sanctions will come into play when information is refused and "publicity of work" is infringed. Vukoje Bulatović notes "public work, open publicity and access to information about all essential societal activities are an indispensable precondition for self-management."[45] Although legislation is doubtlessly a step in the right direction, it remains to be seen whether these laws will in fact increase access and counterbalance governmental pressures on the media in the changed social setting of the 1970s.

"Freedom of Expression"

What is the upshot of all of these integrative developments for an understanding of how Yugoslav media policy in the 1970s will balance social control against the requirements of expressive freedom in this ethnically diversified country? Western journalists observing the scene are divided into two camps: those who believe that a new "political orthodoxy" is asserting itself in the country of the South Slavs and others who claim that the nation's survival justifies the institution of new integration mechanisms. The latter maintain that President Tito at 84 is trying to reconstruct a party strong enough to organize the economy, keep the confederation working, and assure the nation's survival after succession without a reversion to Stalinism.[46]

The previously presented arguments document that it is entirely too simpleminded to evaluate a country's information system as more or less democratic by merely recording the presence or absence of censorship practices. After all, it is well known that every society regulates its information flow by various means. Even on the North American continent, where everyone supposedly has the right to speak, information access is not the same for all groups. In an advertising sponsored media system, for instance, access privileges are disproportionately held by industry rather than by other publics, such as youth, reformers, and old-age pensioners. Evaluation of a country's media system must, therefore, do more than merely record censorship practices. It must inquire into the way in which these practices are *activated*.

Such an inquiry will have to assess a country's level of censorship by considering whether it is legally or arbitrarily defined, under what circumstances it arises, and whether it applies equally to the economic, cultural, and political information streams. A survey of Yugoslavia's information history documents three major conclusions. It shows that censorship has decreased and become legally defined in the past thirty years; that it tends to arise primarily in response to internal, not diplomatic, situations; and that it is unequally distributed across the different kinds of information flows. A brief recapitulation, on which these conclusions are based, follows.

A comparison of Yugoslavia's four information periods, each dominated by its own press law, shows that the amount of subject matter to which censorship practices are applicable has drastically declined in the past thirty years, and that the right to censor has been transferred from the government to the courts. During the period of administrative socialism (1945 to 1950), a centrally organized information hierarchy checked content before publication, and the 1946 press law restricted publication rights to those guaranteeing not to undermine the "constitutional order for anti-democratic purposes." Since then, during the transition, decentralized, and present press periods (1950s to today), precensorship has been abolished and censorship now lies with public prosecutors who may act only ex-post facto, after a broadcast, publication, or film presentation.

Moreover, the revised press and broadcast laws of 1960, 1968, and 1973 have continually restricted and specified the 1946 catch-all Article 11 which punished "the propagation of national, racial or religious discrimination and incitement to hatred on these grounds . . . and the distribution of false or alarming news, detrimental to the interests of the people or the state." While the new articles may still cover too much ground, *Naša štampa* noted in October, 1971, that only three out of ten censorship cases were upheld in the Croatian and Serbian supreme courts in the last quarter of the year, in spite of the fact that the number of complaints had increased. Among these were articles in *Kniževne Novine, Hrvatski Četnik,* and *Student.*[47]

A case study of Croatia's media co-optation, which appears in Chapter 9, illustrates that the situations triggering censorship action have become less determined by diplomatic needs than by the internal workings of the country's decentralized political system. In a detailed study, Frans Kempers, a Dutch scholar, concludes that in spite of periodic reverses and strains, interference with journalists and authors voicing criticism of the Soviet Union has been waning. Djilas was free to criticize the USSR as early as 1956 in various articles after the Hungarian uprising,[48] and in 1968, during the Czech invasion, the Yugoslav media served as one of the major world outlets for that country's "clandestine" radio reports. Yet such criticism is carefully measured in accordance with President Tito's political aims. Kempers concludes: "Whenever the Party leadership considers the moment opportune for criticism of this kind to be aired in the press, one may be sure that such publications point to tensions between Belgrade and Moscow, respectively between Belgrade and some other East European capital."[49]

On balance, however, internal political realities are more important barriers to political expression in Yugoslavia than diplomatic considerations. It is these that local journalists and theoreticians criticize most vigorously and are trying to change. As one Slovenian theoretician points out, "though socialist democracy considers a free, autonomous and self-governing public as a prerequisite for . . . pluralism in politics . . . the media are not yet open forums for all types of discussion in Yugoslavia. Pluralism is to date more freely expressed in the sphere of social self-government than in that of politics. Unfortunately the existing structures of the Socialist Alliance . . . are not assuring the articulation of differing opinions, views and interests, and thus (inhibit) the actual confrontation of alternative political concepts."[50]

Another scholar notes that an "open" communication system presupposes four things: the free flow and exchange of information in all communication channels; open sources of information; availability of all subject matter necessary for self-managing decision-making; and publicity of work of all social and government organizations.[51] Many of these are not yet realized in contemporary Yugoslavia. As previously noted, journalists and others have incorporated access to news sources and the open working of deliberative bodies into the new republican press laws and pressed for equal representation on their supervisory publishers' councils to counterbalance the information monopoly of the government so dramatically illustrated in the Croatian media co-optation by the Dabčević-Kučar faction.

A review of the kinds of information most open to censorship practices reveals, finally, that economic, cultural, and political material is sensitive to scrutiny in this order. Censorship is almost nonexistent in economic reporting where nothing but the publication of economic secrets of "special importance" is prohibited. The fact that there are merely a handful of cases in which this clause was invoked during the past fifteen years indicates that the unfettered exchange of economic information was essential for the self-management system and for coordinating the country's push for industrialization.

The picture is quite different, however, when it comes to freedom of cultural and intellectual expression probing the foundation and working of Titoist socialism. Here two paradoxical trends emerged throughout the twenty years between 1955 and 1975. The present chapter detailed the increased organizational autonomy of the media and publishing houses, the proliferation of journals, and the growth of book and film production, not to mention the exploration of previously taboo subject matter during this period of cultural "laissez-faire." In the 1970s there has been an increased imposition of controls on the way in which political subject matter is to be treated. Many of these controls, it turns out, were activated by informal extralegal cultural bodies, rather than through regular court channels, and applied to communicators, writers, as well as intellectuals. Chief among these were members of the University of Belgrade's Department of Philosophy, which supported the students in their 1968 demands for more jobs and a return to the Marxist goal of social equality. When their exclusion from the party did not lead to their dismissal from the faculty, the communist conference tried to oust them from their teaching jobs by changing the university's statutes and by packing faculty councils with outside representatives.[52] By the end of 1974 their fate was decided and prominent philosophers like Mihailo Marković and Sveta Stojanović are now removed from teaching and work in research institutes.[53]

In summary, it may be said that censorship in Yugoslavia is legally rather than arbitrarily defined, though in the cultural and political spheres extralegal boards or political committees may take on censorship functions under specified circumstances. The situations where such informal censorship mechanisms come into play are sometimes diplomatic, when the regime is engaged in delicate Soviet negotiations, or when some fundamental axioms of Yugoslav Marxism are being challenged, as in the writings of students, philosophers, and literateurs. It appears, furthermore, that censorship is unequally employed in the country's three communication flows. Economic information circulates freely and cultural messages are interfered with relatively infrequently. Only political information is subject to systematic distortion, reflecting the values and outlooks of the League of Communists. How this distortion is introduced and how it affects political content is the subject of detailed analysis in the next chapter. Based on participant observation data, this investigates the national news agency's (Tanjug) operations during Yugoslavia's four information periods.

1　National Bank of Yugoslavia, *Statistički bilten*, pp. 8-9. For further detail on the economics of this period consult Macesich, "Major Trends," pp. 213-235.

2　Gregory Grossman, "Economic Reforms: A Balance Sheet," p. 54ff.

3　Fritz W. Hondius, *The Yugoslav Community of Nations*, p. 335.

4　For further detail consult "Constitutional Changes in Yugoslavia," pp. 1-29, and "The Latest Changes (1971) in the Constitution of the Socialist Federal Republic of Yugoslavia," pp. 1-36.

5　Paul Lendvai, *Eagles in Cobwebs: Nationalism and Communism in the Balkans*, p. 118ff.

6　Bogdan Denitch, "Mobility and Recruitment of Yugoslav Leadership: The Role of the League of Communists," *Working Papers for the International Study of Opinion Makers*.

7　Paul Lendvai, *Eagles in Cobwebs*, p. 150.

8　David Binder, the *New York Times* correspondent in Belgrade, commented on October 6, 1966:
"President Tito said the new 35-member Presidium would be the guiding force of the party. The Presidium includes all but 2 members of the old 19-man Executive Committee. The new members are almost all in their fifties. For the first time there are also representatives of Yugoslavia's smaller minorities, which suffered discrimination in the past. . . . The new Executive Committee which has been downgraded to a purely administrative role is composed of younger Communists. The average age of this group is 45."

9　Stevan K. Pavlowitch, *Yugoslavia*, p. 344.

10　Pavlowitch notes "of the sixty-three personalities elected to the Central Committee at the 1948 Congress, only ten were still among the fifty-two members of the latest presidency (V. Bakarich, Y. Blazhevich, R. Dugonjich, E. Kardelj, L. Kolishevski, Ts. Miyatovich, M. Popovich, P. Stambolich, F. Flahovich — and Tito). Of the nine members of the 1948 Political Bureau, only Tito and Kardelj were left in the new Executive Bureau." *Yugoslavia*, p. 345.

11　Mate Oreć, "Application of International Principles on Freedom of Information in Yugoslavia" in *Mass Media and International Understanding*, p. 388.

12 Secretariat of Information of the Federal Executive Council, The Constitution of the Socialist Federal Republic of Yugoslavia, pp. 24-25.

13 *Yugoslavia Radio-Television Yearbook, 1970*, pp. 395-403.

14 J. T. Crawford, "Yugoslavia's New Economic Strategy: A Progress Report," p. 616.

15 *Jugoslovenski radio televizija godišnjak 1971/72*, p. 440.

16 *Ko je ko u Jugoslaviji*, p. 158.

17 *Ibid.*, p. 68.

18 Bogdan Dečermić, "Spotlight on Publishing," p. 22.

19 *Yugoslavia Radio-Television Yearbook, 1970*, p. 12.

20 Živorad Stoković, "Broj i prosečan tiraž jugoslovenskih listova i časopisa," p. 189.

21 Walter Emery, *Five European Broadcasting Systems*, pp. 67-83.

22 Bruno Begović, "Podaci o tiražu jugoslovenskih i nedelnjih listove u 1964 godini," p. 173, and Živorad Stoković, "Broj i prosečan tiraž jugoslovenskih listova i časopisa," p. 189.

23 Jugoslovenski Institut za novinarstvo, *Tematka struktura sadržaja jugoslovenskih listova*, p. 49.

24 Radio Belgrade's third program is typical of activities in Zagreb and Ljubljana as well. It broadcasts approximately three to four hours in the evening. Chief editor Miroslav Djordjević noted that discussions of burning issues were most popular. Listeners had also learned about electronic music, scientific advances, the newest aesthetic theories, and the impacts of the Soviet and Yugoslav economic reforms in the course of 1969.

25 *Yugoslavia Radio-Television Yearbook, 1970*, p. 252.

26 John McLin, *Eurovision*.

27 Yugoslav Institute of Journalism, *Press, Radio, and Television in Yugoslavia 1969*, p. 82.

28 See the informative article by Bryan, "The Press Systems of Yugoslavia," pp. 291-299.

29 Lukić, *Contemporary Yugoslav Literature*, p. 182.

30 For a detailed account of this meeting consult *Filosofija*.

31 Budislav Šoškić, "Ideological-Political Platforms of Activity of the League of Communists of Yugoslavia: Current Questions Concerning the Social Position and Role of the Information Activity and Media of Public Information," p. 13.

32 Maria R. Haug, "Social and Cultural Pluralism as a Concept in Social System Analysis," p. 298.

33 Maurice Pinard, "Communal Segmentation and National Integration," p. 16.

34 Werner S. Landecker, "Types of Integration and Their Measurement," pp. 19-27.

35 Dennison I. Rusinow, *A Note on Yugoslavia: 1972*, p. 3.

36 Josip Broz Tito, Edward Kardelj, and Stane Dolanc, *Ideological and Political Offensive of the League of Communists in Yugoslavia*, pp. 10, 50.

37 James Feron, "Party Tightening Ordered by Tito."

38 Tito, "Tito Claims Dissidents Crushed as Long Purge Ends," p. 4.

39 "President Tito's Interview with Representatives of the Federation of Yugoslav Journalists," pp. 4-6.

40 Miodrag Avramović, "The Press and the Socio-Economic Reform in Yugoslavia," pp. 2-3.

41 Šoškić, "Ideological-Political Platforms," pp. 2-10.

42 "The Press as an Integral Component of Our Self-Governing Society," pp. 6-7.

43 Tito, Kardelj, and Dolanc, *Ideological and Political Offensive*, p. 103.

44 Robinson, "The New Yugoslav Writer: A Socio-Political Portrait," pp. 185-197.

45 Vukoje Bulatović, "The Right to Information," p. 26.

46 Claire Sterling, "Tito's New Balancing Act," pp. 45-50.

47 "Political Action Cannot Be Substituted for Administrative Action," p. 1.

48 Milovan Djilas, "The Storm in Eastern Europe."

49 Frans Kempers, "Freedom of Information and Criticism in Yugoslavia," p. 323.

50 France Vreg, "Socialist Democracy and Opinion Pluralism," pp. 214-215.

51 Pavle Zrimšek, "Otvorenost kommunikacijskog prostora kao društvena norma," pp. 4-5.

52 Raymond Anderson, "A New Political Orthodoxy Is Asserting Itself in Liberal Yugoslavia"; also Noam Chomsky and Robert S. Cohen, "The Repression at Belgrade University," pp. 32-33.

53 The Praxis Philosophers, "Auf dem Rückweg zum Stalinismus?," p. 1.

CHAPTER 4

Tanjug: Yugoslavia's National News Agency

The previous two chapters demonstrated that a country's mass media are a sensitive barometer of political, economic, and cultural shifts, adapting their structure, content, and filtering processes to changing social conditions. They did not, however, detail the filtering alterations during Yugoslavia's four information periods. Such a study is best done not on a macro-societal, but on a micro-organizational level, where the workings of a country's major news collector and distributor, the national news agency, can be scrutinized. Such an agency functions in two important ways: both as an importer of international information for the Yugoslav media and as an exporter of national news to the rest of the world. In collecting and interpreting this news, Tanjug sets standards for the local media which require further investigation.

In a world where 70 percent of the people[1] lack the most elementary means of getting information about developments either at home or abroad, two urgent problems must be solved: supplying the physical facilities for transmitting words and images, and achieving a degree of quality, accuracy, and total balance calculated to give a fair picture of the life of each country.[2] A UNESCO study of the mass media in developing countries points out that by 1975 the demand for news in Africa, Latin America, and the Near and Far East is three and a half times that in 1955, with the greatest potential demand concentrated in the Near East. Who will provide the necessary programming for these newly emerging newspapers and broadcast stations?

Historical record shows that the establishment of new information networks has usually been with the help of government resources. The European owner-ship pattern is thus being repeated. In a new nation, only the national govern-ment has adequate resources to cover the cost and to provide the consistent leadership for media development. Neither a largely illiterate audience nor the media themselves, lacking customers to pay for services, can provide the counterforce to government, as in the North American system.

Table 8 indicates that the same picture is being repeated in news agency growth and development. In spite of the fact that the most recent information is somewhat outdated, single dependency agencies, mostly financed by govern-

Table 8
The Financial Bases of World News Agencies

1. *Media or Cooperative* (24)

Arab News Agency (ANA)	Italian News Agency (ANSA)
Argentina Press (ANS)	Kyodo News (KYODO)
Associated Press (AP)	Mexico Informex
Australian Assoc. (AAP)	Netherland Press (ANP)
Canadian Press (CP)	Norway Press (NTB)
Ceylon Press Trust	New Zealand Press Ass. (NZAA)
Chile (COPER)	Philippine News (RNS)
Deutsch Presse Agentur (CPA)	Reuter
Finland (FNB)	Ritzaus Bureau (RB)
Hong-Kong Pan Asia	South African Press (SAPA)
India Press Trust (PTI)	Swiss Press (SDA)
Israeli News Agency (INA)	Venezuela Press (PEVE)

2. *Mixed* (21)

Agence Congo d'Information (ACI)	Madagaskar (MP)
Agence France Presse (AFP)	Maghreb Arab Presse (MAP)
Algeria (APS)	Pakistan Assoc. Press (APP)
Athens News (AA)	Poland (PAP)
Austria Press (APA)	Spain (EFE)
Belgian Press (CIP)	Sweden (TT)
Cameroon (ACP)	Turkey (AA)
Colombia (TP)	United Arab Republic (MEN)
Ghana (GNA)	Uruguay (ANI)
Hungary (MTI)	Yugoslavia (Tanjug)
Iran (PARS)	

3. *Government* (34)

Afghanistan (BAKTAR)	Indonesia (ANTARA)
Agence de Presse Brazzaville	Iraqi Natl. Agency (INA)
Albania (ATA)	Ivory Coast (AIP)
Brazil (AN)	Kenya (KNA)
Bulgaria (BTA)	Korea
Burma (NAB)	Laos Press
Burundi (RUDIPRESS)	Mali (ANIM)
Cambodia (AKP)	North Korea (KCNA)
Central America	Portugal (ANI)
China (CNA)	Prensa Latina (Cuba)
Dahomey	Rumania (Agerpress)
German Democratic Republic (ADN)	Senegal
Ethiopian Internatl. Press	Somalia
Gabon (GBI)	TASS
Guinea (AGP)	Thai Press Service
Holy See	Tonga
Hsin-Hua (NCNA)	Tunisia (TAP)

SOURCE: *World Press, Newspapers and News Agencies* (New York: UNESCO Publication Center, 1964), pp. 153-156.

ment rather than by the media in 1964 and today, outweigh multidependency or mixed agencies by more than two to one. Yet the number of mixed agencies has increased in the past thirty years, and these agencies are often found in eastern Europe and the Near East, where the greatest future news markets are developing. Research will have to determine two important questions: whether and what kind of correlations there are between the degree of government control and the degree of news distortion and what kinds of interpretative differences exist between the world reports of commercial and governmental agencies. This chapter will explore the first of these questions, analyzing how Tanjug has adapted its filtering practices as a result of changing government-agency relations throughout Yugoslavia's four information periods. Subsequent ones will discuss the way in which Yugoslavia's Tanjug interprets the world for its media customers and ultimately for its readers and listeners.

Tanjug and the World

International information collection and dissemination is a manufacturing process depending on a tripartite division of labor. In this manufacturing process five global agencies function as news wholesalers which pass on their product to 145 national agencies. They in turn operate as retailers of this information. The five global agencies, which are also among the oldest purveyors, include Reuter's of Great Britain, Agence France Presse of France, TASS of the Soviet Union, as well as the Associated and United Presses of the United States. They are located in the highly developed part of the world where the greatest demand for information exists. With their superior physical and human resources, they are the original selectors and recorders of world events.

Retailers like Tanjug, in turn, have commercial or barter arrangements with these majors whose daily tickers constitute the raw material out of which they fashion their own national news product.[3] National agencies thus constitute the second filtering screen in the international news flow, where information is additionally selected and condensed, eliminating nearly 80 percent of all incoming copy. Media outlets, as customers, finally reduce this trickle once more, tailoring the news product to local reader and listener needs and interests.

As of 1968, the latest year for which figures are available, an operating budget of $4.2 million supported Tanjug's operations. Table 9 indicates that it sold its information to 873 domestic media outlets, 4,000 factory customers, and countless government agencies, including republican information ministries and embassies. Each of these three classes of customers contributes approximately one-third of the agency's total budget, according to company records. In addition, some thousand foreign news agencies, broadcast stations, and newspapers receive its service under barter arrangements. Its daily volume, 40,000-odd words for local and 45,000 for international customers, places Tanjug in eighth place in the international news market, after the five international super agencies, China's Hsinhua, and Egypt's Middle East News Agency.

The Associated Press's (AP) budget, by contrast, is ten times Tanjug's, a 1968 total of about $44 million. The Associated Press produces a million daily words of combined domestic and foreign reports, an output twenty-five times Tanjug's. Its *European A Service* put together in London comes to Yugoslavia on a twenty-four-hour basis via leased telex from Frankfurt. The content of this wire is top of the world and European news, with a Sunday supplement which carries 65 to 70 percent sports and features. Customers include about 8,000 American and international newspapers and broadcasting stations. Associated Press clients number twice those for Tanjug in Yugoslavia and four times as many total all over the world.

The same pygmy and giant discrepancies are also visible in the two agencies' available technical facilities. Major growth in Tanjug's network was not recorded until the independent period, when electronic media and factory subscribers multiplied and more and faster information dissemination became essential. Company records indicate that between 1962 and 1968 three new radio printer channels were added to the one which linked newspapers for the first time in 1954.

Table 9
Relative Sizes of Tanjug and Associated Press (1968)

		Tanjug	AP
Age		25	120
Operating budget		$4,200,000	$44,030,275
World population with access to agency output		40% Eastern Europe, Africa, Asia	65% U.S., Europe, Latin America
Number of Bureaus	Domestic	6	167
	Foreign	0	57
Personnel (fulltime)	Domestic	428	2,200
	Foreign	28	1,000
Technical facilities	Domestic	4 natl. teletype circuits (24 hours)	4 natl. teletype trunks to 4 regional and 50 state circuits
	Foreign	teletype, radio	teletype, radio
Daily output/words	Domestic	40,000	1,000,000
	Foreign	45,000	1,000,000
Total number of customers	Domestic	873 media and 4,000 factory and gov. agencies.	3,801
	Foreign	1,000	4,199

SOURCES: Richard Schwarzlose. "The American Wire Services: A Study of Their Development as a Social Institution," pp. 416, 397, 417, interviews; *Tanjug* (Beograd, 1965), pp. 45, 39, 33.

Tanjug today services the media through four twenty-four-hour circuits fed by the central office in Belgrade and by the six republican bureaus in the provincial capitals. Two of these channels transmit the 40,000 words a day of the general service. The third carries information designed for the republican ministries and government agencies, and the fourth line is used for international hookups like Eurovision or for carrying special services for Slovenian and Macedonian customers transmitted in the minority languages. There are as yet no foreign bureaus, so news abroad is gathered by twenty-eight independent correspondents and purchased from other world agencies. Tanjug's operational size, with its upward of 130 teletype machines and twenty radio-teletype units for world news reception, not to mention its staff of 456, is thus similar to that reached by the Associated Press forty years ago.

The Associated Press's news collection, on the other hand, covering a home country ten times as populous as Yugoslavia as well as most of the rest of the globe, is carried out by an organization totaling 224 bureaus — 167 in the United States and fifty-seven abroad. These bureaus are staffed by 3,200 employees, of whom 2,200 are located in the United States and 800 in New York alone. The overseas personnel includes 275 foreign correspondents of United States nationality and hundreds of stringers who produce stories only infrequently.[4] The Associated Press's foreign news collection and distribution operations are centered in New York.

> From New York radio teletype circuits operating around the clock transmit news both east and west. . . . A transmitter on Long Island beams the signal by radio to Tangiers, where a relay station boosts the signal and beams it to Europe, the Middle East, South Asia, and South Africa. In London, the incoming beam is fed into teletype circuits covering more than 20,000 miles in Europe. In each country, the news is translated into that country's language, and then put on a separate national teletype network (translation into Spanish for Latin American countries is largely done in the New York offices). The file to Asia is beamed by radio from San Francisco to booster relay stations at Manila and other points.[5]

Such overwhelmingly superior financial and technological strength brings advantages both in international penetration and in extension of services. The fifty-seven countries in which the Associated Press has foreign bureaus selling its product contain 65 percent of the world's population.[6] Similar data for Tanjug reveal that it, too, distributes its news quite widely. Of the forty-four countries with which exchange agreements exist, thirteen are in the Near and Far East, twelve in eastern Europe, eleven in Africa, and eight in Latin America. Together these countries in 1963 had a population of 1.4 billion people out of an estimated world total of 3.16 billion.[7] The Tanjug report thus has a potential distribution of 40 percent of the world's population, 25 percentage points less than its American counterpart. What this means for the role of Tanjug in the future world information market will be the subject of a separate evaluation at the end of the book.

The Agency and the Government

With the above description of the agency's physical armor, it is possible to investigate in greater detail how Yugoslavia's three sociopolitical crises affected Tanjug organization and functioning in the thirty years between 1945 and 1975. Much of the material presented here is based on personal observation of agency practices and extensive interviews with top officials in 1963-64 and again in 1969-70. Table 10 summarizes this information and relates it to Yugoslavia's four information periods. It will be used as a convenient guide for the subsequent discussion of the interrelationships between Tanjug's managerial and financial policies and its changing tasks and product.

According to Table 10, Tanjug's formal organization and financing, in line with developments in other media enterprises, became increasingly independent of government staffing and economic support throughout the past thirty years. When the agency was founded by the Supreme Military Command in 1943 and for the following seven years, it was a fully supported budgetary institution in the governmental information hierarchy and was run by an appointed director and editorial board. Subsequently, however, the managerial setup shifted, first to modified institutional independence in 1952, and then to full autonomy. Today Tanjug, like other media enterprises, is run by an elected workers' council of thirty-four, which in turn appoints both the managing board of eleven and the enterprise director.

With these shifts in formal organization and financing came a drastic decline in governmental involvement with information production. Assembled data show that revenues from the state dropped from 100 percent to 60 percent during the transition period, further declining to the present figure of 33 percent during the independent period. According to the director, the mass media presently supply the second third of the agency's budget, with the final third coming from Yugoslavia's burgeoning factories. These have become increasingly interested in trade and economic information, such as the Dow Jones report and international trade statistics, as industrial development flourishes in Yugoslavia's mixed-market economy.

Despite this shift in numbers and kinds of customers, Tanjug, unlike most western agencies, continues officially to work for the government. Why is this necessary? A deputy director pointed out that it is impossible in a country the size of Wyoming, with one-tenth of the United States' population, to cover news collection expenses from media and industrial contributions alone. There were still too few dailies (twenty-three), radio stations (eight major and 162 local), television stations (six), and magazines (seventy) in Yugoslavia in 1971. In addition, the government has placed a ceiling of twenty dinars on the cost of newspapers, which means that press contributions to the agency's coffers are limited. Government participation in financing is therefore inevitable, but the agency today views this contribution as a payment for raw-information inputs placed at the service of a special client, rather than as an incentive to ignore media and industrial needs, which had been its attitude earlier. According to

Table 10
Tanjug's Organizational and Product Evolution, 1945-75

Tanjug Formal Organization	Management	Financing	Operative Tasks	Programming and Product
1945-1950 Budgetary institution in governmental information hierarchy: organization on Soviet line	director's one-man rule, centralized decision-making, director and chief editors appointed by party	ministry of information, 100%	organize home collection & distribution net; establish relations with Reuter & TASS; foreign correspondents to world centers & eastern neighbors	supply foreign and home media; collect world news for government; propagandize socialist order
1951-1962 Institution with independent financing (1952)	modified workers' self-management, no workers' council and director and managing board have full decision making power	Tanjug revenue from government which covers deficits, 60%; media, 40%	penetration of Europe; home desk stagnation; loss of photo and economic news	distribute official texts for government; first attempt to serve new media customers
1963-1970 Media enterprise (1964) full corporate autonomy	workers' self-management, workers' council (34) appoints managing board (11) and director	Tanjug revenues from 3 sources: media, 33%; enterprises, 33%; government, 33%	multiplication of products & services; revitalization of home desk; foreign technical assistance; extension of foreign net to developing countries	increased bulletin production for factories; division of general service into four; more entertainment oriented content
1971-present Media enterprise	same	same	specialization on international areas not covered by media; strengthen federal reporting net	product proliferation under impact of TV & specialty magazines; emphasis on federal reporting

SOURCE: Interviews and company records.

company records, state contributions cover broadcasts to foreign countries as well as Tanjug's daily roundup of foreign press reaction to Yugoslav events, which its foreign correspondents gather in the world's major news capitals.

Changing management and financing practices throughout the four information periods resulted in a concomitant shift in agency-government relations. This shift needs to be spelled out in greater detail to explain the increased variety of Tanjug's news product as well as the specification and decrease of filtering practices. But how can such a shift in control patterns be analyzed and estimated?

According to Dill,[8] there are four major institutional control groups which constitute the managerial environment of any organization in modern society. Chief among these are government regulatory agencies, customers, suppliers, and competitors. In the Yugoslav information setting, the latter are not nearly as important as the former. Customers cannot exert substantial control over the agency because they are dependent on Tanjug for international and federal copy. The global agency suppliers, in turn, lose much of their influence, because product duplication makes it possible for Tanjug to obtain this copy from other sources. Exactly this happened, as a matter of fact, in 1964 when the United Press International canceled its contract and the agency carried on with the Associated Press, Reuters, and Agence France Presse. Competitors, like the Pres Servis, finally do not constitute a strong force, because it is not a news but a feature agency and thus competes with only one aspect of Tanjug's product.

This leaves governmental regulatory agencies as the potential controllers of the agency's corporate environment. Through what channels do these wield their influence and how have agency-government relations changed since the 1940s? In contemporary Yugoslavia there are two government and three party bodies which wield potential power over the media and the national news agency. These are, first, the Ministry of Information and the Federal Executive Council, and second, the League of Communists with its ideological commission and enterprise "aktivs." The power rearrangement between Tanjug and these bodies took two major changes in the past thirty years: the waning of "official" ministry and council control over the agency and the waxing of "informal" mechanisms to keep Tanjug in tune with the League of Communists' outlooks. Each of these trends will now be documented with organizational evidence.

Paralleling developments in other eastern European countries under Stalinism, Yugoslavia set up a Secretariat of Information in 1946, organized on the principle of democratic centralism. The federal office at first had the task of planning and supervising development of a new information network for the country, as well as that of reinforcing the ideological activities of the party. It is difficult to glean from the scanty published material about this period what kinds of authority the secretariat exercised over Tanjug. Interviews, too, did not throw much light on the point. It is known, however, that the secretariat not only carried the Tanjug budget on its books but that this was also planned by the Executive Committee of the government. Such evidence indicates that certain areas of agency autonomy were seriously impaired.

This impression is further strengthened by references from a number of interviewees to the fact that the Tanjug director, as well as the chief editors of the growing number of newspapers, would come to the secretariat for "briefing sessions" on the foreign policy line and that the "play" of certain sensitive stories and selection from government policy statements was defined from above. One editor mentioned, for instance, in 1964 that "six or seven years ago we would have been given this report on the *Social Plan* with the parts that could be shortened mentioned in detail. Now we make our own selection." Lack of autonomy over financing and product composition indicate that, like the party until 1954, the Secretariat of Information in the first ten years played a more overt supervisory role vis-à-vis Tanjug and the mass media than it does today.

As for the present, Vilko Vinterhalter, Federal Secretary for Information, pointed out as early as 1964 that there was no direct supervision of the press.

> The freedom of the press is naturally not yet completely accomplished, because though the Constitution and laws have been proclaimed, freedom must become a living practice. There is no office or officer in the Federal Government who controls information. The Federal Secretary for Information has no power to prevent the publishing of any item in the mass media or to force them to publish anything. The republican officers of the Ministries of Information are in a similar position. Newspapers are economically independent and the only official link with the government is through a tax.

As a result of previously mentioned legal changes in 1956, and unlike its Soviet counterpart, the ministry neither has budgetary control over Tanjug today, nor appoints editorial personnel. Staff members are selected by the news organization itself. Tanjug is thus distinctly more autonomous in these areas than are the Czechoslovak or Polish agencies. But its institutional autonomy naturally is not complete, since it is only a part, although an important one, of the Yugoslav information system. In the present setup the Ministry of Information is the next higher administrative authority where Tanjug files its production plans. Its role today is no longer that of a politico-economic censoring organ. It functions rather as an administrative repository similar to those local government offices to which factories submit their plans.[9]

As dominant purveyors of general cultural, educational, and political values in any society, the mass media have a special legal status in Yugoslavia, as in the United States.[10] The social role of the media is institutionally recognized by requiring that profit considerations be tempered by an awareness and respect for social needs. How does the government see to it that the media balance their own economic needs and self-interests against the larger benefits for society? For Tanjug, the Federal Executive Council, which corresponds to the Cabinet in the British system, has two ways of doing this: first, sanctioning of the organization and executive definition of its goal; and second, appointment of three members to the Tanjug workers' council, who assist with the formulation of general enterprise policy.

The second article of the *Regulations Governing the News Agency Tanjug,* dated March 6, 1962, repeated in later reorganization documents, specifies a four-fold agency role: "Tanjug's task is to give the press, radio, and television news and other informative material; to inform the public abroad about events in Yugoslavia; to cooperate with similar foreign institutions and organizations; and to provide state organs, institutions, and organizations with services from its domain." This is a very broad and general definition of the functions of the agency. It does not specify what these services are to be, and thus leaves the composition of the product up to the agency. It also does not specify the price of the services, the programming of work within the agency, or the direction and character of planning for the future. Finally, it no longer appoints either the director or any other top Tanjug personnel. In all of these areas the organization, like its American counterpart, is autonomous and self-directing.

A second way in which the government can keep an eye on Tanjug is through its right to appoint three members of the workers' council. This is a unique right pertaining only to the media. Other industrial enterprises in Yugoslavia select the total membership of their workers' councils from within their own ranks. Usually for Tanjug, however, these three appointees are public figures interested in the media. In 1969 they were the director of Yugoslavia's Post and Telegraph, the director of the Institute of Journalism, and a government official interested in international affairs. Three other appointees represent the interests of the press, and three speak for electronic media and were chosen by the Yugoslav Radio Television Association.

A further indication of growing Tanjug autonomy is the fact that over the years the number of representatives chosen to the workers' council by the federal government has decreased, while the number chosen by the agency itself has increased. During the transition period, according to the 1960 agency statute, seven members were appointed and eight elected by Tanjug. In 1962, the number of federal appointees had been halved to the present three, with six others representing professional and media interests, while Tanjug itself elected six. During the independent period in 1964, however, the total board members were doubled to thirty-four, of which the agency gained the right to elect twenty-five from its own staff. In addition to their numerical superiority, the Tanjug representatives have an added authority over agency production operations: they alone vote on financing and purchases which do not depart from the general plan.

These changes reflect the agency's increasing self-control over internal operations, corroborated also by the director's evaluation: "The relation between the Agency and the Executive Council is not one based on censorship over what will be published. In this we are perfectly free. But naturally we could not emit policies contrary to the government policy. The director and the nine appointees guarantee this. In addition, the prevailing political philosophy is basically the same for all of us.'' This suggests that in Tanjug, as in western news agencies, the internal process of socialization and homogeneous social composition of top personnel provide what might be called an ''operative outlook.'' Observation furthermore indicates that outlook is structured and reinforced by three League of Communist mechanisms which exert informal control over public information. They are League membership of chief editors and media directors; the existence of party ''aktivs'' within all organizations; and the use of Tanjug facilities for special news-collection jobs.

For Tanjug autonomy, what is the effect of having its director hold a post in top party councils? It has already been suggested that though such an identification of positions might and does provide a potential and theoretical channel for direct control in the Soviet Union, practice is different in Yugoslavia. Here the agency director shares management authority and power with a democratically elected workers' council and management board. In his capacity as party member, the director cannot officially or singlehandedly exercise authority over agency functioning. Rather, he acts as a liaison officer, a channel for information, if this is considered financially or organizationally essential to agency operation. During one of our meetings, Tanjug's chief executive described his job in the following way:

> The role of the director has been defined by regulations and the law. He is both a manager and a political personage who is appointed by the workers' council. He is a man who understands politics as well as journalism. A director is not the life of the agency. He fits into an already established framework. The self-government mechanisms of the collective take care in large measure of the routine operative tasks. His job is rather to find a common language with which to mediate different needs.

Thus Tanjug autonomy is preserved in the areas of personnel, planning, programming, and definition of product.

A second question which needs investigation is whether the Tanjug ''aktiv'' sets policy. In Soviet industrial enterprises, the party secretary, as head of the party organization, is the Janus-faced alter-ego of the director, providing political dominance and control where the director provides technical and operational skills. Thus in Russia managerial and party hierarchies are intertwined to produce a symbiotic power relationship, where one element cannot function without the other.[11] In the Yugoslav enterprise, on the contrary, the party secretary is not the alter-ego of the director; intertwining of power hierarchies is not the rule. Instead, a division of functions exists. The director has charge of management and the party secretary of political education.

In Tanjug the party ''aktiv'' consists of a party secretary and a seven-member secretariat elected annually from the membership. Election is by secret ballot and for one-year, nonrenewable terms. There is no remuneration for time spent on League matters, which comes out of "spare time." As a result, informants commented that "many people who are excellent workers do not want to join, because they do not want to undergo the discipline of attending meetings after hours." As a result, presently only one-third of the membership are party members, and most of these are found in the journalistic sections.

Commenting on the role of the party in the Tanjug enterprise, a secretariat member provided the following insights: "The League of Communists of Yugoslavia has a social role which it fulfills through 'aktivs' in enterprises. These 'aktivs' educate the membership as well as the 'collective' on political and ideological matters. They try to co-opt activists and new blood to both rejuvenate the ranks and to act as a mobilizing force around which new social policies can be implemented." In this role the League of Communists has nothing to do directly with the managerial process of Tanjug, but can and does make suggestions through the proper organs of management. In other words, the party does not lay down rules which others have to follow. While there once was, there is today no difference in enterprise status between party and nonparty members. The party no longer functions as a source of rewards, and top posts can consequently be acquired on merit.

In spite of the persuasiveness of this argument, the crucial question that has to be answered is whether theory and observation correspond. Does top management have autonomy over the day-to-day operation of the agency and is there a division of labor, so that the internal party "aktiv" has an "integrative" and "supportive" rather than a "control" function, even on the level of agency operation? These conclusions were amply corroborated by observation. First of all, party membership alone is not an avenue to responsible posts in Tanjug. These are filled strictly on merit, as a discussion of professional requirements for managers and new employees will substantiate. In spite of this, party interests are still amply represented, with one-third of the agency staff active members of the League of Communists, though not of the organization's "aktiv." The party's position is well known in all Tanjug councils through dual memberships and contact. Thus there are many channels and pipelines between party chiefs and agency management which obviate the need for overt party pressure.

Three additional types of evidence can be adduced to substantiate the declining importance of the party "aktiv" in Yugoslav factories and media enterprises like Tanjug: the composition of the managing board, the unpaid extracurricular nature of the job of the secretary, and the types of issues with which the party "aktiv" is concerned. Attention has already been drawn to the fact that in Yugoslavia operative management is encased in the larger system of worker self-management, which is legally anchored in the workers' council of the factory. The council group meets only once a month and is concerned primarily with the annual plan of production and the distribution of surpluses into various enterprise funds; it spends comparatively little time with maintenance and personnel problems and none at all with routine operations.

The last type of problem, if it falls within its jurisdiction, comes before the managing board (Upravni Odbor) at its twice-monthly meeting. Problems can be ironed out in two other committees: the "agency board" (Agenciski Kollegium), which meets weekly, and the "editorial board" (Redakciski Kollegium), which meets daily. Membership in these working-management committees, as Table 11 shows, overlaps almost completely. Six members from the seven-member agency board are also present at the daily deliberations of the editorial board. Not one of these persons is in the Secretariat of the League of Communists or the Labor Union Secretariat. Observation suggests that the reason for the lack of overlap here is not only the theory about party functioning, but also the practical fact that Tanjug's top-management personnel carry exceedingly heavy administrative loads. For them the average working day includes the obligatory seven-hour shift from 7:00 A.M. to 2:00 P.M., as well as parts of the second shift. Often these key people were at their desks for an extra three hours in the evening between 5:00 and 8:00 P.M.

In addition, Yugoslav "grass-roots democracy" discourages overlap in principle, because the various management organs in the factory and the social

Table 11
Overlapping Membership of Agency Boards

Top Management Personnel	Journalistic Collegium (Redakciski Kollegium) (11)	Agency Collegium (Agenciski Kollegium) (7)	Management Board (Executive Committee) (Upravni Odbor) (11)
1. Director	x	x	x
2. Deputy director	x	x	x
3. Chief editor	x	x	x
4. Technical director	x	x	
5. Economic director	x	x	x
6. Agency sec'y (legal)		x	
7. Journalistic sec'y	x	x	
8. Editor of foreign desk	x		x
9. Ed. for foreign broadcasting	x		
10. Ed. of bulletins	x		
11. Ed. of photo division	x		
12. For. desk shift ed.	x		
13. Sports editor			x
14. Correspondent Ljubljana			x
15. Translator			x
16. Translator			x
17. Technical service			x
18. Technical service			x

SOURCE: Information derived from interviews.

organizations are considered valuable training grounds to extend political awareness. In a total population which is still 45 percent peasant and in which one-third of the working group does not have more than eight years of formal schooling,[12] such opportunities for training are essential to the process of modernization.

The integrative and supportive functions of the party in Tanjug are further attested to by the small size of the secretariat and the kinds of activities in which it engages. The League of Communists is not a mass party like the Socialist Alliance, to which every adult is invited to belong, nor like the Sindikat (trade union), of which most working people are members. It includes only about 9 percent of the total population and unites by invitation persons who show leadership qualities and willingness to spend the bulk of their spare time in civic activities. Even though it wields ultimate power on the national level, it does not bother to do so within individual enterprises. It is therefore to be expected that the union committee is more active in Tanjug than the party "aktiv."

This is indeed borne out by the union's more complex executive structure. It has a secretariat of fifteen members, twice as large as that of the party, and also maintains seven standing committees. These, according to the union president, cover a broad variety of activity spheres, such as culture and education, political and ideological matters, housing, working conditions, petitions and complaints, technical and safety matters, and sports activities. The union's official job is thus to protect the worker's health and safety vis-à-vis the enterprise and to see that his constitutional right to work is upheld. In this capacity, the union alone pressed in 1967 for an equalization of pay between the privileged journalistic and other sectors of the agency. Furthermore, the union has the task of stimulating worker interest in self-management, which is done through lectures, editorial meetings, and by presenting the candidate lists for the election of members to all managing boards.

Finally, not only the burden of duties but also the unpaid nature of party posts limits the activities of the communist League. The present party secretary also happens to be the special editor for diplomatic affairs, a job that keeps him fully occupied as a journalist for a major part of the day. Jiri Kolaja, who has investigated workers' council functioning in two Belgrade factories, found the same state of affairs there.

> The League of Communists acts — or claims to act — on behalf of the people; it functions as a moral integrative institution . . . (in the two factories) there seems to have occurred a certain informal division of labor, in the sense that the League's secretary was supposed to deal more with organizational tasks than was the director, who with his top lieutenants was primarily concerned with production and sales within the framework of the workers' council.[13]

The third and last way in which the League of Communists can influence Tanjug is as a customer. Like other major clients, such as the larger newspapers and industrial enterprises, the League may ask the agency to collect material on a specific topic. A *Politika* editor mentioned, for example, that his paper had run a series of articles on communal reactions to the constitutional amendments of 1969, for which responses were needed from the mayors of major cities. Instead of using their own much smaller correspondent net, the newspaper utilized and paid extra for the services of Tanjug personnel, who routinely make a survey of republican and local responses to important issues.

Along the same lines, the Central Committee's secretariat at the VII Party Congress of the League of Communists in 1964 decided to set up a special Commission on International Workers' Movements. Collection of information on the progress of socialist and communist parties all over the world is of foreign-policy interest to a regime which is trying to become a force in the so-called nonaligned bloc of nations. Just to keep informed requires a widespread and expensive correspondent group, which the party does not have. Tanjug, however, with precisely such facilities, is at once the logical and economical agency to undertake such assignments. A new special editorship with the foreign desk was created and the post filled in the fall of 1964, with two other assistants appointed a few years later. In a positive and active sense, the party frequently, as in this instance, added to Tanjug activities without dominating autonomy. As a customer, it can operate like a market influence and produce such results as new product development and greater efficiency. It can, however, also act as a brake on activities, as in the rare case where a chief editor was asked to resign.

It may be concluded that overt government lines of control, though formally existent, are not usually used to make policy for the agency, except in special situations. They do, however, provide general perspectives for news coverage. The reason for this lack of explicit censorship lies in Tanjug's dual function as supplier of raw information to government agencies, who have to know what is going on, as well as supplier of news to the media. For wise and successful decision-making, the government needs as unbiased a report as it can get. It is therefore interested in supporting Tanjug independence as a prerequisite for the ability of the agency to view the world through glasses which are more or less clear rather than confusingly pink.

Overt control is not needed because there is an informal understanding between top agency personnel and politicians, all of whom belong to a cadre organization in which decisions made at the top must be followed at the base. One of the special editors corroborated this assessment and summed up agency-government relations in the 1970s as follows: "Out of a pronouncedly state agency we have today turned into a house with a more or less independent status. We not only help explain Yugoslav foreign policy, for example, we are not only the mouthpiece of the government as in the past, but we help mold this policy in various ways. The Federal Executive Council includes us in their survey of opinions before policy is made and we can give our own interpretation of these policies without checking with the Foreign Ministry."

Tanjug's Media Fare

With the agency's relations to government clarified, it is now possible to specify and interrelate growing organizational autonomy with changes in Tanjug's information filtering practices during the four information periods. In Table 10 these are conceptualized as changes in the agency's operative tasks and consequently in its news product. To detail these changes, the content of Tanjug services as well as the kind and degree of filtering will now be scrutinized in greater detail. Such an analysis in turn makes it possible to determine the extent to which the agency functions as a media guide for international and federal news interpretations.

Previous chapters already noted that between 1945 and 1950, during the administrative period, all content was censored. This precensorship, which was carried out by an agitprop-type censorship board composed of party and information officials, was all-encompassing, uniform, and heavy. Uniformity was assured both by the intermingling of the two hierarchies as well as by the three operative tasks assigned to Tanjug at the time. Among these were, according to interviews: the organization of Yugoslavia's home collection and distribution network, the establishment of initial relations with foreign news wholesalers, and the supplementing of diplomatic news from foreign missions.

Informants noted that these tasks required the linking of regional information bureaus, which had emerged throughout the war in various republics into a nationwide system that monopolized all news flow to the fledgling press and radio. In Yugoslavia, as in other Cominform states, the only reliable foreign news wholesaler was considered to be TASS, which supplied all eastern European states with the majority of foreign copy at the time.[14] Yet such diplomatic realities as the uncertain fate of the Balkans and Trieste convinced the top leadership that allied thinking also needed monitoring. Friendly wartime relations between President Tito and Prime Minister Churchill determined that this could be best accomplished through contacts with Britain's Reuters and France's Agence France Presse. Consequently, commercial agreements were signed with these agencies as early as 1946, well before they were initiated by other communist states.

Foreign correspondents, moreover, were assigned to such world information centers as London, Paris, New York, Moscow, and to neighboring western and eastern capitals, where they were supposed to supplement information emanating from diplomatic missions. Seven additional representatives thus initially covered Albania, Greece, Bulgaria, Rumania, Hungary, Czechoslovakia, and Poland. They were, however, recalled after the Cominform break which initiated a seven-year information hiatus with the communist bloc.[15] Throughout the administrative period, Tanjug copy was collected into a thrice-daily raw news digest, *Red Tanjug* (printed in red ink), which was designed for perusal by top government and party officials. From it, information for the fledgling press was daily abstracted. Tanjug, like national news agencies elsewhere in the People's Democracies, thus functioned like a government-owned instrument and constituted the lowest control level over the mass media.

Some of this power over media interpretation, however, began to evaporate during the transition period with the abolition of official precensorship and the introduction of the beginnings of corporate autonomy into Yugoslavia's growing press and broadcasting enterprises. Republican Ministry of Information and Tanjug branch offices slowly lost their monopoly over domestic news collection and distribution as newspapers and broadcast stations began recruiting their own news-gathering staffs. As a consequence, company records indicate that Tanjug's home desk stagnated between 1957 and 1961, functioning primarily as a transmission belt for official texts and losing some of its more enterprising staff to the foreign desk, which provided greater journalistic challenge. During the same period, furthermore, the task of economic news reporting was transferred to an independent institute where differing selection criteria were applied. With competition in local reporting from young newspaper staffs and economic reporting emerging from the stranglehold of centralized supervision, the economic and political news streams were for the first separated.

As a result, not only the extent but the degree of information filtering changed in the 1950s. Economic information became less strongly filtered in response to industrial needs, while political information remained under supervision of the League. Throughout this period, interviews revealed Tanjug staff was not permitted to excerpt official texts which were centrally distributed through the agency's "general service" ticker. Word-for-word reproductions of economic plans, government reports, and speeches were deemed vitally important for the political socialization of the multinational population, as well as the coordination of the economy, as it slowly moved from a centrally planned to a mixed-market state. Filtering sources throughout the period became multiplied. The official agitprop bureau was replaced by relevant party councils and the Ministry of Information, while Tanjug management, which was appointed by the Federal Executive Council, acquired greater power over interpretation.

Foreign news, still under the monopoly of the agency by virtue of being the sole repository and gatekeeper for foreign ticker flowing into Yugoslavia, became extended in coverage and increasingly western-dominated, reflecting the country's search for an independent political stance. In the late 1950s, a number of new correspondents were sent to smaller European nations, especially Scandinavia, and coverage of the seven East bloc neighbors, who had ostracized Yugoslavia after its Cominform expulsion, was resumed. By the end of the period, a corps of eighteen covered the world, including such nonaligned nations as India, Indonesia, Egypt, and various other Mediterranean states. The distribution of this corps indicates that the perspectives from which the world was being viewed had also shifted away from TASS. Increasing diplomatic contacts with various western European nations, with whom trade relations were being re-established, reflected the emergence of economic information needs relatively untinted by political ideology. Tanjug's political news product, however, throughout the transition period remained highly official, relatively undiversified, and primarily geared to serving governmental needs for justification of the new Titoist self-management philosophy. Media requirements were as yet secondary, and their ability to influence the agency as customers did not blossom until the mid-1960s when Tanjug, too, became an independent organization unable to count on government to make up its deficits.[16]

Further adaptations in Tanjug's operative tasks and programming, as summarized in Table 10, during the final two information periods indicate that two previously established filtering trends were further reinforced in the 1960s and 1970s. Both the addition of cultural information and the increasingly informal nature of political filtering add up to an overall reduction of the total degree of filtering within the Yugoslav information system. It has already been noted that the growth and stabilization of the Yugoslav press, radio, and television, as well as the proliferation of industrial firms throughout the decade of the 1960s, placed pressures on the agency to provide better written and more timely information for the newly added groups of customers which presently provide two-thirds of the total revenue.

Tanjug responded by diversifying its information product through the addition of cultural and economic services, as well as the creation of industrial and other bulletins utilizing raw information inputs provided by the four global wholesalers. By the end of the 1960s, the agency's four original bulletins had increased to 100, serving Yugoslavia's factories with export-import and world market, as well as management and agricultural, information. Furthermore, a comparative content analysis documents that Tanjug's general service ticker was redesigned and split to serve the needs of the afternoon press and of radio's hourly news broadcasts. Ten years ago the service spent more than half of its 35,000 daily words on official governmental material, often verbatim speech reproductions. Today it has ten major categories of information, much of it geared to interest the average person, which goes out over two additional circuits. As a result, both economic and cultural news flows to Yugoslavia's mass media were not only greatly increased during the 1960s, but also centralized and coordinated filtering criteria in these two streams became virtually nonexistent.

In political matters, too, filtering criteria changed. The previous chapter indicated that the 1960 press law further restricted and specified the areas where divergent opinions would not be tolerated. Moreover, *Red Tanjug*, which used to serve as the *only* source for the official view on foreign relations and domestic federal issues, can today be excerpted so that republican media editors are able to pick out and highlight those points most pertinent to their local League hierarchies. This led to the great variety of media outlooks and interpretations already noted elsewhere.

Interviews show that the source of political filtering during the independent period moved from outside of the agency to internal Tanjug councils. No longer is there overt Foreign Ministry interference with diplomatic interpretations, nor Ministry of Information briefings with agency editors on controversial issues of the day. With the right to elect its own top personnel, Tanjug is free to set its own filtering criteria, subject only to the limitations imposed by internal socialization.

Chapter 7 will provide evidence that these editors who have been with the agency from eleven to twenty years have much greater autonomy in decision-making than is usually assumed. They select all news items to go on the general service wire and determine lead stories; they also assess daily news requirements as well as the handling or format of items. Because of this autonomy, occasional interpretative "slips" on the part of the agency are inevitable. The latest occurred in 1970 when Tanjug's editor-in-chief, Momčilo Pudar, had to resign because he had permitted the publication of a commentary attacking the World Communist Conference in Moscow. Such views were no longer in line with the outlooks of the League of Communists' Executive Committee, which was attempting to re-establish normalized diplomatic relations with the Soviet Union after the Czechoslovak invasion.[17]

During the fourth information period, which commenced at the beginning of the 1970s, data in Table 10 indicate Tanjug redefined its operative tasks once more. This time reduced media usage of agency material became the touchstone for moves to strengthen world coverage and to focus on federal and inter-republican reporting, where media resources proved inadequate. The former led to the extension of Tanjug's foreign correspondent corps beyond Europe to the capitals of Africa and Latin America and to a revitalization of Tanjug's home desk. Today twenty-eight correspondents report from Léopoldville, Dar es Salaam, and Addis Ababa, as well as Djakarta, Peking, Delhi, and Rio.

Why this particular selection of reporting centers? Once again these decisions for a small agency with limited resources are political. Stationing correspondents in some of these countries not only helps conserve scarce monetary resources because exchange agreements pay for Tanjug's correspondents in places like Rio, but also because such positioning helps implement Yugoslavia's policy of fostering friendly relations with African and other nonaligned nations. The agency's home desk, which had languished when it functioned merely as a routine channel for the transmission of official political material, received additional editorial and correspondent personnel in the late 1960s and 1970s in order to cope with increasingly important federal changes, such as constitutional decentralization and interrepublican bargaining. For the first time, twenty-three permanent journalists and forty stringers cover every major Yugoslav town and produce specialized material for morning and evening papers and the broadcast media. All of these, except for *Politika, Vjesnik,* and *Borba,* lack reportorial contacts in other parts of the federation. Yet those media need to keep abreast of such interrepublican issues as social insurance coverage, resource and trade relations, and the sociocultural autonomy of the country's multinational population.

How have these changes affected the extent, degree, and source of the agency's filtering process during this final period in the 1970s? As in the decentralized period, it appears that filtering was primarily aimed at political reporting. Both the economic and cultural information streams move through the agency relatively unamplified and are recorded in specialized bulletins. These have to satisfy the interests of a variety of media and factory customers, differentiated by language, culture, and economic development, who are interested in straight trade and market reports.

The handling of political information has, however, become much more sensitive after the League's return to democratic centralism and its resumption of an adversary role following the Croatian crisis. As a result, the degree of filtering in this sphere seems to have increased, with criteria again more carefully defined from the center. Nationalities, strife, and criticism of social self-management practices have once more become virtually taboo subjects. Though there is no evidence that the agency's management has lost its autonomy over production processes, the 1970 replacement of the agency's chief editor indicates that journalists in responsible positions are more carefully picked and socialized. In such an atmosphere, Tanjug's reporting of federal League activities will per force become one of the major frameworks for media reporting of sensitive, internal political events. Many readers, both within and outside of Yugoslavia, have noted the dampening of opinion variety, as well as the removal of freelance intellectuals from media staffs as a result of these changes.

The cumulative evidence presented in this section amplifies historical evidence about filtering changes already presented in Chapter 3. It indicates that increased financial and organizational autonomy within Tanjug led to three kinds of specific filtering changes throughout the four information periods. The data suggest, first of all, a general decrease in the extent of filtering as the economic and cultural streams became free from overt editorializing. There was also a decrease in the degree of filtering as the press law became ever more explicit and agency personnel were able to excerpt official texts. Furthermore, it suggests, as shall be seen in the next section, that Tanjug editors assumed increased control over the definition of the filtering process itself. Not only have they since the mid-1960s acquired the right in their daily meetings to decide on how filtering criteria were to be applied, but they also grew increasingly free from formal extra-agency interpretative interferences, which previously emanated from the Ministries of Information and Foreign Affairs. How these changes affected the role of Tanjug vis-à-vis the Yugoslav mass media will be the subject matter of the final section.

Customer Relations

In the Soviet Union and many other socialist countries of eastern Europe, the government-financed national news agency, with a monopoly on news gathering abroad and the reception of foreign agency ticker at home, represents simply the lowest or working level of official control over the mass media. These control levels include, in the Soviet Union and East Germany, the propaganda and agitation department of the Central Committee (agitprop), the press department of the office of the Prime Minister, and the national news agency. In these countries, although the executive power is left to the party and the government organs, Anthony Buzek points out "the news agency serves as a convenient channel for quick transmission of urgent, day-to-day instructions of a purely technical nature, and also, of course, for comment, censored and adapted to the official line."[18] Newspapers and broadcast editors, eager to avoid "political error" in reporting and in assessing events, therefore turn to agency material with alacrity, because it is ideologically safe and decontaminated.

The cumulative evidence of this chapter has indicated that there is no such hierarchical relationship between Tanjug and the governmental or League agencies in decentralized Yugoslavia. In addition, while the agency had little autonomy during the period of administrative socialism, observation revealed that it is relatively independent today. Its relationship to Yugoslav power centers in the 1970s can better be described as a "voice among equals." In a decentralized multinational country where only the League of Communists speaks with a single voice, it influences government thinking, as much as it itself is influenced.

This raises the question of the extent to which Tanjug is able to "direct" the Yugoslav media in the 1970s. One way of getting an answer to this question is to check Tanjug's foreign news collection practices, the kinds of news the media buy from Tanjug, and how they use it. In contrast to such neighboring agencies as Četka of Czechoslovakia and PAP of Poland, Tanjug lost its monopoly on foreign news reporting during the 1960s. This is evident from the fact that its foreign correspondents corps has been reduced by one-quarter since 1963 and that its twenty-eight representatives today share this function with forty-one other colleagues working directly for the regional media. One interesting aspect of Table 12 is the concentrated location of Yugoslav foreign correspondents in the four world capitals, the implications of which will be discussed presently. For the moment, it is important to note that Tanjug has strong competition from its media customers, who send their own reporters to those cities where the news is made. London has a representative from six of the seven media; Washington, New York, Moscow, and Paris, from five; Rome and Cairo, from four.

The data also suggest that there is a division of labor between Tanjug and the media which is based on geography and content. The competitive stationing of media correspondents in major world capitals makes Tanjug unable to direct the Yugoslav press and broadcast stations concerning major international happenings. Any similarity of coverage, if it exists, results rather from a similarity of

Table 12
Geographical Location of Yugoslav Foreign Correspondents (Tanjug and Other Media)
(⊗ = stringers)

	Tanjug	Politika (Belgrade, Serbia)	Borba (Belgrade, Serbia)	Vjesnik (Zagreb, Croatia)	Oslobodjenje (Sarajevo, Bosnia H.)	Nova Makedonija (Skopje, Macedonia)	Delo (Ljubljana, Slovenia)	Radio and TV
Total	28	9	9	6	3	3	5	6
(parttime)	7							
London	x	x	x		x	x	x	x
N.Y. or Washington, D.C.	xx	x	x	x	x			x
Paris	x	x	x	x		x	x	x
Moscow	x	x	x	x				x
Rome	x	x	x			x		
Warsaw	x	x	x					
Bonn	x			x				
Cyprus	⊗						x	
Cairo	x	x	x		x			
Algiers	x			x				x
Delhi	x	x	x					
Trieste							x	
Athens	x							
Mexico	x	Latin x America					Latin x America	Latin x America
Brussels	x							
Rio	x			x				
Beirut	x							
Tokyo			x					
Bucharest	x							
Budapest	x							
Dar es Salaam	x							
Jakarta	x							
Leopoldville	x							
Peiping	x							
Laos	x							
Prague	x							
Sofia	x							
Stockholm	x							
Tunis	x							
Vienna	x							
Addis Ababa	⊗							
Berlin	⊗							
Chile	⊗							
Khartoum	⊗							
Rangoon	⊗							
Ulan Bator	⊗							

SOURCE: Yugoslav Journalists' Association, *Bulletin* No. 1 (July, 1964), Belgrade, pp. 60-61. Personal interviews with Tanjug, *Borba,* and Radio Belgrade editors.

background, including party membership and training, on the part of all Yugoslav journalists, not from overt control or censorship. The media are more interested, utilization figures show, in reprinting agency articles from Africa, Latin America, and the Far East, where they do not station their own men, than from the world capitals where they do. Tanjug's special article service instituted in 1964 was designed to give background and serious attention to "third world" information, otherwise ignored by the global agencies. For Tanjug journalists, this service also provides visibility and additional finances. Finally, there is the fact that Yugoslav media may subscribe directly to a foreign news service, thus breaking Tanjug's monopoly as the only foreign news source. In 1971 *Politika,* as a matter of fact, seized an opportunity to buy the *New York Times*'s report, which now flows into its office daily and supplements what Tanjug has to say.

Perusal of Tanjug's product-use figures further corroborates the agency's unmonopolistic position vis-à-vis the media. The economic director mentioned that in 1969 the Slovenian media used 70 percent, Serbia, 60 percent, Croatia, 55 percent, and the republics of Bosnia-Hercegovina, Macedonia, and Montenegro approximately 35 percent to 40 percent of Tanjug's services, filling up the rest of their space with material gathered by their own correspondents or originating from foreign agencies, notably the Associated Press and Reuters. As in North America, Tanjug customers pay a rate based on their circulation for the services provided by the agency. The media of the less-developed republics pay less, but also utilize less agency material, according to the above figures. In addition, a Tanjug foreign correspondent mentioned he found it hard to compete with foreign correspondents from the media because he had to concentrate much of his daily international report on diplomatic and political news for the information of government agencies. *Vjesnik* and *Politika* men are not so restricted and thus write about films, culture, and matters of interest to the average reader, which has tended to depress the use of Tanjug copy.

A careful investigation of the changing role of Tanjug in the Yugoslav information control pattern leads to the conclusion that the agency's influence has been declining since the 1960s. This is a result primarily of the new government requirement for economic solvency. Moreover, the strong pressure to compete for readers and listeners also produces a growing reportorial independence and specialization, both in the press and in the electronic media. As previously noted, this trend ultimately forced Tanjug to diversify its own general service coverage and to keep up with customer demands.

Press direction on the part of Tanjug thus amounts to an informal division of labor determined by differences both in customer character and in technical facilities. Since Tanjug covers a larger part of the globe, the agency supplies the press and electronic media with primarily official federal, economic, and diplomatic information, as well as integral texts of important speeches and communiques. Media correspondents, on the other hand, focus on local and republican issues which are widely diversified in multinational Yugoslavia. They stress human interest in their writing, and thus communicate the strong regional differences in Yugoslav newspapers and broadcast coverage already noted in the previous chapter.

With the increased diversity and improved quality of the agency news product since the late 1960s, it is difficult to understand the decreased media use of Tanjug material. Interviews with customers revealed that media complaints center around three issues: speed of transmission, manner of political presentation, and coverage of secondary events or human interest stories. Customers in Slovenia and Croatia are particularly disturbed by the fact that their readers and listeners frequently hear about major Yugoslav events from international newspapers which can be freely imported, or from Austrian, German, and Italian radio and television stations. Since newspapers have deadlines and competition to meet, speed is essential to them as well. Sending their own men, who report directly and do not have to contend with a complex and relatively slow internal routing system, may save an hour in making a debate available and in addition supplies a "regional angle" to federal happenings.

Lack of human interest material is cited as a second major complaint by the broadcast media, whose services have grown spectacularly during the 1960s. They, in turn, want Tanjug to provide fresh copy every few hours to keep listeners interested and informed of national and international happenings. Uninteresting news presentation is being rectified both through the "foreign article service" which backgrounds topical issues and through diversifying the general service, which is now sent out over four lines instead of two. The doings of international pop singers and human interest stories add to this diversity. Yet, in spite of the agency's desire to keep up with the times and to improve the quality of its information to suit media customers, money and outdated journalistic practices continue to be a major stumbling block to innovation. Consequently channels are sometimes turned over to officialdom quite uncritically.[19]

A third and final complaint came from an interview with *Borba*'s foreign-desk editor, who made the following interesting point. As the media gain experience and get to know their diversified local audiences better, they feel increasingly that Tanjug should be a supplier of information *without comment,* leaving interpretation to the individual papers or stations. This comes close to asking agency personnel to become pure observers and recorders, a difficult professional role to play in Yugoslavia. Such a media request supports the earlier point that the agency has lost much of its interpretative control, except in the sphere of federal reporting of sensitive interrepublican issues. Like the Associated Press, any political influence it wields over the media is a fortuitous by-product of the quantity of Tanjug reports the individual customer chooses to use and of the fact that top media and agency personnel are all party members whose outlooks become modified through League of Communist participation.

Three conclusions about the degree of "self-management" exercised by one of Yugoslavia's most important media enterprises emerge from this discussion. First of all, both the news agency's managerial setup and its autonomy profile indicate that Tanjug is today organizationally self-sufficient following the precepts of grass-roots democracy envisaged by Yugoslavia's ideologues who introduced workers' self-management as a means for decentralizing power. It makes the majority of its operational and resource procurement/disposal decisions without overt governmental interference. It also no longer functions as a junior department in a formal governmental hierarchy.

Moreover, it was noted that its information collection and distribution practices do not serve the purposes of government alone. With the majority of financing today coming from media and enterprise customers, governmental news categories and priorities have given way to a more balanced coverage of world events. Finally, the agency's power to direct the six regional press and broadcast systems in Yugoslavia is severely limited because of competition from media foreign correspondents, free access to foreign news agency copy, and audience participation in media financing. Yet, internal political matters are once again more heavily filtered, and here Tanjug can influence media interpretations informally by setting the framework for the understanding of national events.

As a result of this social and financial transformation, Yugoslav communicators will have to adapt themselves to new realities. In order to follow official exhortations and turn the media into "open forums for debate," they will have to develop a sense of public responsibility and begin to report events balancing governmental versus audience needs in self-managed socialism. How this role transformation occurs and whether it is effective or not will be the focus of the following chapter.

---

1 UNESCO, *Mass Media in the Developing Countries,* p. 16.

2 Llewellyn White and Robert Leigh, *People Speaking to Peoples,* pp. 2-3.

3 Tanjug has commercial agreements with three of the four western agencies, paying approximately $1,000 monthly for these services. It barters its own product for a limited TASS ticker.

4 For further details on the Associated Press's communication layout, consult Charles H. Brown, *News Editing and Display,* pp. 111-113.

5 Edwin Emery, Phillip H. Ault, and Warren Agee, *Introduction to Mass Communications,* p. 305.

6 Richard Schwarzlose, "The American Wire Services: A Study of Their Development as a Social Institution," p. 416.

7 UNESCO, *Statistical Yearbook, 1965,* pp. 15-21.

8 William Dill, "Environment as an Influence on Management Autonomy," pp. 409-443.

9 Pejovich, *Market-Planned Economy,* p. 87.

10 In the United States, the special role of the press in the democratic process is legally recognized by the First Amendment and by acts of Congress which subsidize the transmission of

educational and business communications through preferential third- and fourth-class mail rates.

11 For a more detailed discussion of this point, see Barry M. Richman, *Soviet Management*, pp. 77-93, 200-215.

12 Socijalistička Federativna Republika Jugoslavija, *Statistički Godišnjak, SFRJ, 1971*, pp. 352-353.

13 The same point is noted in Jiri Kolaja, *Workers' Councils: The Yugoslav Experience*, p. 67.

14 Theodore E. Kruglak, "Agerpress, the Rumanian National News Agency," pp. 343-347.

15 For further details on this point consult Gertrude Joch Robinson, "Tanjug: Yugoslavia's Multi-Faceted National News Agency," pp. 50-51.

16 *Ibid.*, pp. 122-123.

17 "Tanjug Editor Quits after Attack on Soviet."

18 Antony Buzek, *How the Communist Press Works*, p. 724.

19 See *New York Times* managing editor Clifton Daniel's address "Coverage of Bay of Pigs Buildup" before the World Press Institute in St. Paul, Minnesota.

CHAPTER 5

Who Mans the Media?

In modern industrial society most social communication is no longer face to face. Instead, messages are mass produced by institutions and rapidly distributed to large and heterogeneous publics. This so-called communication revolution has brought into existence and cultivated a form of consciousness which creates and sustains specific kinds of content while dropping out others. What is selected by whom and why becomes an ever more important and perplexing question. The previous chapters have investigated the social and historical "settings" which affect media performances in Yugoslavia. Here, in contrast, the emphasis will be on the "performers" — those who create the varied media content which fills contemporary newspapers, radios, and television screens.

Many communication theorists have drawn attention to the fact that individuals are linked together in social groups not only by political and property relations, but also by the ideas they share about the world they inhabit. The ideological function of integrating people's beliefs and value systems, which used to be entrusted to the head of the family, the priest, or politician, has in modern society been delegated to the mass communicator. He is the one who generates community consciousness and makes possible the governing of people too numerous and too dispersed to interact in any other way. Consequently, there are today three rather than two organized groups involved in the social communication process: the senders of messages, the audiences which receive and listen, as well as the media men who function as transmitters or selectors. Each group acts in a different communication environment, which helps predict their differing behavior patterns. The participants' bargaining positions, the relative values of rewards exchanged, and the legitimizing of relationships are all determined by this context.[1]

In Yugoslavia, the number of communicators, which may be defined as the editorial manpower responsible for informational and entertainment content in the print and broadcast media, increased from a low of 249 in 1921 to a high of

4,769 in 1971.[2] This constitutes a growth of 1900 percent in fifty years, compared to a growth rate of about 50 percent for the same period in Great Britain and the United States.[3] Such an explosion in numbers is closely linked with Yugoslavia's rapid increase in media outlets and the country's movement from under to middle development in a short three decades.

In spite of their proliferation in numbers and their central position in the social communication process, communicators around the world have been much less studied than senders and audiences. Little is known about their social characteristics such as age, recruitment, career pattern, status, and pay, all of which affect their outlook. We also lack information on the way in which the organization of media enterprises influences journalistic work and values. Nor are there many studies probing the effects of economic development and political setting on professional performance.[4] A number of reasons for this neglect come to mind. Among them is the fact that communicators filling channel roles are less conspicuous than the political and business elites. Both politicians and businessmen wield superior power over message initiation, but they lack the communicator's power over people's minds and outlooks.

In addition, communicators inhabit a shadowy realm between "craft" and "profession," making a determination of whether and under what circumstances they behave as professionals difficult to assess.[5] The variety of tasks performed by media personnel, requiring different kinds of specialization and outlook, are another stumbling block to analysis. There are at least four kinds of mass media manpower: information collectors, information processors, managers, and technicians. Each of these groups has little in common with the others concerning practice, training, and career pattern. And each is represented by a variety of different professional associations.

Finally, there is the very practical difficulty of surveying and classifying such a large, heterogeneous, and loosely organized group of people. Even governmental censuses fail to categorize media personnel in more than the most general terms. The 1970 United States census listed 152,984 persons giving their occupation as editors, reporters, authors, publicity writers, or public relations specialists.[6] Canada's approximately 7,000 communicators are classified with all other types of "authors." How many of these people are employed fulltime in the mass media is difficult to determine. As a result, only the smaller countries with more powerful journalism organizations, like Israel and Scandinavia, maintain more detailed records, as do the Soviet Union and most eastern European countries. Here communicators belong to journalism associations to qualify for health, vacation, and pension benefits.

For many years a dictum of faith has asserted that there are fundamental differences between the journalism corps in communist east European and capitalist west European countries. These differences were assumed to lie in social background, training, and job performance. Yet until recently, precise comparative data to test these assumptions were lacking. Systematic information on the way in which level of economic development affects professional performance has also been unavailable.

To provide a very crude framework to begin to answer these questions, the following chapter will compare the demographic and professional characteristics of Yugoslav and United States communicators. Basic characteristics include the size, distribution, age, sex, and social composition of the two communicator groups. Professional characteristics to be compared are their education, training, level of experience, and salary. All of these provide clues to professional behavior because, as Rosten noted many years ago, a journalist does not operate in a psychological or social vacuum. For this reason, "the social heritage; the 'professional reflexes'; the individual temperament; and the economic status of reporters assume fundamental significance."[7] They in addition to training become one of the crucial sets of "facts" determining the way in which journalists "see" and interpret the world.

Demographic Characteristics

The task of drawing a comparative picture of Yugoslav and United States journalists has been greatly facilitated by the fact that both countries have supported communicator research during the past five years. In Yugoslavia these data come from a 1969 sampling of Yugoslav Journalists' Association membership, whereas in the United States they are the result of a pioneering survey based on a representative sample of 1971 media personnel.[8] Selected comparative data from these sources are summarized in Table 13 referred to throughout the subsequent discussion.

Table 13 indicates that Yugoslavia had 4,235 and the United States approximately 69,000 fulltime employed journalists in the media at the beginning of the 1970s. These figures do not include those people who work parttime as correspondents, freelancers, or stringers. Various studies and interviews with Yugoslav journalists indicate that this additional group may be quite large. Financial pressures force many communicators to write for additional publications, and the volume of material produced further suggests that the total number of those collecting and processing information in the two countries may be double or triple those listed above.

What about the distribution of these communicators? Are there major differences in the way in which more and less developed countries and countries with different political systems deploy their communicator corps? The answer here seems to be a qualified no. Table 13 shows that the majority of journalists are employed by the print media and that irrespective of economic or political differences, the press constitutes the core of most information systems. In Yugoslavia, 57 percent of all journalists work for newspapers and magazines, and another 13 percent, in governmental information posts, prepare bulletins and press handouts. This comes close to the 75 percent of all United States communicators employed by newspapers and magazines. The remaining quar-

Table 13

Professional Profiles of Yugoslav and U.S. Journalists

(in rounded percentages)

Total Number		Yugoslav Journalists 4,235 (1968)	U.S. Journalists 69,500 (1971)
Sectors:			
Newspapers		43	70
Magazines		14	5
Radio		18	10
TV		9	10
Wire service		3	5
Other (gov. info.)		13	
Region:	U.S.		
Slovenia		11	
Croatia	(N.E.)	20	36
Serbia	(N. Central)	51	23
Bosnia-H.	(South)	9	25
Montenegro	(West)	2	16
Macedonia		7	
Sex:			
Male		88	80
Female		12	20
Age:			
20-30 yrs.		16	34
31-40		44	24
41-50		34	21
51-60		5	15
Over 61		1	6
Education:			
Secondary		45	2
High school		14	12
Some college or professional		30	28
College degree		11	58
Fields of study:			
Journalism		8	42
Liberal arts		40	29
Social sciences & history		15	24
Law		33	(.6)
Other		4	5
Journalistic experience:			
Under 5 yrs.		15	36
6-10		27	19
11-20		41	22
Over 20		17	23

Table 13 (continued)
Professional Profiles of Yugoslav and U.S. Journalists
(in rounded percentages)

Total Number	Yugoslav Journalists 4,235 (1968)	U.S. Journalists 69,500 (1971)
Positional distribution:		
Low level editorial	7	1
Rank and file reporters	31	35
Star reporters/content chiefs	37	34
Dept. heads/editors/for. corresp.	18	17
Division chiefs-overall resp.	7	13
Mean annual salary: (in thousands)	(1968)	(1970)
Low level editorial	$1, 2 - 1, 4	$ 4 - 6
Rank and file reporters	1, 4 - 1, 6	6 - 9
Star reporters/content chiefs	1, 6 - 2, 0	8 - 12
Dept. heads/editors	2, 1 - 2, 2	11 - 12
Division chiefs/overall responsibility	2, 3 - 3, 1	13 - 25
	plus 20% bonuses and child allowances	depending on organ- ization size and education

SOURCE: Saveznog Odbora Saveza Novinara Jugoslavije, *Izveštaj o Radu*, Beograd (May, 1969), pp. 151-183. John Johnstone, E. Slawski, and W. Bowman, *The News People: A Sociological Profile of American Journalists and Their Work* (Urbana, 1976).

ter of the corps in both countries contains approximately 20 percent broadcast journalists and a miniscule 5 percent in the wire services. The differences in the distribution of broadcast personnel, 18 percent in Yugoslavia and 10 percent in the United States, are accounted for by differences in the two countries' levels of economic development. In Yugoslavia twice as many journalists are in radio as in television, because radio is better diffused. In the United States, on the other hand, where these rates are nearly equal, television and radio personnel are nearly equally distributed.

In both countries economic rationality and historical impetus cause the media to become concentrated in certain regions.[9] In Yugoslavia level of economic development, cultural differences, and the mountainous terrain provide more media outlets per capita in the richer northeastern republics than elsewhere. The same factors have additionally led to the concentration of print and broadcast facilities in the larger cities, which are at the same time the seats of the six republican governments.

As a result 31 percent of all journalistic manpower is found in the most highly developed republics of Slovenia and Croatia, with only a bit more than a quarter (29 percent) of the total population. Middle-developed Serbia, which contains 43 percent of all Yugoslavs, also has more than its share of journalists (51 percent). In the least developed southwestern republics of Bosnia-Hercegovina, Montenegro, and Macedonia, with the final third (29 percent) of the population, journalists are severely under represented (18 percent).[10]

Even though levels of economic development are much higher in the United

States, and linguistic barriers are less pronounced, similar imbalances in manpower distribution are evident. Most media industries are concentrated in the northeast, which used to be the center of the population. In the twentieth century this trend has been perpetuated through commercial sponsorship. Media headquarters, as well as commercial headquarters, are generally to be found in New York City. Table 13 indicates that the northeast, with its Middle Atlantic states, consequently attracts 36 percent of all United States journalistic manpower, while the north central and southern states have only 23 percent and 25 percent, respectively, and the South trails with 16 percent.

In both countries, moreover, there is also a disproportionate bunching of journalists in urban areas. Though Yugoslavia's 1971 census found that nearly two-thirds (66 percent) of the total population still lives in towns of less than 10,000 population, journalists are primarily located in the republican capitals.[11] Forty-one percent of all Serbian communicators are found in Belgrade, 46 percent of all Croatians live in Zagreb, and over 50 percent of all Bosnian, Slovenian, and Macedonian journalists are located in Sarajevo, Ljubljana, and Skopje. In Montenegro an incredible 85 percent of the total corps is concentrated in Titograd.

Urban over representation is also a feature of United States communicator corps. Here, however, it appears that the greatest over representation is in middle-sized cities between 250,000 and 500,000, where there is a ratio of 2.5 journalists to the population, than in the large metropolises where the ratio is 1.2.[12] The causes of this unbalanced distribution pattern are largely technological: as circulation increases, editorial manpower decreases. In the United States 41 percent of all journalists are found in cities over a million containing only a third (35 percent) of the total population. Another 15 percent work in medium-sized cities, with 6 percent of the population, and the rest (44 percent) are distributed in smaller cities under 250,000. Among these, towns of 10,000, accommodating 33 percent of the total population, have only 4 percent of the journalists.[13]

Turning now to a comparison of the sex and age compositions of the two journalist groups, neither level of economic development nor political ideology seems to have a major effect on sex distribution. Journalism throughout the world is a male-dominated profession, with women in the minority. Differential recruitment seems to operate as effectively in Yugoslavia, where the ratio is about 1 woman to 7 men, as in the United States, where it is 1 to 5. This same 20 percent level is repeated in other highly developed western European countries like Germany,[14] Britain,[15] and Scandinavia.[16] In both Yugoslavia and the United States sex stereotyping and entry difficulties into journalism are furthermore evidenced by the fact that total labor force distributions of women and men are closer to 4 to 1 and 3 to 1 in the two countries.

Differential recruitment is due to a variety of factors: barriers to access in the prestige professions, mechanisms of self-selection, and, most important, outdated work role definitions, all of which have dissuaded women from entering the public arena.[17] Though more detailed breakdowns on the distribution of Yugoslav women journalists are lacking, it has been shown elsewhere that women are most prevalent in the least prestigious media sectors.[18] In the United States magazines have approximately 30 percent womanpower, weeklies, 27 percent, dailies, 23 percent, the wire services, 13 percent, and radio-television, a miniscule 5 percent.[19] Though the print sectors are generally more open, even they circumscribe the location of women. Nearly half (45 percent) of all female United States journalists work in small circulation dailies published in cities of less than 50,000.[20]

As in all of the more established professions, it is found that women tend not to be assigned to the most important news beats and that they have difficulty moving up the managerial ladder. Lubin found that more than 70 percent of United States female journalists cover the less prestigious "soft news" beats like personalities, culture, education, and consumer affairs.[21] Such segregation inhibits later career movement up the professional track to star reporter. Women are also less than proportionately represented in the various managerial levels. In general, the higher the managerial echelon, the fewer women are in evidence. On the top three levels women are less than 1 percent of all day and night, assistant managing, and chief editors in the United States media,[22] though they constitute 20 percent of the total corps.

Naturally these barriers to access and promotion also affect the salary of women staffers. In the United States average yearly pay differentials for equal work have been estimated to be as high as $3,000, while in Canada the figure may be a little less, around $1,500.[23] This is a substantial discount on the female abilities and services provided the media in North America.

In addition to being sex-typed, journalism is also a "young man's" profession. This suggests that the demands of the job, rather than economic or political factors, are most influential in determining recruitment. Table 13 indicates that 60 percent of all Yugoslav and 58 percent of United States communicators fall into the twenty- and thirty-year age groups. The relative youthfulness of the profession is further corroborated by Johnstone, Slawski, and Bowman, who note that United States journalists are 2.7 years younger than the labor force as a whole. In addition, journalists are substantially over represented in the twenty-five to thirty-nine year group.[24] The same holds for Latin Americans.[25]

The fact that people enter journalism relatively late and leave it relatively early is demonstrated by both Yugoslav and United States figures, which show that less than 15 percent of all communicators are below the ages of twenty or above fifty. Late entry in both countries is a result of higher than average educational attainment, as well as historical factors. In Yugoslavia, where a majority of journalists acquire their skill through on-the-job training, these historical factors include a training delay due to World War II. In addition, the political workings of the one-party state indirectly supported late entry in the 1950s by requiring that journalists prove their party reliability first and their professional skills second. These policies have since changed and there are now more young people in the profession. Yugoslav Journalists' Association statistics show that the twenty to thirty year group doubled from 8 percent to 16 percent in the five years between 1963 and 1968.[26]

The relative dearth of journalists in the over fifty group suggests that the profession is both strenuous and frustrating. A very bottom-heavy positional distribution in media hierarchies as well as relatively low average pay scales indicate that a journalist reaches maximum earnings relatively early in his career but usually becomes blocked on the lower hierarchical levels. In later years competent and ambitious communicators have "nowhere to go." According to data in Table 13, about two-thirds (68 percent) of all Yugoslav and the same percentage of all United States communicators are in rank-and-file reporter or content chief positions. These carry either no, or a minimum of, managerial responsibility. Only approximately a third of the total corps are department heads, managing editors, or division chiefs with overall responsibility. Mean annual salary figures, too, show disappointing possibilities for increases in both countries, a factor which will be further evaluated in the subsequent section.

To complete the discussion of basic characteristics, the ethnic and the socio-economic backgrounds of Yugoslav and United States communicators require investigation. In most societies, journalists represent the major ethnic groups. In Yugoslavia there are five of these and since republican borders follow ethnic lines, except in Bosnia-Hercegovina, journalists are usually recruited from the prevailing majority. Serbs and Croats practice in their respective republics, sharing positions in Bosnia-Hercegovina. The same goes for Montenegrins, Slovenes, and Macedonians, which constitute the communicator corps for their respective republics. In the United States, too, journalists largely represent the dominant Anglo-Saxon western European groups. There are only a few Orientals, Spanish-Americans, or blacks in the media today, although equal rights legislation is slowly changing this picture.

It is much more difficult to make a detailed comparison of the socio-economic background of Yugoslav and American communicators, because the data are sketchy. Judging by the fact that Yugoslav communicators have, however, received more schooling than the average population, it is probably safe to say that the majority do not come from worker backgrounds. In Yugoslavia only 24 percent of the total population over eighteen years has some higher education, while twice that number of journalists (41 percent) have taken university or professional courses.[27] A study of Polish editorial personnel found that, among Polish journalists, 80 percent belonged to the bourgeoisie by background rather than coming from worker or peasant origins.[28] American journalists also tend to come from privileged middle- or upper-middle-class social backgrounds. This is not surprising, considering that the majority are white Anglo-Saxon males. According to Johnstone, 62 percent of the respondents' fathers were in the white-collar sector of the labor force, and 35 percent were craftsmen, operatives, service workers, farmers, or laborers.[29]

Professional Characteristics

While it would be quite beside the point to inquire what kind of education and training doctors or lawyers have acquired, great variations in educational background are the norm rather than the exception in journalism. These variations constitute one of the most important barriers to developing a well-defined professional culture. One does not have to earn a college degree or undergo any other kind of certification in order to work as a journalist either in Yugoslavia or in the United States. There is, furthermore, little agreement as to what type of training constitutes the best preparation for the profession. This section will therefore investigate the educational background, work experience, and salary of the two sets of communicators to gain further understanding of their social and professional reflexes.

Table 13 illustrates the great heterogeneity in the field of study followed by communicators. Congruent with Yugoslavia's middle level of development, well over half (59 percent) of its journalists are secondary school graduates, with another third having some university or professional education. In the United States, on the other hand, well over half of all communicators (58 percent) have college degrees. These comparative data suggest that the Yugoslavs are still "professionals in the making," a status which implies a variety of incongruities which will be explored in the following chapter. Americans, in contrast, have attained levels of education which are found only in the top occupational categories.

The implications of these differences in educational levels should not blind us to the fact that journalism corps all over the world exhibit great educational heterogeneity. This heterogeneity expresses itself first in a bifurcation between those with apprenticeship experience and those who have studied, and second, in the fields where majors were acquired. As a result of this segmentation there is a recruitment crisis in journalism, and the merits of a college education versus in-service training are still not clearly established. Heterogeneity in majors raises the question of what constitutes the best educational preparation for journalists. Here the two countries follow different traditions.

In Yugoslavia the major division is between those who immersed themselves in the liberal arts (40 percent) or law (33 percent), and those who opted for social science (15 percent) or journalism (8 percent). In the United States, alternatively, the break is between journalism (42 percent), the liberal arts (29 percent), and the social sciences (24 percent). These differences in fields of study reflect differences in the university organization and educational policies of the two countries.

In contrast to the United States, where land-grant colleges have taught journalism since the late nineteenth century, Yugoslavia, like much of western Europe, does not consider journalism a traditional university course. If it is taught at the advanced level at all, it has been grafted on to existing university departments of political science or sociology, or relegated to institutes. The fact that only 8 percent of all Yugoslavs with university training have specialized in journalism suggests that they, like their United States colleagues, utilize the profession as a bridge to other careers. Among Americans nearly half (42 percent) of all students have combined news and editorial writing with academic concerns.

In spite of these differences in curriculum, the subject matter covered by the two groups is remarkably similar. Interviews elicited the fact that not only is law the most accessible faculty in Yugoslavia, but it also teaches a broad range of topics which are usually incorporated in United States history, political science, and sociology curricula. There are courses in the comparative history of law, political theory, sociology of law, Marxian bases of law, and special topics, like Yugoslav constitutional, civil, and criminal law. All of these acquaint young journalists with the politico-economic structure of their country.

Although type of educational background is a good criterion for determining whether a person will remain in a particular career, a group's career commitment is also expressed by the total number of years spent in the profession. The fact that journalists are not very committed, but switch into other occupations throughout their careers, is amply demonstrated by the small number of communicators who have over twenty years of experience. In both countries less than a quarter of the journalists have spent over twenty years in media professions.

In spite of this general finding, the comparative data in Table 13 indicate that the Yugoslavs are probably somewhat more committed than the Americans. Nearly two-thirds (68 percent) have from six to twenty years of experience, in contrast to only 41 percent of the Americans. Moreover, only 15 percent versus the United States 36 percent of the total group are in the one- to five-year category, where career commitment tends to be lower and the greatest amount of switching occurs. The greater commitment of Yugoslav journalists may be connected with the fact that the majority are members of the League of Communists. As mentioned earlier, such membership is held by only 9 percent of the total population and requires a belief in public service. This additional commitment seems to reinforce the staying power of Yugoslav journalists vis-à-vis their North American colleagues.

While similar data are unfortunately lacking, Johnstone's study indicates that, among United States communicators, the majority of job moves occur within the same medium. There are additional regularized routes of transfer, with weeklies serving as training grounds for dailies, which in turn send their experienced personnel to news magazines and wire services. There is little manpower flow between print and broadcasting. Within broadcasting the movement is clearly toward the more prestigious television.[30] Kruglak also found practically no movement from Agerpress to Bucharest dailies, because the Rumanian wire-service personnel is permitted to contribute to these periodicals in their spare time.[31]

Whether these patterns also exist in Yugoslavia is presently unknown. What is known is that whereas United States communicators may find employment in public relations, business, teaching, economic analysis, or advertising, Yugoslavs often move out of media jobs into government or diplomatic positions. Interviews with Tanjug staffers indicated that, though teaching and public relations are becoming more prevalent, ministries of information in the six republics have attracted journalists, as have Yugoslav embassies. These patterns of job mobility out of the media are particularly well illustrated by the seven ex-directors of the national news agency, Tanjug. Vladimir Dedijer (1943-44) now holds a history chair at Ljbuljana University. Ivo Vejvoda (1943-47) became ambassador to Rome in the 1950s, while Šime Balen (1947-49) is now a director of a Zagreb publishing house. The only woman in the group, Olga Kreačić (1949-54), is presently working in the Federal Ministry of Information. Vjekoslav Prpić (1954-59) became ambassador to Austria, and Jovan Marinović (1959-63) took over as head of information services at the federal legislature. Vukašin Mićunović (1963-67), the last director, left the agency to work for the Federal Executive Council.

A comparison of salary ranges indicates that the majority of Yugoslav journalists are paid relatively low salaries and that the salary differential between the top and the bottom ranks is much narrower in socialist than capitalist countries.[32] According to association data, 45.5 percent of all journalists are junior staff or reporters, 46 percent are content chiefs or editors, and the remaining 8.5 percent, top management. This corresponds fairly closely to the positional distribution of the North American communicator corps, as indicated by the figures in Table 13. Naturally, this hierarchical distribution is partially determined by experience and has effects on salary levels. Consequently, the 24 percent of Yugoslav communicators who have less than ten years experience tend to be on the rank-and-file reportorial levels and to earn the lesser salaries of about $130 monthly. These figures almost exactly mirror conditions in Latin America, where a journalist in Guatemala earns between $60 to $100 monthly. Among the 48 percent in editorial positions with eleven to twenty years of experience, salaries are one-third higher and range between $175 and $200 monthly, plus 20 percent bonuses. Only the 7 percent in top managing positions earn top incomes of around $265 a month and upward. Lawrence Day mentions that when all sources of income were considered, 67 percent of his Latin American journalists earned less than $400 a month.[33] The average comparative figure for Yugoslavia is around $100 less, though the fact that Yugoslav communicators earn an additional 20 percent in production bonuses and child allowances probably offsets this disparity.

In contrast to Yugoslav annual mean salary ranges between $1,200 and $3,100, North American journalists can look forward to nearly five times this income. Rank-and-file reporters make between $6,000 and $9,000 a year, depending on their sex, the size of their organization, and the medium they work for. Print and, within it, news magazines offer higher salaries than broadcasting. This averages out to a monthly income of about $750. Content chiefs and editors make about $1,000 monthly, while division chiefs and those with overall responsibility may have salaries that are double this figure.

In spite of the fact that Yugoslav salaries seem low with respect to United States figures, they are above the mean in their own society. Interviews and statistics indicate that even though a *Borba* editor noted with regret he made only half the salary of a Yugoslav factory director, at 2,500 dinars a month this still represents an income well above twice the industrial average for 1970.[34] In addition, total figures taken in isolation are misleading because they do not reflect the more egalitarian income distribution in socialist countries. In Yugoslavia rents are controlled and minimal, social security takes care of medical, hospital, and retirement needs, and everyone who works receives three weeks of vacation with pay.

Johnstone's $11,133 median income findings for 1969 also place United States journalists into the middle income range of those occupations classified as professional and technical.[35] The average earnings of editors and reporters were considerably higher than those of secondary school teachers ($9,886), slightly lower than those of accountants ($11,969) and sociologists ($11,797), and considerably lower than those of lawyers and judges ($20,139), or physicians and dentists ($20,190). The same middle position is also reflected in Hatt and North's study, which ranks United States occupations on a prestige scale from 96 points for a Supreme Court Justice to 33 points for a shoe shiner. Here communicators are awarded 71 points, almost the same as undertakers or managers of small city stores.[36]

The Two Journalism Corps

The assembled material permits a return to the initial questions and the drawing of some preliminary conclusions about similarities and differences between the journalism corps in communist and noncommunist societies and the impact of a country's developmental level on journalistic work. These conclusions are fragmentary and offered as a first approximation only. Future research will have to systematically compare not two but six countries at varying levels of development and with different political systems, in order to offer more authoritative generalizations. In spite of these shortcomings, even this limited comparison has provided some illuminating insights.

Though it has been assumed that the basic and professional characteristics of communist and noncommunist communicators are fundamentally different, the data presented here suggest that this is not the case. Similarities far outweigh differences. Political ideology does not affect the size, sector distribution, sex composition, or even the social level from which journalists are recruited. Ideology is also relatively irrelevant in determining such professional characteristics as the groups' educational specialization or level of experience measured by years in the profession. Where differences do exist between the social characteristics of Yugoslavs and Americans, these are primarily the result of disparities in the two countries' levels of economic development. These affect the total number of available communicators, their average educational levels, working hours, and salary. It may be concluded, therefore, that the modern mass media everywhere require personnel competent to understand and to explain the complex workings of politics, economics, and culture. To acquire such understanding requires a journalism corps with intellectual awareness and verbal facility, plus stamina. The former are achieved by various kinds of advanced training; the latter is largely a matter of age.

To begin the evaluation, differences in social characteristics resulting from disparities in level of economic development will be explored first because their effects on journalistic work in Yugoslavia and the United States are most easily interpreted. Differences in social and professional characteristics, it was hypothesized, influence the way in which communicators go about collecting and interpreting information in the two countries.

The first and most striking difference is to be found in the comparative sizes of the Yugoslav and United States communicator corps. On the most primitive level the small number of communicators indicates that information is an even scarcer commodity in the less than in the more highly developed countries. In Yugoslavia, the overwhelming concentration on political and economic news at the expense of entertaining features is at least partially explained by the small size of the journalism corps. Figures from highly developed Canada, with virtually the same population, indicate that Yugoslavia's communicator corps would have to be half again as large, or about 6,500 (instead of its present 4,325), to provide its 21,000,000 people with the same quantity of press and broadcast fare Canadians receive. Comparative data from Great Britain further support the contention that the ratio of 1 communicator per 2,500 to 3,000 population is relatively standard in highly developed countries.[37]

Whether the lower sex ratio of women in the Yugoslav media can be attributed to the same causes is, however, unclear. Little is known about the effects of economic development on the sex stereotyping of professions. Data from Germany and Scandinavia, in addition to the United States material presented here, indicate that the level is between 20 percent to 25 percent in these highly developed countries.[38] Though more work needs to be done to unravel these complex interrelationships, it is clear that journalism in communist, capitalist, developed, and developing countries is a predominantly male profession. It is such because everywhere communicators play an important role in the public arena which has traditionally been closed to women.

In addition to affecting the size of the communicator corps, level of economic development also affects their average educational attainment. In Yugoslavia, the data showed more than half of all journalists are high school graduates, whereas in the United States a majority have college degrees. This affects their work in the sense that they sometimes lack the insight to report complex events adequately or, more often, become the uncritical recorders of official explanations. One of Yugoslavia's ministers of information noted in a conversation that effective self-government demanded a communicator corps with good education and high status to ferret out sensitive information and to effectively question politicians. Unfortunately lack of time and inadequate material incentives have seriously hampered the educational upgrading of one-third of Yugoslavia's communicators who are in the forty- to fifty-year-old category. Older journalists in both Yugoslavia and Latin America are unable to return to institutes or to a university for specialized courses, because these often require a minimum of a year's attendance,[39] as well as personal payment for professional upgrading. Few journalists have these extra funds, let alone the time for this endeavor.

Considerably lower salaries for communicators are another effect of differences in level of development. In Yugoslavia the per-capita gross national product is about $850 a year, one-eighth of the American average and roughly akin to that in Mexico.[40] Mean annual salaries are consequently on the order of six to eight times smaller than in the United States. Though journalistic salaries are still above the average paid to other workers in developing countries, they do require a communicator to work overtime or to supplement his income by freelancing. In both Yugoslavia and Latin America, 84 percent of all journalists work between forty-five and fifty-five hours weekly, about fifteen hours more than the average American spends on the job. Consequently, the association is now pressing for a forty-two hour average work week with two-day weekends in Yugoslavia. If productivity and pay can be increased, such a work schedule may become a reality by the end of the 1970s.

In spite of these differences, great and surprising similarities in basic and in professional characteristics were found in the Yugoslav and United States journalism corps. These suggest that many of the "professional reflexes," as Rosten called them, may turn out to be the same for communicators around the world. These similarities start with the fact that irrespective of level of economic development, most communicators are employed in print rather than in the broadcast media. Newspapers everywhere are the agenda-setters for the electronic media, helping broadcast personnel to decide where to deploy their limited amount of recording equipment and mobile crews.[41] Because they are more numerous, papers are also often more influential in reaching national elites. In Yugoslavia, politicians and intellectuals alike read *Politika* in much the same way that the *New York Times* is a staple for Washington decision-makers. Star reporters like Djordje Radenković and Scotty Reston not only earn high salaries, but also belong to a common in-group with the persons who figure in their stories.[42]

The urban-rural, age, ethnic distributions, and socio-economic backgrounds of communicators also show remarkable consistency across political and economic lines. Journalists all over the world are more likely to live in and write for the urban rather than the rural population. They will select their topics with the politically powerful rather than the majority audience in mind. In developing countries of Africa, Latin America, and the Far East, this leads to the emergence of elite-oriented media programming, often in a language which is unintelligible to the general public and dealing with matters which are of little concern to rural villagers.[43]

Another factor reinforcing what might be called the "urban outlook" is the relatively high and homogeneous socio-economic background of communicators in both eastern and western countries. Higher than average social background of parents, although this can only be surmised, will encourage different "perceptions of reality" from those of the average person. What exactly these perspectives are remains to be investigated, but Darnton makes a case that conventions of writing "news" in different countries are affected not only by the professional work context, but also by inherited techniques of storytelling.[44]

The fact that communicators tend to be recruited from the ethnic majorities of their respective countries also reinforces the prevailing elitist outlooks and evaluations of social conditions. For this reason it was difficult, until the late 1960s, to find coherent accounts in the Serbian press about conditions in the autonomous republic of Kosovo-Metohija. The struggles of blacks and Puerto-Rican Americans lack depth and perspective in the United States for the same reasons.

Still another similarity shared by the two communicator corps is the fact that they are highly cohort differentiated. Even among Americans the older personnel who have been in the field the longest tend to have the least advanced education. If they went to college they tended to specialize in developing literary skills. Those in the middle of their career, on the other hand, are most likely to have been trained in journalism, while the youngest journalists tend to be social science majors.[45] In Yugoslavia a similar trend toward greater educational prerequisites, as well as a shift toward social science preparation, has been evident since the 1960s. One-third of all Yugoslav journalists with some advanced training or college degrees studied law, with liberal arts the other preference. Such a shift in educational preparation goes hand in hand with the introduction of specialized coverage, such as space technology, production and trade trends, as well as science, health, and medicine, which are now staples in both national and international reporting.

Though the differences in the social and professional characteristics of the Yugoslav and United States communicator corps are not nearly as great as anticipated, it must be remembered that social background alone is not a sufficient criterion for determining the way in which a journalist will behave in a particular country. To acquire a complete picture of "professional reflexes," the work and social settings in which the communicator operates also need investigation. Work settings teach the novice the concrete rules for selecting newsworthy events and for reporting these events, while the social setting defines the way in which the communicator interacts with senders and receivers in the mass communication of messages. The subsequent chapter will focus on the way in which "news values" are defined in Yugoslavia and the United States, and how the social role of the journalist is affected by a Marxian and a libertarian world view.

---

1 Singelmann, "Exchange as Symbolic Interaction," p. 420.

2 Bjelica, *200 godina*, p. 166.

3 Jeremy Tunstall, *Journalists at Work — Specialist Rorrespondents: Their News Organizations, News Sources, and Competitor-Colleagues*, p. 12.

4 See in particular a number of articles in Jeremy Tunstall, *Media Sociology: A Reader*, and Chapters 6 and 7 in David Chaney, *Processes of Mass Communication*.

5 Examples of this dilemma abound and account for the lack of discussion of journalism in textbooks about the professions. See, for instance, Penn Kimball, "Journalism: Art, Craft, or Profession?," pp. 242-260.

6 U.S. Bureau of the Census, *Statistical Abstract of the United States*.

7 Leo Rosten, *The Washington Correspondents*, p. 150.

8 John W. Johnstone, Edward J. Slawski, and William Bowman, *The News People: A Sociological Portrait of American Journalists and Their Work*.

9 *Ibid.*, Chapter 2.

10 Yugoslav Journalists' Association, *Izveštaj o radu*, p. 68.

11 See data in Table 1, Chapter 1.

12 Johnstone, Slawski, and Bowman, *News People*, Table 23.

13 *Ibid.*, Chapter 2, pp. 18-30.

14 Marion Marzolf, "Daring to Go Ahead: The Modern Woman Journalist in Western Europe." Also, Elizabeth Berg, "Women in German Broadcasting," pp. 19-20.

15 Tunstall, *Journalists at Work*, p. 13.

16 Stockholm Journalists, *Stockholms-journalister: a report by Journalist forenings utredning om foretagsdemokrati*.

17 Cynthia F. Epstein, "Encountering the Male Establishment: Sex-Status Limits on Women's Careers in the Professions," pp. 965-982.

18 Gertrude Joch Robinson, "Communicator Studies: The State of the Art."

19 William Winslow Bowman, "Distaff Journalists: Women as a Minority Group in the News Media," pp. 99-100.

20 *Ibid.*, p. 105.

21 Joann Lubin, "Discrimination against Women in the Newsroom."

22 Bowman, "Distaff Journalists," Table 3.9.

23 Gertrude Joch Robinson, "Women Journalists in Canadian Dailies: A Social and Professional Minority Profile," p. 19.

24 Johnstone, Slawski, and Bowman, *News People*, Chapter 2, pp. 11-12.

25 Lawrence J. Day, "The Latin American Journalist: A Tentative Profile."

26 Compare Yugoslav Journalists' Association, *Bulletin No. 1*, pp. 38-39, with figures in *Bulletin No. 3*, p. 171.

27 Socijalistička Federativna Republika Jugoslavija, *Statistički Godišnjak SFRJ, 1975*, pp. 90, 503.

28 Aleksander Matejko, "Newspaper Staff as a Social System," p. 173.

29 Johnstone, Slawski, and Bowman, *News People*, Table 2.10.

30 *Ibid.*, Chapter 4.

31 Kruglak, "Agerpress," p. 347.

32 Salaries were converted at the 1968 dinar to dollar conversion rate of $1 = 12 dinars.

33 Day, "Latin American Journalist," p. 155.

34 Socijalistička Federativna Republika Jugoslavija, *Statistički Godišnjak SFRJ, 1971*, p. 274, lists a dinar median pereonal income of approximately 1100 monthly with 63.9 percent of the total population making between 1001-1200 dinars.

35 Johnstone, Slawski, and Bowman, *News People*, Chapter 8.

36 Paul Hatt and C. C. North, "Prestige Ranking of Occupations," pp. 278-279.

37 Tunstall, *Journalists at Work*, p. 13.

38 Marzolf, "Daring to Go Ahead"; Berg, "Women in German Broadcasting"; Stockholm Journalists, *Stockholms-journalister*.

39 Mary Gardner, "Journalism Education in Guatemala," p. 7.

40 Richard F. Janssen, "Workers in Control: Yugoslavia's System of Letting Employees Manage Business Works Surprisingly Well," p. 36.

41 Halloran, Elliot, and Murdock, *Demonstrations and Communication*, Chapter 5.

42 Robert Damton, "Writing News and Telling Stories," p. 183.

43 William Hachten, *Muffled Drums; the News Media in Africa*.

44 Darnton, "Telling Stories," p. 192.

45 Johnstone, Slawski, and Bowman, *News People*, pp. 200-201.

CHAPTER 6

Journalists in Conflict

Anyone interested in describing the unique aspects of a particular occupation must be aware that professional behavior is influenced by at least three sets of variables. Among these are a group's personal characteristics, its work setting, and the legal and political norms imposed by the larger society. The previous chapter supplied a professional portrait of the Yugoslav communicator. It remains to analyze the work and the social contexts in which information production occurs in the country of the South Slavs.

In spite of the fact that United States communicator research is of relatively recent vintage, and has been limited to a few subgroups and to restricted aspects of their lives and work, various assumptions about the relative importance of the three sets of variables have been made. In the earliest studies, like Leo Rosten's[1] on Washington and Theodore Kruglak's and Leo Bogart's[2] on foreign correspondents, it was assumed that the social characteristics of communicators are most important in determining a communicator's "professional reflexes." Since then it has become apparent that why journalists agree with their paper's outlook and how they learn to report are all part of the on-the-job socialization process. Breed's[3] classic study, which made this point first, has since been amplified by Lee Sigelman's[4] and Gaye Tuchman's[5] work on routinization and the ritual of "objectivity" in reporting, and by George Gerbner's[6] analysis of the institutional pressures on mass communicators.

Most recently a trend has emerged indicating that legal and societal variables are the most important determinants of a journalist's definition of his or her social role. The research of Jay Blumler,[7] Bernard Rosko,[8] and John Johnstone[9] comes to mind here. All of these authors agree that journalistic roles are more strongly determined by structural than by personal characteristics. The political organization and culture of a country and its media organization have a greater impact on how communicators define their social role than does training. Such a finding suggests that communicator roles and news values are not the same all over the world, and that professional indexes are not universally applicable.[10]

To determine how independently Yugoslav communicators carry out their work in the 1970s and how they define their social role, this chapter will investigate the process by which journalists have become separated from other power groups and what kinds of role definitions emerge from Titoist media philosophy. Since communicators depend on the patronage of message senders, and Yugoslav journalists, in particular, have historically been beholden to politicians in their country, it is legitimate to inquire into the extent to which they function today as independent communicators rather than as party apologists. Information to answer these questions emerges from a study of Yugoslavia's history of journalism and from observation of the changing role behavior among Tanjug's editorial staff.

The Yugoslav Journalists' Association

According to Wilenski,[11] who analyzed the history of sixteen of the oldest professions, including law and medicine, there are five clearly discernible stages in the process by which an occupation changes into a profession. First, the occupation becomes fulltime. Second, professional schools are established to teach a systematic body of knowledge. Third, a professional association develops to press the group's interest. Fourth, persistent political agitation for job protection ensues. Finally, a formal code of ethics is drawn up to eliminate the unqualified, reduce internal competition, and emphasize the service ideal. Codifying an occupation and providing its practitioners with specialized skills guarantees public acceptance and the evolution of independent values and outlooks among the new professionals. Moreover, providing a bulwark such as a professional organization also affects task performance.

Yugoslav journalists passed through Wilenski's developmental stages approximately a century later than journalists in western Europe. The reasons for the delay are varied, but one point stands out clearly — the foreign occupation of much of present-day Yugoslavia until the late nineteenth century. Marjanović[12] notes that as a consequence journalism did not become a fulltime occupation until after the 1848 European revolution, when political, scientific, and literary journals were for the first time permitted to print in the local Slav languages. *Slovenija* and *Slavenski Jug*[13] both appeared in 1848, and *Šumadinka* followed in 1850 in Serbia. Even after the Serbs routed the Turks and the Obrenović and Karadjeordjević dynasties took over, journalists remained the handmaidens of power and had little chance for developing a professional image. They were generally treated as servants of the state and printed what officials wished to disseminate. Only at the turn of the century, under Alexander I, did the Serbian press law provide some brief initial conditions for freedom of the press and a professional association, while Croatia and

Slovenia had professionals well trained in Austria. Yet these early developments were, so to speak, nipped in the bud when the 1914 war erupted and the dictatorship of the 1930s emerged.[14] The Axis invasion from 1941 to 1945 simply reinforced previous historical trends which made Balkan newspapers and news agencies transmission instruments for government information and propaganda.[15]

Throughout this period and well into the 1950s, professional training for journalists was neither codified nor uniform. Danilo Zlender notes that in postwar Yugoslavia there were three distinct changes in the direction of professional training closely related to the League of Communists' doctrinal shifts already mentioned in Chapter 2. First, training was carried out with a Marxian theoretical orientation on the Soviet model. Then, during the period of reorientation in the 1950s, formal training stagnated and fragmentary in-service was the norm. Only in 1960 were academic centers created to put journalistic training on a more professional footing and to lay the foundation for a distinction between journalistic and party roles.[16]

In 1948, the Yugoslav party viewed journalism as a purely political function. The Belgrade Academy of Journalism and the Zagreb School of Journalism at that time trained 400 candidates for various foreign policy and propaganda posts. The political orientation of these schools is reflected in the fact that a majority of the journalism candidates had no reporting or writing experience.[17] Zlender mentions additionally that the curriculum was mainly theoretical and "not assumed to incorporate the daily experience of actual journalism." Candidates were selected for their political and ideological steadfastness. Great emphasis was placed on Marxism-Leninism, the history of diplomacy, and national and world history and literature, all topics familiar to functionaries trained under the Soviet system.[18] Both schools were closed in 1952 after the break with the Cominform brought the administrative period of centralized government to an end.

In the next eight years, while the party redefined its role in line with economic and governmental decentralization, a stagnation occurred in the formal program of journalistic training. Although Yugoslav chroniclers view this period with regret,[19] it gave journalists a chance to acquire professional competence. Editors and writers lost many material advantages accruing to them as party functionaries, yet they gained genuine craft experience throughout these years which prepared them for a more independent role in the 1960s. In the larger newspapers,

new recruits insufficiently qualified for certain specialized columns by reason of their former studies or occupations, had first to spend two to three months in the local news section where they were instructed in the fundamental principles of journalism before being transferred to other sections. The journalists' associations also resumed the task of organizing short-term courses for complementary vocational training wherever it was deemed profitable. At the same time discussions were held within the associations concerning the best method of journalistic training, but opinions differed greatly on the subject.[20]

The third period ushered in a full-fledged academic program of journalism training in the 1960s. Yugoslav universities today emphasize both practical skills and a social science approach to the media. The Belgrade Institute of Journalism (1960) functions as an advanced trade school under the auspices of the professional association and as a research center, while three new departments of journalism are to be found in the universities of Ljubljana (1963), Belgrade (1969), and Sarajevo (1970). Each of these departments today graduates communicators with both theoretical knowledge and practical experience who view themselves as experts. This strong professional emphasis is readily observable in the curricula, which contrast sharply with what went on in the earlier party schools.

The Institute of Journalism has recently organized intensive three-month and year-long correspondence courses on specialized topics like news and feature writing, international news coverage, radio presentations, and sports reporting. It also initiates surveys and seminars on topics of special interest. In the 1970s, inefficient newspaper distribution, the effects of "sensationalism," and the level and quality of criticism in the media were studied. Various symposia concerned themselves with the role of the media in self-government, the sociological aspects of communications processes, the media and international understanding, and the impact of satellites on broadcasting. They reflect the increasing empirical orientation of communication analysis in Yugoslavia.

The departments of journalism at the three universities, on the other hand, are broadening the academic bases of the profession along social science lines, similar to those in American universities. Since they are incorporated into the faculties of sociology and political science, undergraduates follow general courses for the first two years and specialize in the last four semesters. The journalism curriculum includes public opinion and mass communication theory, theory and practice of journalism, Yugoslav media organization and media law, international press history, and, in Ljubljana, Slovenian language and literature. Many of the 210 advanced students studying in 1971 received stipends from the media and combined their studies with practical work. In contrast to those in the United States, students in Yugoslavia have no difficulty finding employment upon graduation, because advanced degrees are still scarce in journalist circles.[21]

Contrary to the Soviet Union, Czechoslovakia, Poland, Hungary, and East Germany, Yugoslavia has taken the first step on the road to teaching a systematic body of journalistic knowledge, emphasizing mass communication rather than political perspectives. Though predictions about trends are as yet premature and Yugoslavia's university-trained journalists number not more than 600 to 700, a beginning has been made in upgrading both practical and theoretical talents. This upgrading is along lines reminiscent of those in Great Britain, where communication has become a legitimate university course at Leeds and Cardiff. In both Yugoslavia and England, communication graduates are among the journalistic elite and join both government and media agencies in top positions.[22]

In addition to specialized knowledge, Yugoslav journalists have acquired a second bulwark differentiating them from League functionaries and protecting them against arbitrary bureaucratic encroachment from other power centers. They are now members of a separate professional organization. The new Yugoslav Journalists' Association, with branches in the republics and autonomous provinces, split off from the larger trade union organization in 1959 to agitate more effectively for the needs of mass communicators. Chief needs, according to the 1969 statute, are increased professionalization, regional coordination, and improved information access, called "publicity of work" in Yugoslavia. The eight major tasks of the Yugoslav Journalists' Association are:

(a) to coordinate and assist the work of republican associations in fulfilling the basic aims and tasks of journalism;

(b) to work for the successful performance of journalists' activity, to develop the responsibility of journalists in professional work, and to protect their repute;

(c) to accept, take initiatives, and engage in the solving of professional questions of journalists and journalism;

(d) to take part in preparations, that is, to cooperate with competent organs in drawing up legal and other provisions in the sphere of journalists' activity and to take initiative in this sphere;

(e) to support and organize ideological-political and professional exchanges of views;

(f) to cooperate with the Yugoslav Institute of Journalism and all institutions dealing with the study of journalism and the training of journalists;

(g) to cooperate with affiliated and interested organizations and associations in the promotion of journalism in order to implement consistently the principle of the public character of work;

(h) to represent Yugoslav journalists in the country and abroad and to protect their professional interests.[23]

As a federal umbrella organization, the association has, from the start, agitated for and supported increased self-government at all media institutions and encouraged journalistic interpretative independence. Bogdan Osolnik, chief editor of Yugoslav Radio-Television Belgrade, told a group of visiting journalists in 1963: "When the state administration or any other body assumes the role of interpreter of truth as well as of the interests of society, there is always the chance that all this could work against the individual, against his elementary human interests, and of course become a means for dehumanization and enslavement."[24]

The changing social setting in which the journalist has worked since the

1960s has brought about a concomitant change in the way in which he is supposed to view his role. The association participated in this new role definition by analyzing the public's information needs and by insisting on the elimination of the most serious Stalinist aberrations of bureaucratic power and secrecy. It formulated the public's "right to know" clause which is incorporated in the 1963 constitution and proposed new press and broadcast laws specifically abrogating prepublication censorship. It also agitated for the separation of jurisdiction over press law infringements. Today journalists and other publicists are judged in open court for libel and other press law infringements instead of having to submit to government or party committees. This gives them increased protection and permits the judging of their ideas only *after* they have been publicized.

Since the new journalistic role, which is supposedly based on the freedom to report, also carries with it the responsibility to select content which is both popular as well as socially relevant, the association has also become concerned with the protection of journalists who must ferret out controversial material. For the first time, a code of ethics has been developed; it will be discussed at greater length in the next section. Today articles demanding the upgrading of working conditions, a shorter work week, better retirement benefits, and the protection of media autonomy dot the pages of *Naša štampa,* the official journal of the association.

All of these developments indicate that mass communicators as an elite group have become distinguished from both governmental officials as well as party and trade union practitioners during the 1960s. They have updated their "symbol broking" skills through systematic communication studies and specialized in-service training. They have also banded together to agitate for job protection, professional standards, and the ideal of serving the public through responsible reporting. As a result, communicators in Yugoslavia seem to be in a state of flux with new roles and outlooks emerging. To test the assumption that changing social and work settings affect the way in which journalists go about their jobs, the subsequent section will investigate changing role behavior among Tanjug's editorial staff. This was observed during two periods in 1964 and 1969, both before and after the introduction of workers' self-management.

A Case Study in Role Behavior

With Yugoslav journalism in a general state of flux, what changes are reflected in Tanjug editorial personnel? Have they undergone the same shift in training procedures as their compatriots? And what has the effect of institutional liberalization been on their professional outlook? Tanjug's organizational history revealed that, during the war and immediately after its founding in 1943, the chief editor and most personnel were appointed with approval of the secretariat of information, and centralized organization under the director was the rule. Interviews also showed that, at its inception and during the crucial years when the agency was the only source for allied news about Yugoslavia, Tanjug drew on the services of the most experienced men in the political establishment. Ivo Ribnikar, editor of the prewar paper *Politika,* was its first director, and Moša Pijade, the party theoretician, its chief editor.

Even after the end of hostilities, the information and political power elites remained merged. Scarcity of trained journalists forced Tanjug, like other media, to make do with personnel without explicit professional qualifications, while administrative fiat during the period of "administrative socialism" encouraged the recruitment of politically "safe" and trustworthy men for the growing wire service. During the 1950s, state financing perpetuated this relatively inefficient personnel program which worked against journalistic expertise and standards. In addition, government communiques, which could not be altered, militated against reportorial excellence. Like staffs everywhere, Tanjug had to train its own personnel in the absence of journalism schools.

Tanjug training throughout the period was haphazard, like that of Yugoslav journalists in general. Promotion in the agency, too, did not yet proceed on purely professional lines, since party appointments could upset the pattern. Only toward the end of the 1950s did a division between the information and political elites slowly emerge. This came about as a result of agency decentralization of power to the various desks and departments, and the communist party's role shift from "governor" to "adviser" after 1956. Interviews revealed that this change in emphasis produced changes in working practices which ultimately elicited a more professional outlook. Tanjug's working editors at this point, for the first time, received the right to select freely from official documents, to handle the general service wire without prior consultation of appropriate ministries, and to have a say in the recruitment of new personnel.

In the 1960s three other factors contributed to the development of a professional outlook among Tanjug's editorial staff: (1) the increased need for financial independence after the 1965 economic reform, (2) administrative changes in the wage system, and (3) new organizational practices. Company records indicate that financial independence with its concomitant loss of government handouts, as well as the devaluation of the dinar, made increased efficiency one of the top priorities. In 1965 network charges, foreign service costs, and the maintenance of technical equipment suddenly jumped by 60 percent, severely overstraining company resources. As a result the agency took two drastic actions. First, it invested only 9 percent of gross income in capital funds, using the remaining 6 percent to bolster salaries and cushion the shock of adaptation. Second, there was a staff cut from 525 to 456, which is approximately 85 percent of the original number. This was affected not from the top down, but by the working units themselves, which decided on the basis of competence who should be retained. New recruits, no longer selected by the personnel department, now apply for job openings in public competition. Young journalists wishing to work in correspondent and top editorial jobs today must have the equivalent of a college degree, preferably in the social sciences or journalism, as well as knowledge of a foreign language.

The second prominent role change which also encouraged a more professional outlook is the new flexible wage system. This determines salaries on the basis of individual effort and the success of the enterprise as a whole.[25] Since the 1960s, workers' councils in industry, the media, and Tanjug calculate wages on the basis of position held. This determines 80 percent of the salary *(startna osnova),* and there are in addition bonuses for overtime and quality. One form of incentive is thus reintroduced into a system which otherwise grants every citizen a secure job irrespective of how well he or she performs. Agency records indicate that in spite of the fact that material expenses doubled between 1963 and 1969, income tripled in the same period. Such growth was possible because Tanjug productivity per employee tripled and a whole new range of news services was introduced. Chief among these were technical and financial bulletins for factories, business guides, publication of books, a tourist daily in English and German, more aggressive photo distribution, and the development of a specialized broadcast service.

New organizational practices encouraging greater independence among agency personnel included staff rotation and the establishment of a fund for professional education and retraining. In the past, promotions and selections for desirable foreign correspondent posts were made by the managing board and the director. Today there is open competition here, too, on the basis of competence, knowledge, and language experience. As a consequence the managing board simply approves the nominee selected by his own working subgroup. Coveted foreign correspondent jobs can also no longer be held for more than four years since a rotation policy gives everyone qualified a chance to upgrade his talents. Though many of the top staff have been with the agency for ten to twenty years, comparative records show that they have not held the same position for nearly as long as their American counterparts in the Associated Press. While such a policy forestalls the kind of bureaucratic inbreeding so prevalent during the period of administrative socialism, it does limit the development of specialized expertise. Yet in a small organization like Tanjug and with fewer resources, it is perhaps more economical to build up a journalist corps with a general level of competence. Such a strategy permits interchangeability of personnel, which is not possible with a few star reporters.

Finally, Tanjug's regulations concerning professional education were designed to secure adequate staff competence to meet the growing needs of the agency. Leaves of absence and shorter working hours were granted to attend special seminars and language courses at the Institute of Journalism, in which journalistic and technical skills are improved. In return, the beneficiary is required to attend classes regularly and to reimburse the agency in the event of course failure. A questionnaire administered to the top editorial personnel of Tanjug's editorial department and to the special editors of the foreign desk reveals that half of them, ten out of twenty, have taken advantage of special language courses to further their careers. This is a high percentage for such a small group in leading positions and underlines the practical concern with increasing professional skills and competence.

Noting administrative changes alone, however, does not answer the factual question as to whether Tanjug's editors have changed their outlooks and today work increasingly as independent journalists. Personal observation of news-room functioning elicited at least five points which corroborate that these editors are first and foremost journalists. It has already been noted that promotion and rotation of the staff occur on the basis of competence. Recently the post of foreign correspondent to Moscow fell vacant and was filled by competition among a group of three staff contenders. It has also been mentioned that agency recruitment is handled through public application. In the past years classified ads run in the Belgrade papers turned up twenty-five applicants for various openings. Both of these practices preclude staffing only on the basis of political steadfastness.

Interviews also elicited the fact that sanctions, except in very rare cases, are imposed for journalistic, not party, reasons. Editors are punished for doing an inadequate reporting job, rather than for failing to toe the party line. Thus, for instance, a staffer reported a nonexistent shipping line between Rijeka and Bulgaria. Jadrolinija, the involved enterprise, protested the error, which Tanjug had to admit. The punishment, meted out by his peers in the home desk, was loss of salary, which for severe errors may be as high as 80 percent of the monthly take-home pay. In another case, the night-shift editor of the Skopje branch lost 25 percent of his wage for not checking on the reported seismographic strength of the second earthquake tremor in 1964. The figure he gave would have implied many deaths and substantial damage to new buildings, neither of which occurred.

Finally, it appears that Tanjug editors turn to their own peers for advice on journalistic interpretation rather than to an outside source. In answer to a questionnaire asking whom they queried in case of need, all respondents listed first their immediate colleagues and, as a last resort, the chief of the foreign desk. However, few journalists could remember consulting the latter recently. The editor for foreign correspondents recalled consulting the chief on a fluid foreign policy situation in Bangladesh where various interpretations of events were possible. His advice to the correspondent stationed on the spot was to follow and report developments and let the interpretation emerge from the events.

All of these indexes taken together substantiate the conclusion that Tanjug journalists, like their colleagues in the media, are beginning to see themselves as practitioners of the reporting trade and, in fact, act as such. If they are also involved in party work, time considerations and the exacting nature of their jobs force these activities into their leisure hours. Questionnaire data corroborate that few Tanjug journalists participate actively in political organizations. Instead they write books and articles to supplement their income. The same conclusion emerges from the 1969 Yugoslav Journalists' Association data which note that only 19.3 percent of all journalists engage in party, trade union, or Socialist Alliance activities.[26]

Titoist Media Philosophy

Having covered the complex social matrix in which communicators work, it remains to find out how journalists define their social role in the 1970s. It has already been suggested that communicators are only one among three groups engaged in the social communication process; they play a channel role between the potential sender and receiver groups. To the extent that they fulfill the expectations of these groups and effectively select and translate messages, they retain both sender patronage as well as audience recognition. Yet such a general description does not provide much insight into how communicators view their social roles in a given country.

Researchers have approached this problem from two perspectives, either by developing media typologies[27] which describe very general, abstract role types, or more recently by providing descriptions of how journalists themselves define responsible professional practice.[28] A most interesting United States survey focused on communicators' conceptions of the functions of the media in American life and on their beliefs regarding the role of the journalist in gathering information. This study found that in the United States two stances with different philosophical bases are prevalent. The "neutral" and "participant" role conceptions pit "proponents of a professionalized, objective, restrained and technically efficient journalism against those advocating a socially responsible journalism."[29] The majority (79 percent) of all American communicators combine aspects of these two stances, with only 10 percent and 11 percent, respectively, adhering to the pure "neutral" or "participant" role definitions.

Unfortunately similar empirical data on Yugoslav definitions of communicator roles are lacking. It is therefore necessary to devise a two-step comparative approach. This deduces a journalist's role conception from the country's general media philosophy and then searches for empirical evidence supporting or denying these deductions. Since Titoist media theory has not been explicitly worked out anywhere, it is useful to develop its rationale by comparing it with Leninist press theory. Such a comparison helps to differentiate the two and to clarify the ideological assumptions underlying communicator behavior in Yugoslavia.

Wilbur Schramm, in his discussion of the Soviet media, notes that Leninist communication theory is quite under developed in comparison to that provided by the libertarians, because it constitutes an integral part of the Marxist theory of the state and society. Instead of searching for theoretical underpinnings of the Soviet media, their actual working must therefore be analyzed. Four characteristics seem to be most salient: the media are controlled by the state, they are closely integrated with other instruments of power, they are used instrumentally to convey the word of the party, and they are characterized by strictly enforced responsibility.[30]

Titoist communications theory differs from this description in several important ways. This raises the terminological question of whether it should still be considered a variant of Leninism or, in fact, constitutes a wholly new form of media organization. Though others may disagree, this writer believes that the Yugoslavs have developed a new theory. This conclusion is further corroborated by Raymond Nixon's 1965 assessment of world press freedom, where he notes that "the decentralization of controls over the Yugoslav press has reached the point where the system can be described as 'mixed' with a 6 rating rather than one of absolute party or government control."[31]

Where and how, then, does Titoist press theory differ from Leninism? To begin with, there is the matter of state control of mass communications. In Yugoslavia, as has been seen, the print and broadcasting statutes of 1956, 1965, and 1968 established financial and operational media autonomy which guaranteed freedom of speech and the citizen's right to know. Bogdan Osolnik, one of Yugoslavia's most influential journalists, describes the new system in the following way. In a democratic self-governing society, the media have three vital functions. First, they must supply "objective and comprehensive social information" so that each citizen and self-governing unit can develop a responsible outlook on matters of practical concern. This information must come from a variety of sources rather than from restricted governmental or party bodies. Second, the media must act as "public forums" and criticize "negative phenomena and trends within society." Finally, they must serve as a means for "social education" by spreading elementary knowledge "for following and understanding the socio-economic process."[32]

As public forums, the media are supposed to be mirrors of events, reflecting quite clearly economic, political, and cultural realities. Media integration, with other instruments of power, is therefore not overt in Yugoslavia. There is no merging of media, party, and governmental hierarchies, though informal control does exist. The Tanjug organizational study indicates that top editorial posts are always held by party members, though they no longer combine these posts with nonjournalistic activities. Long years of journalistic practice and party membership rather than the formal intermingling of the information and party elites provide the common framework for interpreting national and international events.

The instrumental use of the media in Yugoslavia is counterbalanced by the media's financial independence from government and by the citizen's right to know. To inform themselves, Yugoslavs may organize magazines, factory papers, or local radio stations. These are supposed to collect information from a variety of sources in addition to government and party bodies. Historical evidence indicates that they do this quite freely in economic and cultural matters, but that the media are indeed used for the transmission of official political information, particularly when there are internal or diplomatic pressures. Though Tanjug data suggest that editorial autonomy is quite extensive, it is not as broad as publisher autonomy in the United States. Here Sulzberger can make decisions about *New York Times*'s political coverage which differ from the government outlook. Such is not the case in Yugoslavia, where a publisher's council of a paper monitors "socially responsible reporting." What this means in any particular instance depends on how the republican party leaders interpret the issues.

What are the implications of such a theory for the definition of communicator roles in contemporary Yugoslavia? In a system of linked rights and responsibilities, the journalist must balance the right to publish against a duty to his own social conscience. The Yugoslav Journalists' Association notes that he must record the facts as he sees them, "analyzing social processes and contradictions with the help of his own views and attitudes."[33] This means, as President Tito mentioned in an interview on Brioni June 17, 1969, that "simple transmission is not presently required of a journalist. On the contrary, he is expected to be creative, to make a constructive contribution to our social development." Instead of identifying with Leninism, which attaches the media to the party apparatus and makes the journalist a mere transmission belt for the party line, Yugoslav self-managed democracy defines him as a socially responsible yet independent recorder of events who should provide independent and nonpartisan sources of comment and criticism in contemporary Yugoslavia.

What evidence is there of the extent, range, and substance of freedom of criticism in contemporary Yugoslavia which would substantiate the contention that the communicator no longer functions as a simple cog in a press system run by the party to disseminate party views? Such evidence is exceptionally difficult to gather systematically and to evaluate analytically. There are no adequate comparative criteria for assessing the degree of freedom of a particular media system. Even Nixon's index is qualitative and based on the opinions of a panel of informed judges. These merely note that Yugoslavia's media freedom is "intermediate with tendencies appearing to favor a controlled system at the present time."[34] Theory, too, cannot be used as a yardstick for practice. There is left the alternative of presenting various illustrations of press criticism to provide a sketch rather than a proof of the Yugoslav journalist's extent and kind of critical independence.

Illustrations of the degree of criticism possible in the economic realm include the following examples. In the spring, when vegetable prices drop, journalists visiting local restaurants provide astounding calculations of the profits produced on cabbage simply by chopping it up into slaw. When veal is scarce in Belgrade, while the Adriatic coast seems to feel no such hardship, the reader finds articles denouncing the distribution system. The papers also keep their readers informed on which restaurants water their wine, what factories are wasting scarce foreign currencies by buying too many foreign patents, and how the communes are pressuring successful firms to merge with unsuccessful ones. Descriptions of embezzlement and corrupt directors running their workers' councils are a standard feature in the campaign to strengthen workers' self-management.

The breadth and substantial nature of cultural criticism is evidenced not only in the press and publishing but also in literary and philosophical magazines and in film. Socialist realism, never firmly established in Yugoslavia, was officially denounced as early as the 1950s, ten years before cultural liberalization became a fact in eastern Europe. Translations of Joyce, Proust, and Faulkner soon led to experimentation with modern styles and stream-of-consciousness writing. By the 1960s, Yugoslav films, especially those by Makavejev and Pavlović, took the lead in probing controversial human dilemmas and such taboo subjects as social and economic inequality. There is, furthermore, evidence that the breadth of literary themes increased dramatically in the 1960s. Novels published in the past few years often paint a gloomy picture of Yugoslavia's partisan war and its impact on human values. Others probe such themes as crime, mental disorder, and the rift between generations, usually not permitted in socialist societies.[35] Humanist philosophers, gathered around such magazines as *Praxis, Naše Teme,* and *Filosofija,* challenge the correctness of such basic Marxist assumptions as the belief that socialism automatically solves all problems of alienation, that self-management principles contradict market relations, and that the cult of the personality interferes with the democratization of government.[36] They also reject dogmatic adherence to dialectical materialism as a means for justifying the status quo rather than discovering novel solutions to societal problems.[37]

The narrower framework for political criticism is indicated by the handling of the Djilas and Mihaijlov cases. Both of these indicate that party tactics are debatable, but substance is sacrosanct. Why is this so? The answer lies in the way in which differentiation and integration needs are balanced in Yugoslavia's mass media system. Chapter 3 noted that ethnic and economic diversity lead to differentiation and pluralistic reporting so that integration can be achieved only on the political level of "common causes." Among these are criticism of capitalism, espousal of the virtues of self-management, the need for the withering away of the state apparatus, ethnic equality, and confederation.

When any of these basic tenets are challenged, as in the case of then vice-president Djilas and Mihaijlov, who advocated an opposition party and an opposition press on the grounds that these are not precluded by Marxist principles, or when ethnic differences become the wellsprings of a nationalist movement, political freedom of expression is drastically curtailed.[38] Yet, in spite of these limitations, the extent and range of political criticism is considerably larger than in any of the other eastern European communist states, where the following report about a car accident involving the son of a Presidium member would never have been printed.

According to accounts in *Borba,* which is closely associated with the party, and *Politika,* the biggest Yugoslav newspaper, Mr. Sekulic was driving his father's car at high speed one night and struck a pedestrian. Though serious injuries usually mean a few days' detention in jail, he was released after only three or four hours, during which the police say he confessed to the accident. Under a headline entitled "Why Mr. Prosecutor?," a *Borba* article notes that the public prosecutor supposedly telephoned the release order. Such a headline and the accompanying article provide one of the bolder examples of criticism within the relatively large and flexible limits of political press freedom in Yugoslavia. One knowledgeable foreign correspondent evaluates these limits in the following way:

> Newspapers such as *Politika* and *Borba,* formerly dependent on official subsidies, are approaching full financial independence. The press, in turn, under the goad of competition, and with leaders calling insistently for freer and broader public debate — and complaining sometimes because this is not sufficiently forthcoming — manages to mirror a considerable range of the controversy that takes place in the Government and the party.

> Criticism of official policies and agencies, revelations of mismanagement and corruption, and the airing of radically varying views on the desirable extent of economic reform and democratization appear regularly.

> There are limits. President Tito is not criticized, although ideas he is known to favor are not necessarily immune. Foreign policy questions are treated with some caution. Important government and party figures are not attacked by name, although it sometimes is apparent that criticism of a policy has a particular official as a target.[39]

By the 1970s, larger social issues also received public scrutiny. In 1971, the weekly news magazine, *NIN,* published the first statistics on Yugoslavia's poor, a fact otherwise ignored in socialist societies. It turns out that one-third of the total population, including private farmers, unskilled workers, gypsies, and others, fall into this category. Major newspapers, like Zagreb's *Vjesnik u Srijedu,* raised questions about the steadily mounting emigration of skilled workers to western Europe, while *Politika* and *Borba* covered and analyzed the effects of new election procedures. Among these were such previously taboo subjects as deals made on candidates' lists and political in-fighting between designated candidates.

"Apologists" and "Critics"

A decade after the promulgation of a new media philosophy integrating the press and broadcasting into Yugoslavia's system of self-management, how is the communicator handling the contradictions stemming from his professional need for greater autonomy and the policy needs of the League of Communists to be the vanguard and guiding elite in a socialist state? Can he, in fact, live up to the official exhortations and make the media into open forums for discussion? To what extent is the Yugoslav communicator, as in the American "fourth estate" ideology, able to choose a more adversary role by speaking his mind, criticizing inefficiency in government, and stimulating public opinion?

Two categorical answers have traditionally been given to these questions. The first and most prevalent argues that the journalist is not able to function as an adversary in communist society, because a political system based on democratic centralism must use the journalist as an apologist for party policy. Such an "apologist" role, in turn, runs counter to the individual reporter's need for independence in the expression of his own views. Antony Buzek puts it this way:

> The desire of journalists for a truthful independent and effective press comes into direct conflict with the party and its leadership. The conflict is, however, much deeper than even the rebellious communist journalists realize. The party can make concessions only in marginal, harmless areas of press activities. It cannot afford to relax its control and direction because this would lead inevitably to inquiries, first into connections, between the present leadership and past crimes or "mistakes," then into the role of the party, and finally it would lay open to question the whole political and ideological system of communism. [40]

A second and more positive evaluation maintains that, even within a one-party system, journalistic independence is possible if the party is run on a decision model which assures minority rights of dissent and tolerates differences of opinion. [41] Such an interpretation is particularly relevant for Yugoslavia, where communism is being built in a more pluralistic setting.

Both of these arguments are oversimplified, because they fail to recognize that journalists do not define their social roles in mutually exclusive categories and that the extent of criticism need not be the same in all information streams. Johnstone's study of United States' communicators disproves the belief that the majority of journalists view their function as being exclusively "neutral" or "participatory." It shows instead, as previously mentioned, that they embrace aspects of both the objective and the interpretative reporting stances. Yugoslav evidence mentioned in the previous section indicates that in pluralistic communism the degree and extent of possible criticism varies in the cultural, economic, and political spheres.

In the Yugoslavia of the 1960s, this pluralism emerged as a result of important constitutional and economic changes. Rudi Supek notes political control was transferred from the executive to the legislative branch of government, and, as a result, the party's influence became more informal.[42] Increasing strife among nationalities heralded the fact that the League of Communists became less monolithic, encompassing a variety of republican points of view about economic progress, social change, and how to deal with ethnic cleavages. In addition, constitutional, economic, and political changes favored what Benjamin Ward calls a "democratized society" made up of a variety of interest groups.[43] Six republican communist parties, each containing conservative as well as liberal branches, legislators, mass organization spokesmen, directors of economic enterprises, intellectuals, and communicators, vied for power and used the mass media to publicize their often conflicting views on current issues.

All of these shifts strengthened journalistic independence and made it possible for communicators to function as both critics and apologists. The media are consequently relatively open forums for debate on cultural and economic topics in contemporary Yugoslavia, though, in the political realm, "advocacy" reporting is probably the norm. The reason for this differentiation lies in the fact that the League itself vascillated between two modes of operation in the past fifteen years. During the 1960s, well into 1967, in fact, democratic pluralism with assured minority rights of dissent was espoused by the more liberal League factions in Slovenia and Croatia. After the Croatian crisis of 1971, the federal leadership, however, went back to the democratic-centralist tradition, where the minority has no rights vis-à-vis the majority. In the 1970s, therefore, communicators, as a potentially independent but weaker interest group in Yugoslav society, must adopt a more circumspect "apologist" role in the interpretation of the domestic political scene.

For the journalist, the contradictions inherent in Titoist media philosophy lead to severe role conflict and insecurity in political reporting, as the following passage from the professional journal *Novinar i novinarstvo* indicates. Here Franc Setinč comments:

> The one and the other say to us that we are shallow, that we oversimplify, that we readily misinterpret certain examples. In short, that we uncritically accept a logic of thought which does not include all of the facts of societal working. . . .
>
> This is a sharp judgment, which is perhaps not completely true. However, there is a grain of truth in it. But if we ask who is guilty, I would not agree with those who find the guilty one only among journalists. The truth is, we share the guilt. The causes for this should be looked for in our narrow-mindedness, in our deviation from the common goal, expressed in our writings, in false professional solidarity, etc. But guilt lies also in other places. We ask ourselves whether this judgment does not apply to various groups, assemblies, conferences and so forth. . . .
>
> How shall we overcome this disparity? In my opinion the solution lies in further democratization of our society, so that the call for a tribunal where different thoughts and points of view can be expressed, can be made real. . . .
>
> Journalists are yet not able to inform objectively, to participate in discussions, but have to reproduce the spirit of this discussion in a pre-determined mechanical sense. Or maybe these discussions are not always fully open to the public, so that the journalist cannot see what is going on. Sometimes it is the first, sometimes it is

the latter. It seems to me that the struggle for the open point of view is not yet won. Because of that journalists come up against many obstacles.[44]

The document reveals eloquently how difficult it is for the journalist to fulfill his independent reporting function in a communist state where access to important meetings is often curtailed. It also shows that journalists themselves feel that the range and extent of political criticism should be enlarged. In answer to the question "to whom are we responsible?," one reporter commented that "we do not want to be degraded once more to the level of mechanical, technical collector, and middle-man of information." In Yugoslavia of the 1970s, bolstered by federation membership[45] and republican access laws, the new professional in the public dialogue wants to become an equal partner who "reflects reality as it is" and adds "interpretation" to his "transmission" function.[46]

The extent to which the risks involved in critical political reporting force communicators to choose the safer "apologist" rather than the "critical" roles is indicated by two Yugoslav studies. These show that journalists as a group are less influential in contributing to policy decisions and also less critical than other groups in Yugoslavia's policy-making elite.

All of these elites were asked a series of questions on whether the Yugoslav press is critical enough of various administrative injustices, mistakes by high officials, and abuses by enterprises which together yielded a "freedom of criticism" index. Table 14 indicates that although the mass communicators, according to the dictates of Yugoslavia's new media policy, should have a special occupational interest in encouraging governmental criticism, they show one of the lowest criticism scores of all groups. Intellectuals, as expected, were in first place with a score of 78, while League of Communist members and trade union officials placed second. Only public administrators and legislators, like communicators, opted for less press criticism and scrutiny of government agencies.

In explaining these findings, Allan Barton notes that it might be argued that the mass communicators' low score is misleading: "since to score as favorable to criticism they have to say that the press (their own institution) is not critical enough of various abuses."[47] It turns out, however, that even on an item formulated differently, namely, the penalty for a political attack on a prominent figure, mass communicators fall well below the scores of intellectuals and federal administrators in tolerance for criticism. Doubtlessly they feel that since their group is low man on the influence scale, they prefer not to draw attention to themselves.

A second study[48] by the Yugoslav Journalists' Association provides evidence that the majority of communicators choose the safer "apologist" role in political reporting. The 1969 membership survey contained a series of questions probing journalists' thoughts on the role of criticism in self-governing socialism. While a large number answered the more neutral social background questions, only 139 out of a possible 4,206 responded to the questions investigating critical stances. This small group turned out to be made up of the older and more settled group of journalists between thirty and fifty years of age.

While no general conclusions can be drawn from such a small sample, the answers do serve as indicators of how the minority of outspoken journalists feel about their critical role. It turns out that fully 20 percent of this minority admit that they reluctantly wrote critical articles. Among the approximately 80 percent who do write them, this activity was justified on two main grounds: to mobilize public opinion and to help work out social problems. Only 13 percent

Table 14

Freedom of Criticism Scores of Various Yugoslav Elites

(in percentages)

Freedom of Criticism	Mass Organization	Legislature	Federal Administration	Economic Administration	Mass Communication	Intellectuals
Totals	(76)	(65)	(90)	(81)	(101)	(104)
Press not critical enough of:						
(a) Injustices to individuals by government agencies	54	63	51	56	54	77
(b) Bureaucratic attitude of government agencies	68	71	66	69	51	73
(c) Mistakes by high officials	83	75	80	80	87	93
(d) Abuses by enterprises	59	59	62	66	52	68
What should be the punishment for political attack on a prominent figure?						
No penalty	22	22	48	25	39	52
Freedom of criticism index: total score	44	34	34	42	33	78

SOURCE: Allen Barton, ''Determinants of Leadership Attitudes in a Socialist Society,'' *Working Papers for the International Study of Opinion Makers,* II, Columbia University (1970), p. 10.

of the "critical" journalists felt they should indulge routinely in criticism as part of their professional duty. Moreover, most of those who felt they should criticize, the survey indicates, came up against severe problems. Twenty-five percent of all respondents noted their articles were not published, and more than 33 percent mentioned that they had various types of troubles as a result of critical articles. These included authoritative rejoinders, conflict with the criticized persons, and sometimes even court battles. Because of the risks involved, almost half, or 48 percent, of those journalists willing to criticize admitted that they did not take every opportunity they saw to write critical reports. The survey concludes "these data do not testify to exceptional militancy among our journalists, nor do they testify to sufficient tolerance by those criticized."[49]

Recent official remarks on the way in which press criticism has been exercised shed further light on why communicators are returning to the safer role of the apologist. In the 1970 ideological-political platform, the Yugoslav journalist was accused of "alarmist presentation of conflicts of interest in society," of "destructive criticism," and of assuming "the right to speak on behalf of all public opinion." President Tito summed up this outlook in the following remarks: "I am not satisfied with the work of our press during the recent past when we had a very difficult situation, when there were many negative things which they however further dramatized. And today when we have gone forward toward better things, the press continues in its old place. It continuously registers only negative things, things which will irritate people, as if it wanted to discourage us from believing that we can ever escape our difficulties."[50]

These are certainly strong statements coming from a leadership which in principle favors using the media for a two-way exchange of information between the government and the people.[51] Taken together these trends seem to represent yet another downward drift toward a narrower definition of "social responsibility" and "freedom of speech" in the government's shifting attitude toward these issues. Whether such a curb of the media is justified in the light of Yugoslavia's rapid decentralization or constitutes an attempt to cope with the increasingly acrimonious nationality crisis requires a separate discussion. For the present, the question of where the Yugoslav public receives its foreign news and what kind of a picture of the world this news presents will be investigated.

---

1 Rosten, *Washington Correspondents,* Chapter 1.

2 Theodore Kruglak, *The Foreign Correspondents;* Leo Bogart, "The Overseas Newsman: A 1967 Profile Study," pp. 293-306.

3 Warren Breed, "Social Control in the Newsroom: A Functional Analysis," pp. 326-336.

4 Lee Sigelman, "Reporting the News: An Organizational Analysis," pp. 132-151.

5 Gaye Tuchman, "Objectivity as Strategic Ritual: An Examination of Newspapermen's Notion of Objectivity," pp. 660-679.

6 George Gerbner, "Institutional Pressures upon Mass Communicators," pp. 205-248; Edward Epstein, *News from Nowhere.*

7 Jay Blumler and John Madge, *Citizenship and Television*.

8 Bernard Rosho, *Newsmaking*.

9 Johnstone, Slawski, and Bowman, *News People*, Chapter 7.

10 Oguz B. Nayman, "Professional Orientations of Journalists: An Introduction to Communicator Analysis Studies," pp. 195-212.

11 Harold Wilenski, "The Professionalization of Everyone?," pp. 137-158.

12 Steven Marjanovich, "The History of the Yugoslav Press and Printing," p. 30.

13 For further details on the origin of the press in Serbia, Croatia, Slovenia, Montenegro, Bosnia-Hercegovina, and Macedonia consult the detailed study by Bjelica, *200 Godina;* Skerlić, *Istorijski pregled;* Horvat, *Povijest novinstva Hrvatske;* Lapajne, *Razvojne smeri;* and Vatoveć, *Development of Slovene and Yugoslav Periodical Journalism*.

14 For a contemporary account of the imposition of the dictatorship consult Svetozar Pribićević, *Dikatura kralja Aleksandra,* which was first published in French in the 1930s.

15 For greater details on the names, dates, and places where partisan papers were published throughout the war years, consult Vojno Istorijski Institut, *Bibliografija izdanja*.

16 Danilo Žlender, "The Training of Journalists in Yugoslavia," pp. 35-43.

17 Dushan Timotijevich, "The Training of Journalists in Yugoslavia," pp. 57-69.

18 For a criticism of the Russian curriculum consult *Sovietskaya Pechat*, pp. 36-42.

19 See Žlender, "Training of Journalists," p. 37, and Timotijevich "Training of Journalists," p. 90.

20 Timotijevich, "Training of Journalists," p. 91.

21 For further details consult France Vreg, "Adekvatno naučno, a ne pragmatističko obrazovanje novinara," p. 5; and Sergije Lukač, "Novinarstvo na fakultetu političkih nauka u Beogradu," p. 7.

22 Tunstall, *Journalists at Work*. In Great Britain, in contrast to the United States, where 145 journalism faculties trained 31,000 young journalists in 1969, only 30 percent of national specialist reporters were found to be graduates. Paul V. Peterson, "Journalism Enrollment Tops 31,000 for 145 Schools," pp. 893-895.

23 Yugoslav Journalists' Association, *Bulletin*, No. 3, p. 25.

24 Bogdan Osolnik, "On the Principles and Mechanisms of Information in Yugoslavia and the Social Role of the Media," p. 8.

25 For a more detailed description, see Svetozar Pejovich, *Market-Planned Economy*, p. 99.

26 Yugoslav Journalists' Association, *Izveštaj o radu*, p. 166.

27 Fred Siebert, Theodore Peterson, and Wilbur Schramm, *Four Theories of the Press*.

28 Johnstone, Slawski, and Bowman, *News People*, Chapter 7.

29 *Ibid.*, p. 2.

30 Siebert, Peterson, and Schramm, *Four Theories*, p. 121.

31 Raymond B. Nixon, "Freedom in the World's Press: A Fresh Appraisal with New Data," p. 10.

32 Passages quoted from Bogden Osolnik, "Sredstva informisanja kao integralni elemenat samoupravnja i neposredne demokratije u Jugoslaviji." Paper presented to International Association for Mass Communication Research Congress, Hercegnovi, Yugoslavia, Sept., 1966.

33 Federation of Yugoslav Journalists' Association, *Bulletin*, No. 3, pp. 16, 38, 7.

34 Nixon, "Freedom in the World's Press," p. 6.

35 For further detail see Vasa D. Mihailovich, "Serbian Fiction 1965," pp. 281-283, and "Yugoslav Literature since World War II," pp. 149-161. Also E. D. Goy, "The Serbian and Croatian Novel since 1948," pp. 58-84.

36 W. N. Dunn, "Ideology and Organization in Socialist Yugoslavia: Modernization and Obsolescence of Praxis," p. 11.

37 Svetozar Stojanović, "Contemporary Yugoslavian Philosophy," p. 298.

38 Gustav Adolf von Arnim, *Eine Strukturanalyse der Presse der Volksrepublik Jugoslavien, 1945-1963*, pp. 256-281.

39 Richard Eder, foreign correspondent in Belgrade, "Mihajlov Is Given New 4½ Year Term by Belgrade Court."

40 Buzek, *How the Communist Press Works*, p. 258.

41 Svetozar Stojanović, *Kritik und Zukunft des Sozialismus*, pp. 85-87.

42 See the discussion in Rudi Supek, "Power Structure of Statist and Self-Governing Socialism," p. 10. Also Branko Horvat, *An Essay on Yugoslav Society*, pp. 190-192.

43 Benjamin Ward, "Political Power and Economic Change in Yugoslavia," pp. 568-579.

44 Frank Setinč, "About the Dilemmas of the Role of the Journalist in Changing Public Opinion," pp. 3-11.

45 Professionalism is not viable by itself, but it plays an important role as a countervailing source of rhetoric and criteria of action. See Philip Elliott, *The Sociology of the Professions*, p. 149.

46 Sergije Lukač, "Profesionalac Danas-Sutra," p. 9.

47 Allan H. Barton, "Determinants of Leadership Attitudes in a Socialist Society," p. 8.

48 Manojlo Gluščević, "Neki indikatori mišljenja i ponašanja komunikatora testiranih na fenomenu društvene kritike," pp. 15-17.

49 *Ibid.*, p. 17.

50 Josip Broz Tito, "Štampa treba da prati mere i da pruža pomoć," p. 1.

51 The 1969 debate on the Yugoslav Journalists' Association revision of the 1964 code of ethics (see Appendix 1) indicates that the social and moral duties as well as the question of professional immunity remain ambiguous to this day.

CHAPTER 7

News of the World

The Mass Media as ''Myth-Makers''

After discussing the societal factors determining Yugoslavia's mass media structure and who controls the press, radio, and television in self-managed socialism, the following three chapters concern themselves with the media's symbolic dimension. They inquire how image making and reality filtering is accomplished by Yugoslavia's myth-makers and explore the way in which the media select dominant perspectives, order these, and attach values to them. An understanding of the processes leading to reality interpretation clarifies both how a country's world perspectives evolve and what its news values are, as well as what its audiences will pay attention to and find important and good.

Throughout this discussion it is assumed, as noted in the introduction, that the process of human communication has at least two unique characteristics. First, human beings take account of only a limited number of the hugely complex events which make up reality. Second, the process of ''taking account'' is one in which raw sense data acquire meaning and are converted into processed ''information about.'' Thayer notes that ''information, not data, is the raw material for thinking, decisioning, problem solving, attitude development, learning, and all of the specifically human activities that concern us about our own psychological functioning and the behavior of people.''[1] Meaning, in other words, does not reside in messages, but in what people do to or with the information to which they pay attention.

All communication processes can be analyzed on four different levels: the intrapersonal, interpersonal, organizational, and technological. Since news production is a group activity which occurs in a primarily bureaucratic setting, the frame of reference here will be largely organizational. It will concern itself with the way in which groups of people confronted with a specific operating

A shorter version of this chapter has been published under the title ''Foreign News Selection Is Non-Linear in Yugoslavia's Tanjug's Agency,'' *Journalism Quarterly,* XXXVII (Summer 1970), 340-351.

situation work out lines of action which link them to each other and to the larger environment. Such a study assumes that the work setting and the way in which people interpret this setting affect their behavior. The mass media must therefore be studied both as organizational units and as producers of symbolic content which shapes the way in which reality is perceived in different societies.

Many researchers have stressed the important role of the media as symbolic legitimizers of the basic values and outlooks of their particular societies. Their centralized organization and wide distribution of programming make it particularly easy to produce and disseminate legitimations which integrate the disparate symbol universes characteristic of modern society. Peter Berger and Thomas Luckmann note that the media participate in all four levels of the legitimation process. They contribute on the linguistic level by transmitting certain ways of talking about human experience, using the vocabulary of democracy or social self-management, as the case may be. They also participate in the distribution of prevalent legends, maxims, and folk tales which represent the selected historical experience of their people. On another level, they make available explicit theories by which various institutional sectors such as the legal, educational, and political systems are legitimated. They finally help structure the all-encompassing frame of reference which relates man to the cosmos. Here history, past, present, and future, is ordered. "With regard to the past [the symbolic universe] establishes a 'memory' that is shared by all the individuals socialized within the collectivity. With regard to the future, [program records produce] a common frame of reference for the projection of individual actions. Thus the symbolic universe links men with their predecessors and their successors in a meaningful totality." [2]

The most accessible data for a symbolic investigation of mass-produced communication are its distributed performances or media content. The analysis of programming such as newscasts, articles, dramas, films, musical performances, and educational shows, provides insights into three disparate aspects of how meaning is created. It produces a map of reality filtering indicating the set of events that a particular society is paying attention to as well as transforming from raw data into functionally useful information. They also provide a record of how this transformation is accomplished and what systematic criteria mold a nation's unique perspective or outlook. Programming, finally, constitutes a contact point between producers and audiences, indicating that communication, or "symbolic exchange" as Lin calls it, requires more than mere information flow. The receiver must not only decode the information transmitted but also "understand" it by reacting in some manner. [3]

Each of these aspects of meaning creation will be the focus of a separate discussion. Chapter 7 investigates what Tanjug, Yugoslavia's foreign news gatekeeper, pays attention to among the multiplicity of world events and how organizational context affects meaning. Chapter 8 analyzes how Yugoslavia's characteristic news values have evolved, and Chapter 9 discusses the role of the media in nation building. Whether the "alternative realities" presented by Yugoslavia's six networks tend to feed or undermine common outlooks among the country's multicultural and multinational population will be evaluated here.

International Gatekeeper

The international scene today is made up of more than 150 states and territories which are stratified along political, economic, and ideological lines. Nations, in turn, are represented by statesmen who, depending on the power status of their country, may play an important role in the international community. Since it is well known that action is based on the actor's perception of reality, it is important to investigate the image of international reality to understand international behavior. How this collective image is shaped is not known in any precise detail, but it is known that the mass media with their ubiquity and perseverance have a disproportionately strong influence on this image, because few individuals are able to test it from firsthand experience.

According to John Galtung and Mari Ruge,[4] there are at least seven steps involved in the chain from world events to personal image. Among them are media perceptions and images as well as personal perception and images, with selective distortion entering each link. This study is confined to selectivity between only two links in the chain, namely media perceptions and media images. Even such a confined study is much more complex than anticipated, considering that international news production is not a single but a three-tiered process. Selection and distortion would have to be studied first at the level of the five global agencies with their large staffs,[5] budgets, and technical facilities. These function as wholesalers. Then it would require investigation on the level of the more than 100 national agencies which serve as middlemen or retailers of information, not to mention at that of the local media, which are the ultimate institutional customers for foreign news.

Such a far-ranging study is clearly beyond the capacities of a single investigator, and therefore this study is an analysis of how one national agency, Tanjug, fashions its world perception from already assembled global news inputs and converts them into foreign news images to be passed on to the Yugoslav mass media. In the following chapters the processes by which events become "news" in this country will be investigated from two points of view. The first will use foreign desk processing of information to clarify institutional procedures as unique selection "settings" for meaning development. The next, in contrast, utilizes a comparative content analysis of Associated Press and Tanjug foreign news tickers to elucidate differences between socialist and capitalist perspectives, and thus aims at specifying some of the general principles shaping foreign news content.

Almost twenty years after the initial study by David Manning White,[6] "gatekeeper" research continues to bewitch communication analysts. This is all the more remarkable since various studies have shown that news selection is not a linear chain of individual decisions made by the wire editor. As early as 1956 Walter Gieber pointed out: "As a 'gatekeeper' in the channel of telegraph news, the wire editor appears to be passive. . . . He operates within the temporal orientation of a publishing cycle. . . . The press association has become the recommender of news to the wire editor and thus the selector of telegraph news."[7] John McNelly's "intermediary communicator"[8] study uses the same step-by-step decision model, inserting merely a few extra positions to describe the flow of an international news story. Abraham Z. Bass correctly points out another shortcoming of this adaptation: it cannot differentiate between key decision-makers and other functional roles performed by newsmen. He concludes: "The place of importance is not there (with the wire editor) but at the central news desk, the wire agency editor equivalent."[9] In his reformulation, the emphasis is for the first time on the complex operations of a group of people working as a unit in news processing. Yet, the nature of their interrelationships, the regulation mechanisms within the desk, and the degree to which technical and organizational variables mold the news are not further described because the gatekeeper model provides no framework for such explication.

Another weakness of the theory derives from its suggestion that the individual gatekeeper in the news channel makes private decisions, as the housewife does in the supermarket. This is, in fact, not true, as Lewis Donohew's[10] work suggests. He found that the publisher's attitude, the "organization outlook," is most strongly correlated with the finally selected content. The model has also created misconceptions when applied to news processing in nonwestern countries. In communist societies, for instance, the individual gatekeeper easily becomes identified with the "censor," and political management of the news is then assumed to be the result of overt blue penciling by a Glavlit-type agency. In Yugoslavia's Tanjug agency such a hypothesis is misleading, as the discussion in Chapter 4 has already indicated.

To take account of all of the above-mentioned facts, an altogether different kind of theory must be sought — one which incorporates complexity and pinpoints crucial decision junctures. In addition, it must encompass news processing as a set of nonlinear feedback relationships between task positions structured so as to operate efficiently in a specific technological setting. It is proposed that a cybernetic model[11] most adequately describes the organizational news selection process, and this chapter intends to test the efficacy of such a theory in the case study of Tanjug's foreign news desk.

Cybernetics as an orientation is a source of considerable misunderstanding for many social scientists interested in change. Wilbert Moore,[12] for example, objects to the use of all concepts of equilibrium or stability, arguing that to include such ideas as a central part of social theory is to preclude the possibility of dealing with change. He seems to believe that stability and change are inherently contradictory. The difficulty here is not merely semantic, but overlooks the fact that at least one category of stability depends upon and is the consequence of change. Just this kind, called "ultrastability," the capacity to persist through a change of structure and behavior, is of prime importance to cybernetics.

That organizations as well as biological organisms exhibit ultrastability and act like self-regulating systems is a fairly recent insight. From a cybernetic point of view, any large-scale formal social organization is a communication network. It is assumed that it can display learning and innovative behavior.

> Any social organization that is to change through learning and innovation, that is, to be ultrastable, must contain certain very specific feed-back mechanisms, a certain variety of information, and certain kinds of input, channel storage, and decision-making facilities. This can be stated in the form of an axiomatic proposition: that complexity of purposeful behavior is a function of the complexity of the communication components or parts of the system. More specifically, every open system behaving purposefully does so by virtue of a flow of factual and operational information through receptors, channels, selectors, feed-back loops and effectors.[13]

If news selection is a stabilizing behavior pattern, as the theory suggests, a process by which a group of journalists responds to raw news inputs by appropriate processing action, foreign desk operation, should be explainable by looking at the variables suggested by Cadwallader.

Three sets of variables seem to be most important in determining an organization's adaptive behavior pattern: (1) channel layout, (2) storage capacity or institutional memory, and (3) a "program" which indicates the degree of consciousness an organization has of its own behavior.[14] The structure of the communication network or channel layout is important because its configuration determines the direction as well as the quantity and type of information flowing through an organization. In addition, every system whose behavior is purposeful and therefore predictive must have mechanisms for selective storage and recall of information. Continuing adaptive behavior is predicated on information about past acts. Memory thus operates as a kind of negative feedback, introducing biases which change the probability of various kinds of future acts in terms of present and past successes and failures. In order to innovate, the organization, finally, must be able to analyze information. Operating rules determine what can and should be done, by whom, when, and why. They indicate how conscious an organization is of its own behavior.

It will be shown that the foreign desk's structure of positions constitutes Tanjug's channel layout. Its institutional memory is found in the agency morgue, while the program is expressed in company directives. The degree of the organization's consciousness of its own behavior can be derived from the number and kind of monitoring centers developed in the agency to facilitate information feedback on news processing.

In the remainder of this chapter, Tanjug's news inputs and organizational processes within the foreign desk, as well as crisis-situation functioning, will be scrutinized to determine the relative importance of decision-makers versus other variables in news interpretation and to illuminate processes of censorship in the Yugoslav system where media content is generally subordinate to the diplomatic goals of the League of Communists.

Selection and Processing

In general, the study of self-regulating systems explores the ways in which some output is maintained in a more or less invariant equilibrium, or steady state, in the face of disrupting external forces. Company records of foreign news reception and utilization, Table 15, indicate that Tanjug news processing is a relatively invariant selection of an average of about 1.6 million words monthly from about 10 million words of news input. The table also indicates that selection limits variety and that approximately 364,000 words are daily reduced to approximately 55,000 words of processed information. This means that about two-thirds, 66 percent to be exact, of all incoming material is weeded out and discarded.

Reduction, it appears, is not primarily a result of censorship restrictions but of agency selection practices, available transmission channels to the provinces, and market considerations. As Scott Cutlip has suggested, the information capacity of transmission channels is a necessary but not a sufficient determinant of news processing.[15] It is, in fact, one out of three variables which according to

Table 15
Monthly Utilization of All Tanjug Foreign News (in millions)

Month	Number of Words Received	Number of Words Discarded	Number of Words Used
1	9.5	7.9	1.5
2	8.7	7.1	1.6
3	9.7	8.1	1.6
4	10.5	8.4	2.1
5	10.8	9.1	1.7
6	10.2	8.6	1.5
7	10.3	8.8	1.4
8	9.5	8.6	1.3
9	10.3	8.6	1.7
10	11.1	9.2	1.8
11	11.1	9.5	1.6
12	9.7	8.3	1.4
Output	121.4	102.2	19.2
Total Daily (thousands)	264.2	209.3	54.9
Foreign Agencies	244.9	207.3	37.4
Correspondents	14.4	1.1	13.3
Monitoring	4.9	.2	4.7

SOURCE: Table 7 *Mesečni Bilten o Radu Agencije*, Godina III, Broj 13 (1963). Table 8 *Mesečni Bilten o Radu Agencije*, Godina IX, Broj 2 (1969).

the cybernetic theory must be taken into account. In addition, the relatively limited capacity of the Yugoslav mass media, which can absorb only 36,000 words per day of combined home and foreign news, must be borne in mind. Moreover, newsprint scarcity limits all papers to from eight to twelve pages each, and the electronic media are restricted in both numbers of stations and broadcast hours.

Furthermore, Table 15 indicates that Tanjug has three major categories of news suppliers: foreign agencies, its own correspondent corps, and the monitor-

Table 16

Sources and Monthly Utilization of Tanjug Foreign News
(in thousands)

Agency	Words Received	Words Used	Percentage Used
AP (USA)	1,488	250.7	16.8
AFP (France)	1,275	213.3	16.7
Reuter (England)	1,685	255.8	15.1
TASS (USSR)	1,336	230.2	17.2
China News	533	87.5	16.4
IIS (Mexico)	47	13.9	29.4
PAP (Poland)	54	1.5	2.7
MTI (Hungary)	25	1.0	3.8
CTK (Czechoslovakia)	43	1.4	3.3
ADN (Germ. Fed. Rep.)	71	1.2	1.6
BTA (Bulgaria)	42	1.7	4.0
YOM	23	0.1	0.4
MEN (Egypt)	300	26.9	8.9
ATA (Albania)	79	2.6	3.3
ANS (Argentina)	67	2.0	2.9
MAP (Morocco)	67	5.2	7.7
KDO (Japan)	4	0	
USIS (USA)	192	29.3	15.2
GNA (Ghana)	4	0	
Monitoring	149	142.6	95.6
Foreign correspondents	433	398.8	91.9
Total words	7,926	1,666.1	21.0

Sources and Utilization by Geographical Area (thousands)

Agency	Words Received	Words Used	Percentage of Used Total
Western & USIS	4,641	749	45.0
Socialist & Russia	2,187	237	14.2
All others	.514	138	8.3
Foreign correspondents	.433	398	24.0
Monitoring	.149	142	8.5
Total words	7,926	1,666	100.0

SOURCE: *Mesečni Bilten o Radu Agencije*, Godina IV, Broj 1 (Jan. 1964).

ing service in the Belgrade headquarters. It also reveals that the western agencies dominate the origins of foreign news flowing into Tanjug. Associated Press, USIS, Reuters, and Agence France Presse provide about 4.6 million words, or 60 percent, of all incoming information. About 28 percent originates from the socialist agencies in the Soviet Union and other eastern European countries, and 6.5 percent from the European alliance plus six other small countries with which Yugoslavia has news agreements. Tanjug's monitoring provides less than 1 percent and its own correspondents write only 5.5 percent of the total or raw material news, though their copy, as shall be seen, figures large in the finished information product.

The evidence seems to suggest that Tanjug's international news is interpreted from a foreign point of view. This is an erroneous conclusion, as Table 16 indicates. While foreign agencies provide most of the raw material for national agencies, they are also most severely edited. Only 3 to 18 percent of their material is generally used, while the articles from Tanjug correspondents move through the agency in essentially unchanged form. Interestingly, the size of the foreign agency source, rather than its political outlook, is the primary determinant of the degree of its utilization. The Associated Press, Reuters, Agence France Press, and TASS reports are all used approximately 18 percent, a surprising figure since it has often been assumed that TASS continues to dominate eastern European news inputs.

The giants, then, though they are the most prolific source of international information, are used relatively sparingly. The copy of national agencies fares even worse, except for China's Hsin-Hua, which because of Yugoslavia's particular ideological involvement with this country is treated like one of the majors. Mexico's IIS and Egypt's MEN show utilization figures of about 9 percent, while the rest is closer to 3 percent. This suggests that Tanjug uses the world services to provide perspectives on the international discussion agenda, whereas copy from national agencies plugs specific news holes not serviced by the Yugoslav correspondent net.

Tanjug's own staff copy, in contrast, reaches the wire almost unchanged. Here the use figures are 92 percent for the correspondent net and 95 percent for monitoring. Both of these inputs do not require scrutiny or selection because they are essentially company-sponsored. Tanjug foreign correspondents cable the "top of the news," a daily press roundup, and economic and developmental trends in the country where they are stationed. This material is clearly more in tune with the interests of Yugoslav media customers than much of the other news exchanged by smaller agencies. Sources and utilization data in Table 16 indicate that approximately one-third of the agency's daily ticker is company produced by Tanjug foreign correspondents and monitoring. Another 45 percent of the copy originates from western sources, 14.2 percent from the socialist block, and 8 percent from all remaining national agencies. It may be concluded that Tanjug does not accept any raw news sources uncritically, but produces through processing a news mix in which Yugoslav priorities are reflected.

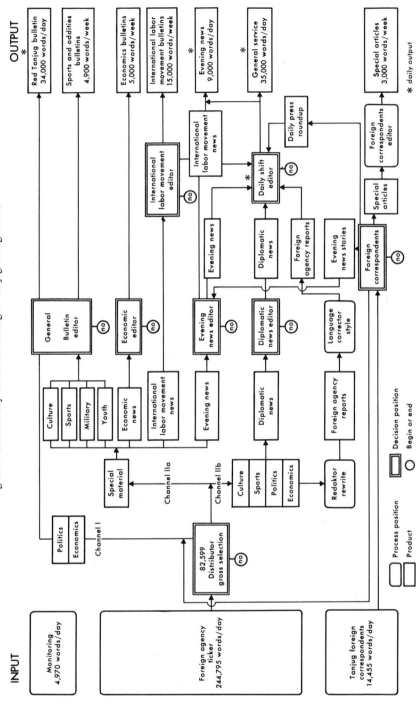

Figure 5. Channel Layout and Processing of Tanjug Foreign News

INPUT

Monitoring
4,970 words/day

Foreign agency ticker
244,795 words/day

Tanjug foreign correspondents
14,455 words/day

OUTPUT

Red Tanjug bulletin
34,000 words/day *

Sports and oddities bulletins
4,900 words/week

Economics bulletins
5,000 words/week

International labor movement bulletins
15,000 words/week

Evening news
9,000 words/day *

General service
35,000 words/day *

Special articles
3,000 words/week

* daily output

82,599 Distributor gross selection — no

Politics
Economics

Channel I

Special material

Channel IIa

Channel IIb

Culture
Sports
Politics
Economics

Redaktor rewrite

Culture
Sports
Military
Youth

Economic news

International labor movement news

Evening news

Diplomatic news

Foreign agency reports

Language corrector style

General Bulletin editor — no

Economic editor — no

Evening news editor — no

Diplomatic news editor — no

International labor movement editor — no

International labor movement news

Evening news

Diplomatic news

Foreign agency reports

Evening news stories

Daily shift editor — no *

Daily press roundup

Special articles

Foreign correspondents — no

Foreign correspondents editor

Process position

Product

Decision position

Begin or end

Source: *Mesečni Bilten o Radu Agencije.* Godina III, Broj. 13 (1963), Tables 7 and 8, p. 16.

A recent study by Karl Rosengren[16] indicates that the process of news selection operates not on one but on three levels with what he calls selective, quantitative, and qualitative gatekeeping occurring in succession. Selective gatekeeping refers to the process by which the wholesale news passes the gate and becomes retail ''news.'' Quantitative gatekeeping pinpoints interpretative activities which tend to give more play to events high on news factors. Qualitative gatekeeping notes the way attention scores are applied. A news flow diagram of Tanjug's foreign desk and the processing practices, Figure 5, corroborates this three-step procedure and locates the six decision positions where selection takes place. These differ considerably from the additional five where flow-through occurs. According to this chart, the distributor does selective gatekeeping and decides what passes the gate, while the special editors do quantitative gatekeeping and determine the amount of space to be devoted to certain preferred hard news categories. The shift editor, finally, is responsible for qualitative gatekeeping, determining the daily attention score to be attributed to different events. The distributor, four special editors, and the shift editor together determine what may be called product composition and mix.

It takes fifteen minutes to process an average story for the wire, although other products like the feature and special article services and bulletins naturally take longer — sometimes six to eight hours, as is the case for *Red Tanjug,* which is published three times daily for the information of governmental agencies and media news editors. It takes a few days or a week for the bulletins.

In the first processing stage, the distributor eliminates two-thirds of all incoming foreign agency material. Six selection criteria are presently applied:[17] (1) Illegible material is thrown out. (2) Stories about sports unknown in Yugoslavia, like baseball, are eliminated. (3) Stories about the private lives of public personalities, local or foreign, are ruled out by the press law, as is (4) purely propaganda material from small agencies, like that of Albania. (5) Speeches given in extenso by minor politicians of smaller foreign countries are also discarded because of space pressures. (6) By far the greatest bulk of information is, however, eliminated under the relevance rule, which discards redundant material from other world agencies failing to amplify already selected items.

Tanjug's gross selection, it will be noted, is from the beginning structured along certain ideological lines. It favors hard news over soft news, and channels economic news, political news, and information about relations among socialist countries to specially designated editors. In adddition, the criteria operate in favor of large versus small countries and make a strict differentiation between the public and private lives of government officials, which will be further documented in the next chapter's content analysis.

Two other inputs bypass the bulk channel. Foreign correspondent and monitoring reports are immediately routed either to the bulletin editor, who includes them, unedited, in his *Red Tanjug* output, or to the special foreign correspondent editor. In the second processing stage, foreign agency information selected by the distributor is further routed along two different channels. *Red Tanjug* copy goes to the general bulletin editor, who classifies it, without much editing, according to country and subject matter. His output provides interested government agencies with an essentially unvarnished look at the outside world.

The copy designed for the Yugoslav media, on the other hand, flows through a separate channel consisting of a number of other positions. While the general news which is self-explanatory receives little editing, other material is more intensely processed by four special editors. The diplomatic, international labor movements, evening, and economic editors scan their material and write a specified number of daily news items and reports, thus contributing to the further digesting of this part of the incoming news. Their workload includes the writing of three items of fifty to 150 words, plus one 200-word report covering the most important event in their area of competence. It is here that decisions are made to give more space to those items which are high on given news factors, such as elite versus other nations, structure versus people orientation, all of which will be corroborated in the following chapter. On the day of the 1968 United States elections, for instance, the special editor for diplomatic affairs wrote a report on President Nixon and his foreign policy views which took precedence over a report from Greece. In spite of the fact that the mass media feel that Tanjug should confine itself to merely reporting the facts, the agency's diplomatic editor noted in a conversation that some editorializing is necessary to make a fact understandable: "In the past this sector leaned heavily on the hand-outs from Protocol," he noted. "But now 95 percent of the time we want to give political commentary and direction to the diplomatic coverage, rather than merely state a fact. Visits of foreign dignitaries are placed in the context of what their aims are and what their countries mean to Yugoslavia."

While these four editors occupy decision positions, their colleague, the foreign correspondent editor, has primarily coordinative functions. Interviews indicated that he manages the foreign correspondent net by tabulating and transmitting the 100 monthly special articles which are independently chosen and signed by the staff. He also monitors output mix through evaluative circulars and through daily telex contact inquiring about top newsbreaks all over the world. He is thus an important feedback source. Foreign correspondents whose special reports have not been sold to the provincial press are told to select other types of subject matter and to write with audience interests in mind.

In response to a question about how a staffer knows what international events to report, this editor commented that "correspondents never rush into premature conclusions because they are bound by three principles of reporting: (1) to cover all daily events in a foreign country objectively, namely, to give the facts; (2) to follow events and see them in a historical perspective; and (3) in those places where we depend on foreign agencies, to cover the daily events for us,

because their resources are greater than ours. The correspondent must emphasize processes and trends . . . in a way which is interesting to our press."
Here, too, the salability of the news enters as a content criterion and modifies ideological perspectives.

The daily shift editor's central position in foreign news processing is based on five vital decision-making and coordinative functions which together establish the kind of attention to be paid to different occurrences. Karl Rosengren calls this "qualitative" gatekeeping. The shift editor makes the final item selection for the media wire and, in conjunction with the chief of the desk, sets the agenda and thus the priorities and play which different news occurrences will receive on a given day. He characterizes his work, which is a multistep filtering operation, in the following way:

> My job consists of giving material from news agencies abroad to the Yugoslavian press. Whether something is released or not depends on my political decision. I have one assistant who gets all of the material [distributor] and from time to time he tells me what is going on, and on controversial material it is up to me to say how the material is to be interpreted. . . . If it is okay, I initial it and it goes on the general service wire. . . . Coordination in our desks works informally.

> In the morning the editor of the desk will consult with me, as well as various special editors, about the topic of the day. If the Kollegium agrees with our interpretation and choice, he will return and say nothing. I do not wait for him to tell me what to do. The Home Desk colleague sits right next to me and we regulate traffic as we see fit.

The daily news editor also functions as a monitor for the foreign correspondent input. If, for instance, there is a French presidential election, the shift editor requests a longer report from the Paris correspondent. To adjust the output mix, he may not use the story sent by Athens or Rome on the same day. Criteria for selection here are based, as shall be seen, on economic and geographic considerations and follow the general requirement that journalists select and report processes and trends in world affairs which reinforce prevailing Yugoslav outlooks on nonalignment, the Sino-Soviet conflict, or the Soviet Union's role in the socialist world.

The daily shift editor functions as a feedback channel for customer wishes. If the Belgrade daily *Borba* wants an item repeated or greater coverage of a particular happening, this editor relays the information to the distributor and adjusts the item mix to suit these needs. The shift editor serves as an informal dispensary of information to the major political power centers of Belgrade. He noted, "I inform the President, Cabinet, and Ministry of Foreign Affairs about matters which might interest them."

In a very simplified way, one can view the activity within the foreign desk as directed toward fulfillment of an output goal of eighty to 110 items a day. Control is exercised by the editor of the shift. In his capacity as censor, he monitors the output mix. As discriminator, he checks if the requisite number of items is going on the wire, and, as decision-maker, he chooses which reports are to be transmitted. With established standards, the shift editor can work quite independently and will turn for advice to his superior, the editor of the foreign desk, only when something extraordinary happens, for example, the assassination of President Kennedy. As Joseph Litterer[18] has pointed out, the decision-maker can then either initiate a new program to bring performance back into line or turn to the goal-setter for redefinition of the standard.

To complete the picture of editorial positions and their functions in foreign news processing, only the activities of the chief of the desk remain to be described. The foreign news editor, like his American counterpart, is not ordinarily involved in the selection process or in product composition. He organizes working shifts, of which there are four, keeps informed on special editors' reports, coordinates the activities of his desk with those of the home news, and consults with the shift editor on the top item. Product emphasis, which story will be selected for primary consideration, is thus his domain. Under ordinary conditions, the daily meeting of the editorial board (Kollegium) takes cognizance of his suggestion. Though few editors could recall instances of asking the chief for advice on interpretation, he informally provides guidance and contributes to product clarification.

Tanjug's Memory

In addition to the above-mentioned processing positions, there is a further variable, organization memory, which also affects news selection. The way in which this occurs, however, is not yet well understood. Considering that psychologists find it difficult to assess the effects of memory on a person's perception and action, it seems an almost impossible task to chart group responses to institutional memory. Therefore, the present analysis should be viewed as a first attempt at unraveling a very complex set of interrelationships. It does not pretend to be authoritative or final, but intends to draw attention to questions which require further investigation.

Organization memory, as Max Weber has pointed out, is to be found in the minds of individual job occupants and in directives and files. Both of these sources store different kinds of information for the future guidance of organization behavior. According to information theory, the probability of novelty, and thus an institution's capacity for learning, depends on the size of possible information recombinations as well as on available material resources. These resources are people and records which together store three basic kinds of information to facilitate routine daily functioning: routine procedures; information on how to reach higher authority when unprecedented judgment is needed in crisis situations; and access to precedents, providing historical perspective.

Routine information, like personnel and financial records and knowledge of the state press and economic laws, is found in the agency's administrative sector, while the definition of journalistic output and processing procedures is laid down in Tanjug's goals, plans, and directives, as well as the departmental production plans which are formulated yearly. Very generally the agency's documents of incorporation require it to perform three tasks, "to give the press, radio and TV information . . . to inform the public abroad about events in Yugoslavia . . . and to give state organs . . . services from its domain."

Information which contributes to adaptation in stress or crisis situations, on the other hand, is stored in organizational programs for action, which have probably grown out of trial and error. Interviews elicited the fact that stress in the foreign desk results from at least three sets of occurrences: insufficient knowledge for the interpretation of a particular news event; heavily increased information inputs; or extension of reportorial activities beyond the usual routine. All of these will be discussed in detail in the section analyzing the effect of the John Kennedy assassination on Tanjug foreign desk operations.

The third type of information access to precedents is required to ensure historical perspective and continuity in foreign news reporting. This kind of information is to be found in Tanjug's morgue (Dokumentacije). Because, according to Benjamin Whorf,[19] the conceptual structure determines how an event will be interpreted, institutional memory or method of information storage provides important clues to the probable meanings which will be attached to different classes of events. What Tanjug selects for permanent storage thus provides guidelines for future interpretations of the world. There is first of all Tanjug's own product, which provides past stands on issues. Among the material filed is 70 percent of the general service. *Red Tanjug,* as well as all weekly and monthly bulletins, foreign press reaction to Yugoslavian matters, and all special reports from its own foreign and domestic correspondents.

There are, in addition, forty-seven Yugoslav newspapers and special publications which cover all aspects of Yugoslav life. These are perused for two major classes of information: comments on Tanjug reporting, which provide one source of feedback on product quality, and material filling gaps in Tanjug reporting.

Special reference services, finally, provide background perspectives on international foreign policy trends, biographies of important personalities, and general information. Most of them, interestingly enough, come from England. *Keesing's Contemporary Archives* is a British weekly diary of important world events. *Reuters* and *Munziger's Biographies* come from London, as does one of the encyclopedias. The other encyclopedia is Russian, while the *Who's Who* is American. No foreign papers are regularly kept or read in the Dokumentacije because of a shortage of staff. In addition, the chief of the section pointed out that there is no need for such perusal because foreign press reaction to Yugoslav affairs is habitually cabled by Tanjug correspondents as part of their daily report.

A content analysis of how material in the morgue is organized reveals that it is filed in a system of ten registers, five on national and five on international matters, which together cover approximately 60,000 different items. Three of these registers file foreign affairs matters organized geographically by continents: Europe, the Americas, and Asia and Africa. The fourth covers international organizations and the fifth, bilateral accords. Each of the country entries is again subdivided into personalities and problems, such as governmental contacts between Yugoslavia and a given state, demographic material, internal political matters, economic structure, colonies, and foreign policy relations of the country with Europe, Asia, Africa, and America.

Registers six through ten classify information about Yugoslavia in the following way: (1) President Tito's speeches since 1945 and what was said about him in the world press; (2) Important government personnel-description of position and major speeches; (3) Yugoslavia's administrative structure; (4) Economy by branches of industry; (5) Education and culture.

The organization's memory structure provides geographic and problem-oriented background perspectives for news selection, rather than an overtly ideological classification. Communist parties throughout the world are item 26 in the register on international organizations, while important party congresses and the activities of McCarthy are mentioned as subitems under the general headings of internal politics in the Soviet Union and the United States.

Karl Deutsch suggests that "in mapping the structure of preferences and priorities which govern the transmission of information within an organization, one obtains a rank order scale . . . and thus a map of its internal value system."[20] The number of item entries under a given country may provide a crude measure of news attention or selection interest clarifying the agency value system. Appendix 2, citing entry totals for the foreign policy registers, suggests that Yugoslavia's view of the world is molded by four additional factors. In the first place, entry totals of 70 to 99 which are recorded for such countries as the German Democratic Republic (72), Austria (78), Albania (82), Greece (92), Bulgaria (92), Korea (93), Czechoslovakia (98), Poland (99), and Rumania (99) indicate Tanjug's interest in other eastern European socialist states or neighbors with whom border disputes have had to be adjudicated.

Second, in the 100 items class are a group of countries with whom Yugoslavia has had either historical friendship or enmities, such as Algeria (116), Turkey (117), Hungary (120), China (138), West Germany (177); or has had close political ties in the drive for the development of a nonaligned bloc, such as Japan (114), India (140), and Egypt (166). Third, entries of 200 or more are registered for Italy (209), France (227), Great Britain (229), and the United States (262), which are not only traditional world powers but also important trade partners. Fourth, the Soviet Union is in a class by itself with 450 entries, far surpassing the news attention paid to any other country.

Tanjug's selection interest, it may be concluded, is thus additionally determined by such factors as (1) a sympathetic concern for countries with a similar political structure and the importance of geographical proximity; (2) historical relationships of friendship or enmity; (3) trade and world power priorities; and (4) the Soviet Union, with which an unusually stormy filial relationship has existed since the Cominform break in 1948. Studies by John Galtung and Mari Ruge support three of these points, while the impact of economic and historical[21] relationships has not been previously documented. They note that foreign news is patterned by factors of cultural proximity and relevance, which increase the meaningfulness of an event, as well as by reference to elite nations and people. The increased governmental interest in Africa and South America is not reflected in these item totals. President Tito's trip to Africa in 1961 rated only eight entries, and Mexico, Chile, Canada, Argentina, and Brazil have between thirty and forty. World trouble spots, too, are low in agency interest; Cyprus (54), Cuba (67), and Korea (93) rated fewer entries than did socialist neighbors.

News production, the cumulative evidence suggests, is indeed a function of inputs, organizational processes, and memory variables. As has been seen, two systems of foreign news processing occur in Tanjug, each of them following a different channel with different capacities. The first involves foreign news selection for media customers; the second, for government agencies. To produce the general service, information is generally subjected to a triple screening process by three sets of editors: the distributor, special editors, and the editor of the shift. As already noted, only foreign news collected by the Tanjug staff itself and monitored information fail to go through the first, or selective, gatekeeping process where gross selection takes place and where national agencies fashion their country's world interpretations along a few relatively simple lines. Since the agency's foreign correspondents have already internalized these priorities, their reports are not nearly as severely edited as foreign agency material. Only 7 percent instead of 66 percent of the total is discarded.

It has been demonstrated that channel layout determines the news output's composition, continuity, emphasis, and style, while the "program" laid down in goals, plans, and directives provides detailed product specification. Storage in the organization morgue affects Tanjug's future behavior and news interpretation by emphasizing various geographical, economic, historical, and problem-oriented perspectives. Ideological values are but one of many factors influencing interpretation. Such a finding raises the question of the impact of other news factors posited by Galtung and Ruge, a point returned to in the subsequent chapter.

The evidence also supports the fact that news selection and processing is an agency controlled activity not formally linked with another governmental or party committee. Table 17 indicates that the scope of the foreign desk's decision-making power is much greater than ordinarily assumed. It extends to four areas: the determination of lead stories, the selection of all news items to go on the general service wire, the determination of daily news requirements, and the handling or format of items. In these respects, the Yugoslav journalist differs little from his American colleagues of the Associated Press, who also enjoy great desk autonomy.[22] Overt or institutionalized government blue-penciling is not a part of foreign news processing in the 1970s, though it had been fifteen years earlier. This suggests that coordination of agency news interpretation with Yugoslav diplomatic priorities comes through informal channels.

It is finally evident that, contrary to the authoritarian structuring of TASS, Tanjug's operations are decentralized. Table 17 summarizes the relationship of various agency councils to processing decisions. It shows that the editorial board (Redakciski Kollegium) does not ordinarily determine news priorities. These are brought before it by the foreign desk chief. Its daily meetings, chaired by the editor-in-chief, serve instead as a correction mechanism evaluating the previous day's product emphasis and scope. The weekly agency board meeting and finance department are even further removed from content determination. Interviews revealed that their monitoring covered such areas as resource allocation and product marketability.

These institutionalized feedback loops are supplemented by informal feedback channels, like telephone calls from customers and government sources, consultation between desk editors, and research in the morgue, all of which additionally serve to monitor output and to clarify content. The evidence

Table 17

Organizational Factors Affecting Foreign News Processing

Channel Layout	
Position	Product Authority Area
1. Distributor, shift editor, special editors	Composition continuity
2. Foreign news editors with shift editor	Emphasis (play)
3. Foreign news editor	Clarification
4. Redaktor, language corrector	Style
Organization Memory	
1. Goals, plans, directives	Specification
2. Dokumentacije (morgue)	Geographical and problem-oriented perspectives for background
Organizational Sensing Centers	
Agent	Monitoring Area
1. Foreign desk	Product composition Product continuity
2. Redakciski kollegium (editorial board)	Product emphasis Product scope
3. Agenciski kollegium (agency board)	Resource allocation for production
4. Finance department	Product marketability

overwhelmingly leads to the conclusion that government agencies are only an auxiliary source for content determination, but that there may be other bureaucratic pressures which temper what Gieber refers to as a reporter's "craft orientation" — his ability to tell a story as he sees it. How do these bureaucratic pressures differ in North America and Yugoslavia and how are they related to censorship?

The Kennedy Assassination: A Case Study in Crisis Management

According to Buzek,[23] there are three types of censorship in communist countries: direct prepublication censorship by a censoring organ like Russia's Glavlit, journalistic self-censorship, and censorship in the form of advice and instruction. That the last two types of censorship occur in any society, and can therefore not be used to distinguish communist from noncommunist countries, is overlooked by this study.

For the purposes of comparison, William Albig's broader definition of the

Figure 6. Social Censorship Levels

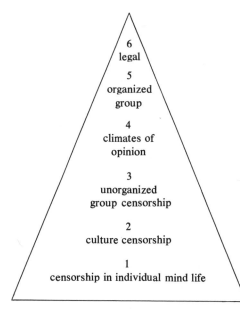

6. Local, state, and national laws, direct and indirect.

5. Nonlegal but formal regulations like TV codes, and so on.

4. Ideologies and developed and cultivated pressures like "Agnewism."

3. Group standards and values restricting communication.

2. Norms and values of culture.

1. The Freudian censor.

Source: William Albig, *Modern Public Opinion*, p. 241.

term seems more useful. "Censorship is the process of restraint on freedom of thought and communication by the minds of individuals, by climates of opinion, or by the process of deleting or limiting the content of any of the media of communication."[24] There are six censorship levels in any society, according to Albig, which he pictures in a pyramidal chart, reproduced here as Figure 6.

Antony Buzek's three kinds of communist censorship, it will be seen, can be incorporated into and are clarified by Albig's scheme. Prepublication censorship by a censoring organ falls into level 6; journalistic self-censorship refers to level 3; and advice and instruction is covered by level 5. Neither in the United States nor in Yugoslavia is there an agency whose sole function is censorship of journalistic reports. Both countries, however, have laws, like the first and fifth amendments to the Constitution or the press law, which regulate the expression of ideas. Chapter 3 has already noted that these are more stringent in Yugoslavia.

The second type, journalistic self-censorship, which Buzek describes as censoring everything to which the party organs could object, starts with the journalist himself. Studies by Walter Gieber[25] and Warren Breed[26] indicate that this is not a purely communist phenomenon. Wherever he is, the journalist has to get the "hang" of his paper's "line" in order to do his job effectively. Interviews in Yugoslavia and Breed's research on the North American continent reveal that the same mechanisms for learning and internalizing journalistic status rights and obligations are operative in both countries.

In his "Social Control in the Newsroom," Breed found that editorial censorship in America is not contained in directives because these would interfere with the professed value of freedom of expression. Instead, it emanates from three sources: the fact that other journalists serve as a model for the newcomer, blue-penciling by editors of higher status, and an informal assimilation of the interests and affiliations of top executives. In Tanjug, also, there are no written directives laying down an organizational policy for "interpretation." Instead, the analysis of foreign news processing suggests that here socialization processes involve journalistic colleagues, shift or desk editors who check all stories going on the wire, foreign desk meetings, and house organs as means for picking up the agency "outlook."

In what way does censorship in Yugoslavia differ from the indirect pressures experienced by an American journalist writing about a controversial topic? Two additional practices were mentioned throughout interviews which are not usually found in the North American continent: censorship by other government agencies which supply speeches and reports already shortened for publication, and censorship in the form of advice and instruction from extra-agency sources. Thus the chief editor mentioned that official resolutions are usually not changed, though programs like the seven-year Social Plan (Sedmogodišnji društveni plan) can today be independently excerpted by the agency. On the matter of advice, another man pointed out, "Ten years ago it was very difficult because we did not publish everything. We had in practice to explain to the Ministry how we were going to play an event. Now, if I am in doubt, I contact the Foreign Secretary directly and the rest of the time we go ahead on our own.''

Since Yugoslavia no longer possesses a formal censoring organ like the Soviet Union's Glavlit, it would be interesting to know how frequently advice is sought on interpretation by different editors. Interviews suggested that the special editors as a group could rarely recall occasions where they even consulted the foreign editor, expressing themselves quite competent to handle their jobs independently. The shift editor, on the other hand, mentioned that he solicited outside advice from personal contacts in the Foreign Ministry or other government agencies about twice daily, and sometimes much more frequently when a situation warranted it.

One such situation of foreign desk ''crisis'' which required governmental assistance with interpretation and new adaption patterns was the reporting of the Kennedy assassination. The author's first study visit to Belgrade in January, 1964, almost coincided with this tragedy, and its effects on the agency were still fresh in the staff's mind. One informant noted:

> The first news came from U.P.I. But since Tanjug was not a customer it could not use this version and had to wait for AP confirmation. Immediately our own correspondents in the U.S. were alerted. After one hour, the first version about Oswald, that he had lived in the USSR and was married to a Russian wife, was received. According to the director's judgment, this was an important point, because it brought another power into the picture. The director decided it was inopportune to spread this fact immediately, so it went only into the internal bulletin *Red Tanjug* and was held up for general publication throughout the night. The Ministry of Foreign Affairs was informed and the correspondent in Washington consulted. On the following day there was a report from him stating ''in the United States there are rumors that the assassination may be a Communist plot.''

Here was a situation which could not be handled routinely and where program reformulation as well as a change of executive function occurred. First of all, the assassination dominated foreign news content. Within the desk, editors worked no longer in regular shifts, but overtime to handle the increased selection load and to digest the unusual flood of material. The Associated Press and USIS filled their wires twenty-four hours a day instead of their customary eight. In addition, extra personnel were engaged and coordinated with researchers in the morgue to provide background material on Kennedy and Johnson.

Changes in executive function transferred the department's responsibility for play and handling to the next highest decision centers. The editor-in-chief and the director of the agency personally activated communication channels to President Tito and top governmental leaders, which like Washington's ''hot line'' are only invoked in an emergency. As a result of these consultations, Oswald's Russian connections were not reported for at least ten hours.

Delaying information is not a common occurrence in Tanjug, whose journalists are proud that the usual processing time for a news item is fifteen minutes. The interviewer was told that such a drastic measure is justified only under two circumstances: the extreme political delicacy of an event like the Oswald case, or insufficient or conflicting information. Delayed reporting in the second instance permits confirmation of the facts, avoiding professional embarrassment.

Table 18
Foreign Desk Crisis Operation
(standard: words/day)

Criteria	Steady State	Crisis Situation
Average input (words/day)	264,220	264,220
Average output (words/day)	17,500	17,500
Average output (items)	80-110	80-110
Organizational structure		
1. No. of editorial positions	8	16
2. Work flow through positions	Normal	for. desk plus ed.-in-chief & director
Interactions of staff		
1. No. of vertical interactions; personnel interacting with other desk members	8	14
2. No. of horizontal interactions; editors interacting with editor-in-chief and director	0	2
3. No. of personnel interacting with outside agency sources	3	5
Decision rules for filtering information		
1. No. of positions involved	5	7
2. Location in desk or out	in	out (editorial board)
3. Positions determining stringency of application	2	4
4. Final decision-maker	editor of shift	ed.-in-chief or director
Mix		
1. Proportion of home to foreign news items	1/3 to 2/3	1/3 to 2/3
2. Content of foreign news output	diversified	overwhelmingly one subject

The evidence confirms that there is no basic change in structural organization between "steady state" and "crisis" functioning in Tanjug's news-processing sector. To maintain the same output when input increases, the information capacity of the foreign desk is simply enlarged. As Table 18 shows, this is accomplished by involving more positions, changing the work flow, increasing the numbers and kinds of staff interaction, and transferring product decision-making to higher organizational levels.

The analysis of the Kennedy crisis elucidates that foreign desk positions were staffed with two editors instead of one. The processing channel involved the editor-in-chief as well as the director, usually not part of the layout. The amount of desk personnel interaction increased because of personnel increases. Possibly as many as six extra editors were assigned to the shifts. Although usually only three, the diplomatic, international labor movement, and daily editor, have contacts with government sources, the chief editor and director actuated additional contacts high in the administration. Moreover, final decision-making on content was removed from the foreign desk to the editorial board, and the foreign news mix showed a concentration on the assassination, which is not usually the case.

While censorship has been a topic of great research interest in the United States, it has usually been very narrowly defined. Inquiries have focused on the suppression of material and activities presumed to have a degrading effect on public morals. The more common indirect pressures, be they censorship in the individual mind-life, culture censorship, or unorganized group censorship, have remained largely uncharted until recent Agnew attacks and President Nixon's evident dislike of the media produced a rash of studies re-emphasizing the need for an independent news establishment.[27]

An attempt has been made here to view different kinds and levels of censorship as one of the environmental factors determining the way in which Tanjug adapts its operations. The analysis of agency foreign news processing has shown that censorship is not nearly as important a variable in the determination of product content as are market and organizational factors. Most criteria used at the feedback points refer to market, resource, and internal desiderata. In this respect, Tanjug is closer to a western agency like the Associated Press than is usually assumed.

Cybernetic Analysis

In assessing the diagnostic and predictive advantages of the cybernetic model, various points stand out. First of all, it appears that contrary to the traditional gatekeeper model it is able to encompass all aspects of the news-selection process while emphasizing the crucial point — that it is an activity carried out in a bureaucratic setting. The model shows that while decision-makers are indeed present and necessary, they do not make up their minds in a vacuum or as a result of personal whim. Their psychological makeup is not as important in determining their judgment as the task to be performed, the equipment at hand, and the goals of the company.

Second, the model explains control interrelations in the foreign desk by pinpointing crucial feedback loops where output information modifies ongoing news production. Three junctures in the net stand out most vividly: the positions of the distributor, daily editor, and foreign desk chief. The model, in the third place, aids with the differentiation of journalistic functions based on operational task descriptions. It establishes criteria for flow-through positions which do not materially alter content and decision positions which do. It shows how the distributor contributes to gross selection, and how the special editors and the shift editor affect quantitative and qualitative gatekeeping.

Fourth, the model draws attention to the crucial role or organization memory in foreign news interpretation, a factor usually overlooked in most analyses. While the task network supplies criteria for news composition, emphasis, and style, the memory provides some of the value perspectives through which all events are viewed. Among these are a sympathetic concern for geographically and ideologically similar societies, an interest in political and economic partners, and the necessity for a small country to be informed about the "super powers."

The model also contributes to an understanding of Yugoslav censorship by pointing out that it is not the primary but one of many environmental factors determining the way in which Tanjug adapts its output content. The analysis of foreign news processing indicated that advice from government sources is primarily sought by the daily shift editor, while in agency councils monitoring output, market and journalistic considerations predominate. No one could recall an instance when a Tanjug interpretation aroused government's ire, except in the extraordinary case of Czechoslovakia in 1968. Here the agency misjudged the governmental line and remained overly critical after the Ministry of Foreign affairs had toned down its attacks.

Most important, the cybernetic model permits accurate prediction of future desk behavior. It supplied hypotheses about crucial variables such as content output, mix, and volume, as well as operating procedures which aided in the analysis of what may be called "crisis functioning," the behavior of the foreign desk under input stress and interpretative uncertainty.

Last, it must be noted that the model is an effective tool in cross-cultural research. It draws attention to system variables irrespective of the society in which these are embedded, and thus helps generate truly comparative data. While gatekeepers and their behavior doubtlessly are a factor in any news channel, this study clarifies and minimizes their importance in two ways: It turns out that most gatekeepers like Gieber's telegraph editor occupy flow-through positions. The handful of journalists who actually make decisions affect content in different ways: through gross selection, interpretation, and determination of balance and mix. None of them are the "king pins" they were originally thought to be. Their decisions are made not so much on individual assessments of newsworthiness as on a cluster of values, including such journalistic and organizational criteria as item output, efficiency, verisimilitude, and speed.

While Tanjug's news selection activities and scope of editorial interpretation are similar to those found in a western agency, these conclusions are not to be interpreted as saying that there is no difference in foreign news perspectives, content, and emphasis. What these differences are and how they reflect the Yugoslav and American images of the world will be investigated in the next chapter.

---

1 Thayer, *Communication and Communication Systems,* p. 29.

2 Berger and Luckmann, *Social Construction,* p. 103.

3 Nan Lin, *The Study of Human Communication,* p. 57.

4 John Galtung and Mari Holmboe Ruge, "The Structure of Foreign News: The Presentation of the Congo, Cuba, and Cyprus Crises in Four Newspapers," pp. 64-90.

5 The Associated Press lists around 250 foreign correspondents in fifty-seven bureaus, while TASS may have as many as 500 in ninety-five bureaus, according to Mark W. Hopkins, *Mass Media in the Soviet Union,* p. 282.

6 David Manning White, "The 'Gate-Keeper': A Case Study in the Selection of News," pp. 383-390.

7 Walter Gieber, "Across the Desk: A Study of Sixteen Telegraph Editors," p. 432.

8 John T. McNelly, "Intermediary Communicators in the International Flow of News," pp. 23-26.

9 Abraham Z. Bass, "The Internal Flow of the News at United Nations Radio: Refining the 'Gate Keeper' and Intermediary Communication Concepts," p. 8.

10 Lewis Donohew, "Newspaper Gatekeepers and Forces in the News Channel," pp. 61-68.

11 A more detailed paper by the author surveys the history of the gatekeeper theory. Gertrude Joch Robinson, "Twenty-Five Years of 'Gate-Keeper' Research: A Critical Review and Evaluation."

12 Wilbert E. Moore, *Social Change,* pp. 9-10.

13 Melvyn L. Cadwallader, "The Cybernetic Analysis of Change in Complex Social Organizations," p. 398.

14 Karl W. Deutsch, "On Communication Models in the Social Sciences," pp. 346, 380.

15 Scott Cutlip, "Content and Flow of AP News — From Trunks to TTS to Reader," pp. 434-436.

16 Karl Erik Rosengren, "International News: Methods, Data and Theory," pp. 1-44.

17 In the early 1960s there were eight criteria, two of which have since been dropped. Originally stories about film and pop personalities as well as about music festivals were not covered by Tanjug. Today film and music festivals are part of its reportage.

18 Joseph A. Litterer, *The Analysis of Organizations,* pp. 233-235.

19 Benjamin Lee Whorf, *Language, Thought and Reality;* see Whorf's chapter on "Language, Mind and Reality."

20 Deutsch, "On Communication Models," p. 365.

21 Galtung and Ruge, "The Structure of Foreign News," p. 70.

22 Schwarzlose, "American Wire Services," pp. 153-154.

23 Buzek, *How the Communist Press Works,* pp. 132-135.

24 William Albig, *Modern Public Opinion,* pp. 240-244.

25 Walter Gieber, "How the 'Gatekeepers' View Local Civil Liberty News," pp. 199-205.

26 Warren Breed, "Social Control in the Newsroom: A Functional Analysis," pp. 326-336.

27 The Network Project, *Office of Telecommunications Policy: Notebook Number Four;* and Harry S. Ashmore, "Broadcasting and the First Amendment: Report on a Center Conference," pp. 19-66.

CHAPTER 8

A Picture of the World

One of the most important insights emerging from the focus on the symbolic dimension of social relations is the realization that "a society cannot be conceptualized solely as an instrumental organization designed or developed in order to solve the difficulties of collective life. Every society is also an expression, an affirmation of the value and meaning of life in that mileu."[1] David Chaney has noted that such a conceptualization draws attention to the fact that human beings often find relations meaningful over and above their manifest or utilitarian function. Mass communications content, viewed as one form of social expression, sensitizes us to the fact that collective life cannot be explained by economic and political categories alone. "Meaning" or interpretation of experience must also be taken into account.

It has generally been hypothesized that national cultures are differentiated from each other through unique patterns of values, expressive norms, and symbolic rituals. The mass media emphasize some of them but not others, yet how they do this is not well understood. This chapter investigates one pattern of values, namely, those which come into play when events are selected to become "foreign news." To make this analysis more comprehensive, Yugoslav and United States selections will be juxtaposed to better understand the differences between what citizens find meaningful and good in the two countries. In speaking about meaning in this context, we are not interested in the psychological question of how meaning is attached and communality of meaning emerges between individuals, but rather in what is considered a meaningful representation of world events to two groups of people living in differentiated societies on opposite sides of the Atlantic.

Such a perspective assumes from the outset that there are no neutral media systems anywhere in the world. They, like the school and church, reinforce the general principles and outlooks, often called "ideologies," accepted by the society in which they are embedded. As early as 1922, Walter Lippmann[2] noted that every editorial office has its rules according to which events are classified as news. Such news, he claimed, must arouse the emotions of readers and provide a chance for identification. More recently George Gerbner and James Halloran[3] emphasized that a particular society's news values are absorbed by the journalist in the practice of his profession. No matter what his lofty ideals may be, these values will be tempered by the economic and political realities in which selection and reporting occur. Gerbner notes:

> There is no fundamental non-ideological apolitical non-partisan news gathering and reporting system. . . . The basic ideological and political choices are inherent not in party-partisanship but in the total operation of "news values," and of standards of reporting. These choices are evident in press systems where ideological plurality is maintained through more than one source and method of press support. The choices are not so apparent but they are made, nevertheless, without public debate, vote, and often in the name of "freedom," where either the commercial press, or a one-party press, preempt the field of daily journalism.[4]

Very little is known about the structure and content of foreign news and about the principles which contribute to variations in outlook. According to Fred Siebert, three different philosophies direct and limit the world press and information systems: the autocratic, the commercial, and the mixed, or social responsibility, theories.[5] Various investigators have scrutinized the impact of these on media content in a variety of countries.[6] Few researchers have, however, raised the more fundamental question about the impact of ideology on news agency flow itself, which is at issue here. No one knows in great detail what constitutes the idiosyncratic balance and mix of an autocratic, a commercial, and a mixed news agency service.

To investigate this question, an attempt was made to collect the tickers of three different news agencies to find out how they reported the world on the same day. Two of these were obtained, with the Associated Press's European service representing a commercial flow, and Tanjug's general service ticker representing a "mixed" rather than an "autocratic" service. The TASS ticker was not available for October 26, 1966, so that comparative comments are based on the more general findings of Theodore Kruglak and Mark Hopkins.[7] The content analysis reported in this chapter consequently emphasizes differences between the commercial and mixed news agency contents and uses TASS data merely to illustrate already mentioned points, rather than to develop additional testable hypotheses.

What is known about the symbolic or meaning dimension of these different kinds of international news flow? One of the first writers in the field, Einar Östgaard,[8] observed that their content tended to stress governmental over human information, higher ranking over lower ranking countries, personified over process oriented descriptions, and conflict over cooperation. John Galtung and Mari Ruge[9] systematized some of these scattered findings and laid the foundation for a differential theory of news values. According to these writers, there are twelve news factors which make certain events more "newsworthy" than others. The majority of these supposedly have to do with the psychology of perception and are, therefore, claimed to be culture free. They relate to such things as selectivity, frequency, and intensity. Others, however, like preoccupation with elite nations and people and a tendency toward personification and negativism, may be culture bound, relating only to the commercial flow. Karl Rosengren,[10] in a lucid 1973 summary of methods and data, takes issue with this formulation. He concludes from a test of two of Galtung's variables that a theory of news values must be couched in economic and political rather than in psychological terms. The subsequent comparative content analysis is designed to investigate differences in foreign news interpretation between Yugoslavia and the United States and to test some of these theoretical predictions.

Three specific emphases will structure the discussion throughout. How do Tanjug and the Associated Press through selection, treatment, and emphasis help define significant realities for their respective societies? What is the difference between their agendas of public discussion? And, what are the dominant values from which realities, policies, and actions are viewed in Yugoslavia and the United States? Answers to these questions will illuminate why certain kinds of events are selected in one system and not in the other and how characteristic foreign news perspectives emerge from differing ideologies and news organizations.

Subject Matter: What Becomes "News"?

Twelve years ago George Gerbner suggested that the mass media structure the meaning of life for their milieu by doing three things: they select the daily items for public discussion, they order these into an agenda, and they make available dominant perspectives from which realities, priorities, and policies may be viewed.[11] Such recent investigators as Maxwell McCombs and Donald Shaw[12] have discovered that there is a correlation between what the media select and play and what the public considers important. Consequently, whatever news agencies like Tanjug or the Associated Press select for coverage will become the international discussion agenda on which their local print and broadcast customers base their own content choices and from which the Yugoslav and American citizens ultimately fashion their own picture of the world.

To make comparative observations about differences in agency selection patterns, extra-media data are necessary. What was the universe of happenings from which Tanjug and the Associated Press chose certain items to become "news" while they totally ignored others? To determine what happened on October 26, 1966, a date arbitrarily chosen to compare international coverage, *Facts on File,* a digest of data on current events, was consulted. Its introduction notes that information is gathered from periodicals, official national and international publications, as well as international news agencies. In spite of the fact that this publication does not provide pure extra-media data, it has the advantage of aiming at completeness. Karl Rosengren notes that a source of this nature can provide a legitimate substitute for independent data, especially if the analysis focuses on data from a limited number of news channels.[13]

World happenings on October 26, 1966, covered the spectrum from the Beatles to Vietnam.[14] Two political conferences dealt with the international implications of the war. The first, composed of three nonaligned nations (Yugoslavia, India, and Egypt), urged an immediate cessation of Vietnam air strikes without preconditions. The second, or Manila, conference, composed of seven nations engaged in the Vietnam fighting, pledged reciprocal withdrawal of their troops in case Hanoi ceased infiltration. In Africa, a Katanga cabinet shift made Mobutu both president and prime minister while it demoted Mulamba to the defense department. In Europe, de Gaulle insisted on a NATO headquarters move and the elimination of French troops from this organization. In South America, the Mexican and Honduran presidents met to plan economic and political cooperation. The American President Lyndon B. Johnson made a surprise visit to the United States fighting troops in Kam Ran Bay, while Emperor Haile Selassie of Ethiopia addressed the Congress of Evangelism in Berlin.

In the economic, cultural, and United Nations realms, Lisbon played host to Common Market ministers debating Spanish participation, while Rome was the scene of the 37th Congress of Socialist Trade Unions. Various eastern European countries concluded trade agreements. In Skopje, there was a conference on earthquakes, while an Atlas rocket and a communications satellite for the Pacific were launched from Cape Kennedy. Moscow celebrated the moon-orbiting of its Luna 12 at the same time that Peking was disturbed by Red Guard activities. At the United Nations, South Africa lost its mandate over much of the continent. The Soviet Union and the United States showed willingness to cooperate on limiting the spread of nuclear weapons, and members shelved a request to deal immediately with continuing Arab-Israeli unrest.

October 26, 1966, finally, also had its share of disasters, sports events, and human interest stories. Forty-three men lost their lives in the Oriskany aircraft fire off Vietnam. The Italian and Adriatic coasts were inundated by floods, and three French fishermen drowned in a mountainous tidal wave. The Moscow military district general had a serious automobile accident at the same time that a group of departing Chinese students tried unsuccessfully to lay a wreath on Stalin's tomb. In London, one of the Beatles took up the Indian sitar and a famous pop singer died. Germany lost a submarine at sea while England entrusted the Earl of Mountbatten with a check on prison security after the escape of a Soviet spy. Great Britain was also the scene of the world heavyweight boxing championship, while eastern Europe and the continent hosted soccer teams from all over the world.

What did Tanjug and the Associated Press select from this plethora of events? Was there any overlap of coverage? What types of content were stressed and what kinds of facts were omitted by the two agencies? Treatment of the same themes provides insights into the degree of mutuality of the world discussion agendas in socialist and western countries which has not been previously noted and systematically investigated. A clearer understanding of omissions, on the other hand, illuminates Yugoslav-American news perspectives which are determined as much by what is said as by what is not.

What kinds of events did the mixed and commercial services select for emphasis and play? A comparative analysis of discussion agendas will have to cover three things: the size of the news flow, the categories of information covered, and those areas where overlap does or does not occur. A purely quantitative comparison indicates that the mixed flow is much smaller than the commercial one. This is clearly a result of differences in size and resources between a national and a global agency. Table 19 indicates that Tanjug's coverage of world events both in terms of items and words is about one-third that of the Associated Press. Of the 139 items in the October 26, 1966, Tanjug general service, ninety-six were about foreign affairs, bearing out the 2:1 foreign/domestic product mix specification noted in the previous chapter. Of the Associated Press's 337 items on the same day, 235 were equally concerned with world matters. Tanjug published approximately 174,100 words against twice that many, 334,000, of the Associated Press.

What were the general types of subject matter covered by the two agencies and how were these classified? It is well known that most social researchers develop content categories without regard for replication or comparisons.[15] Since this study has emphasized comparability, it was decided not to create new categories but to use the 1953 International Press Institute scheme utilized for a comprehensive study of foreign news flow among the United States, western Europe, and India. This study used fourteen categories to define agency subject matter: war, politics, foreign relations, defense, economics, culture, education-science-technology, judicial, social, human interest, crime, disaster, sports, and religion.[16]

Table 19
Content Analysis [a]

	Tanjug General Service	AP European Service
Total number of items	139	337
Total number of foreign items analyzed	96	235
Number of inches (without headline)	435	860
Number of lines (4 per inch)	17,410	34,400
Number of words (10 per line)	174,100	344,000

[a] Items are not necessarily about different subjects, as some long stories were broken up into two to four items in the Associated Press's European service. In Tanjug this was not the case. The agencies' own item numbering was used for identification.

The similarities and differences in agency emphasis will be inferred from subject categories as well as geographic coverage. These can be measured in two complementary ways: by item ranking and computation of percentages. Ranking emphasizes the similarities of Tanjug and Associated Press subject matter, while percentages highlight significant differences. Only the two taken in conjunction give an accurate comparative evaluation of the two services' differing emphases. Item ranking in Table 20 indicates that Tanjug and the Associated Press are similar in the types of subject matter covered as well as geographical areas emphasized. The differing percentages of news items devoted to categories and world regions, however, modify these similarities and indicate Tanjug's considerably wider geographic spread.

A comparative classification of topics covered indicates, contrary to expectations, that both Tanjug and the Associated Press give priority to the same *kind* of news categories, though they do not pay an equal amount of attention to each of these. Both in Yugoslavia and in the United States "hard news" categories such as foreign relations, politics, economics, war news, education-science-technology, and sports dominate the world discussion agendas. They take up 88.8 percent of Tanjug's and 71.8 percent of the Associated Press's total coverage. However, such general figures taken by themselves obscure the stronger hard news emphasis in the mixed versus the commercial news flows, which is demonstrated by a closer look at Table 20.

Table 20
News Categories Covered by Tanjug and Associated Press

Tanjug			Associated Press		
Categories	No. Items	% of Total	Categories	No. Items	% of Total
1. Foreign relations	22	23.0	1. War	48	19.1
2. Politics	16	16.7	2. Foreign relations	33	14.0
3. Economics	14	14.6	3. Economics	29	12.3
4. War	12	12.5	4. Politics	25	10.6
		(66.8)			(56.0)
5. Educ., sci., tech.	11	11.5	5. Sports	23	9.8
6. Sports	10	10.5	6. Educ., sci., tech.	14	6.0
		(88.8)			(71.8)
7. Judicial & U.N.	4	4.2	7. Human interest	13	5.5
8. Social measures	3	3.0	8. Religion	12	5.1
9. Disasters	3	3.0	9. Defense and Nato	9	3.8
10. Defense and NATO	1	1.0	10. Judicial and U.N.	8	3.4
11. Human interest			11. Disasters	7	3.0
12. Religion			12. Social measures	5	2.2
13. Culture			Misc. (Corrections)	5	2.2
14. Crime			13. Culture	4	1.7
			14. Crime	3	1.3
Totals	96	100.00		235	100.0

Here Tanjug's greater hard news emphasis is evident from two factors: the greater proportion of total space these categories assume and the absence of human interest and other types of "soft" reporting. To begin with, Tanjug's four categories of foreign relations, economics, politics, and war include two-thirds of all stories, 66.8 percent of the total. In the Associated Press they make up only a little more than one-half, or 56 percent, of the total content. In addition, it appears that Tanjug does not cover human interest, religion, culture, and crime for the Yugoslav reader, while the Associated Press devotes 13.6 percent of all its stories to these topics. The lack of culture and human interest reporting does not mean that these kinds of stories are not to be found in the Yugoslav press. Since the 1960s, as Chapter 3 demonstrated, there has been an increase of this type of coverage, but it is usually written by the media rather than by Tanjug reporters. Moreover, it turns out that while the Yugoslav agency covers eastern Europe for economic agreements, the Associated Press covers this area solely for sports events, further illustrating the greater hard news outlook of the mixed service.

In determining whether the mixed and commercial agencies ever talked about the same events, a comparison of agency news items, Appendix 3, reveals that thirty of Tanjug's themes match sixty-nine of the Associated Press's. This represents an overlap of 31.3 percent of the total Yugoslav foreign output and 29.4 percent of the American. Nearly one-third of all material in both agencies thus covers the same subject matter. Since this is considerably higher than chance correlation, one may reasonably ask how it came about, considering that the ideologies in the two systems differ. News values are government/party sponsored for Yugoslavia's mixed service and government/business enunciated for the commercial United States agency.

The previous chapter and Galtung's analysis suggest that ideology operates in conjunction with other factors in determining selection. Among them are news inputs, editing procedures, and competitors' estimates of newsworthiness which must also be taken into account. Events occur and, irrespective of an agency's political outlook, reports about them pour into headquarters from correspondents and other news services. It has also been noted that though Tanjug's foreign desk has considerable freedom to select details, its journalistic ethic prevents it from generating a foreign discussion agenda totally unrelated to world happenings. In addition, the amount of coverage a particular occurrence receives from the five international news gatherers will leave its mark.[17] Moreover, certain events where value structures of the two societies are not in conflict will also have a greater chance of being reported in both the mixed and the commercial services.

According to Appendix 3, eight themes fulfill these requirements and therefore appear in both discussion agendas. They are:

(1) Vietnam: the progress of the war; the implications of the Manila troop

pull-out promise to a settlement of the conflict; President Johnson's visit; and the disastrous fire on the aircraft carrier *Oriskany*.

(2) United Nations activities: the great power willingness to cooperate in stopping the spread of nuclear weapons; General Assembly criticism of South Africa's mandate over large parts of the continent; Chinese inability to gain Formosa's seat on the UNESCO council; and United States consideration of the Czech-Polish nuclear inspection proposal.

(3) Technological and scientific matters: America's Atlas rocket and Pacific communications satellite launching; Moscow's Luna 12 moon orbiting; and the conference on earthquakes in Skopje.

(4) International sports events: a Bulgarian-Portuguese soccer tie; Poland's victory in the European national championships; the World Club Soccer final in Spain; and the Danish-Israeli match in Copenhagen.

(5) The Congo: Mobutu's power consolidation.

(6) The NATO headquarters removal from Paris.

(7) International economic affairs: such as West Germany's support of Spain's Common Market membership and the 37th Congress of European Socialist Trade Unions in Rome.

(8) Disasters: such as the floods in Salerno.

A closer scrutiny of this common agenda substantiates a study by Gerbner which showed that the socialist media tend to view realities and evaluate priorities and perspectives in terms of substance and promise, rather than in terms of a power contest. Consequently, coexistence, disarmament, and colonial liquidation are selected not mainly to illustrate aspects of big power strategy, but as the essential prerequisites for a better life now. From this perspective, conflict is seen as delaying and played down and instances of agreement played up for their readers.[18]

The eight selected common themes illustrate that Yugoslav and United States discussion agendas resembled each other on the urgency of a Vietnam war settlement which could have engulfed others in a world conflagration; United Nations activities designed to curtail the spread of nuclear weapons; NATO and defense questions which may herald a redistribution of military power on the European continent; developments in science and technology which have universal applicability; and sports, which provide a peaceful outlet for competitive instincts.

Table 21, which subsumes these themes under the appropriate fourteen subject categories and records length as an indication of proportionate interest, however, indicates that though a bit more than one-third of each agency's content is alike, this similarity of outlook extends primarily to minor rather than to major discussion categories. Of the four well-represented topics encompassing more than 50 percent of all Yugoslav and United States ticker reports, only one, the topic of war, belongs to a major international news category. This substantiates the frequently noted discrepancies between the mixed and commercial discussion agendas on such crucial issues as foreign relations, economics, and politics.

Table 21
Length of Theme Coverages in Tanjug and Associated Press
(in rounded percentages)

Theme and Subject Category	Tanjug (435 inches)			Associated Press (860 inches)		
	No. Items	Length	% of Total in Category	No. Items	Length	% of Total in Category
Vietnam war	11	49	100	28	97	58
UN debates — judicial	3	24	75	7	35	88
Sports	4	18	36	10	29	43
Educ.-sci.-tech.	6	38	55	7	25	50
Congo nuclear inspection	2	9	13	7	26	28
NATO-defense	1	2	100	5	17	56
Trade Union Cong. Common Market (Econ.)	2	14	14	3	14	10
Floods — disasters	1	3	33	2	6	29
Totals	30	157		69	249	

Emphasis: What Is Important?

Having established the fact that Tanjug presents a greater hard news emphasis for its media customers than the Associated Press, it is necessary to investigate differences between the mixed and commercial news flows. Such differences, according to Einar Östgard, may arise from extra or intramedia factors. The former refer to structural hindrances to international news flow and various types of censorship along the transmission chain from world events to the reader's personal image about these events. The latter have to do with the fact that audiences in different countries are familiar with various aspects of reality and therefore develop conceptions of what is "meaningful" and "consonant" with previously established outlooks. They also develop ideas about what constitutes "continuity" in reporting and how the composition of a newspaper or broadcast report ought to be fashioned. In general, it may be assumed that: "The news concerning people, things or issues with which those receiving the news are the most familiar, finds its way through the news channels more easily than news concerning unfamiliar persons, things, or issues. . . . The greater the possibility of identification with the news, the greater will be the news flow."[19]

The subsequent section covers those aspects of reality which tend to make events meaningful for a Yugoslav versus a North American or western European audience in order to gain a better understanding of the foreign news values which are operative in the two societies.

According to John Galtung and Mari Ruge, the international news flow, as transmitted by a large capitalist agency, has been structured by the following four news priorities: it overrepresents elite nations, concentrates on elite people, tends to present events in personal terms as due to the actions of specific individuals, and overstresses negativism. The authors describe the preoccupation with elite nations and people as quite understandable since the elite can be used as a model to tell about everyone. Furthermore, personification is a direct outcome of elite-concentration and speaks to the westerner's need for meaning and identification, as well as his cultural idealism which pictures him as the master of his own destiny. Negative events are frequently selected because they are less ambiguous and are unexpected. They thus fulfill the "novelty" criterion.[20] Each of these points will be separately investigated to acquire a clearer picture of the mixed news flow as represented by Tanjug's general service and to discover the attention focuses and subject matter treatments which differentiate its news values from those mentioned above.

To determine whether a small socialist country like Yugoslavia pays attention to the same numbers and kinds of nations around the globe, items on the two tickers were classified as to the countries they covered. Table 22 indicates that Tanjug's coverage of world events does not suffer from the elite myopia

Table 22
Comparison of Most Heavily Covered Countries

	Tanjug		AP	
	No. Items	% of Total	No. Items	% of Total
United States	14	14.6	47	20.0
Internationaland	9	9.4	38	16.1
Vietnam (T) Great Britain (AP)	8	8.3	30	12.3
U.S.S.R. (T) Vietnam (AP)	6	6.3	18	7.7
Subtotals	37	38.6	133	56.1
Group of 10 countries (T) West Germany (AP) (Berlin)	with 3 items each 30	31.0	15	6.4
Group of 7 countries (T) Italy (AP)	with 2 items each 14	15.4	14	6.0
Group of 15 countries (T) China (AP)	with 1 item each 15	15.0	9	3.8
Subtotals	59	61.4	38	16.2
U.S.S.R. (AP)			8	3.3
Totals	96	100.0	179	75.6

prevalent in the Associated Press. Its most numerous references, thirty-seven items or 38.6 percent of its space, go to the United States, international organs (UN and NATO headquarters), Vietnam, and the Soviet Union. The same countries, with Great Britain substituted for the Soviet Union, receive 133 Associated Press item references, constituting 56.1 percent of its total coverage. Interestingly enough these priorities have remained the same for the western agency which in 1953 confined United States world interest to Korea, where another war was being waged, UN and NATO headquarters, Great Britain, and Japan.[21]

Though Tanjug agrees with the Associated Press that events in western

Table 23
Countries Covered by Agencies

Countries	Tanjug Total Items	Tanjug % of Total	AP Total Items	AP % of Total
Yemen	2	2.2		
Brazil	3	3.1	38	16.1
Internationaland [a] (E)	9	9.4		
Senegal	1	1.0		
Sudan	1	1.0		
United States [b] (E)	14	14.6	47	20.0
W. Germany (& Berlin)	3	3.1	15	6.4
Indonesia	2	2.2		
Mexico	3	3.1		
Bulgaria	3	3.1	2	0.9
Burma	1	1.0		
France (E)	3	3.1	6	2.6
Vietnam	8	8.3	18	7.7
Italy	2	2.2	14	6.0
Chile	1	1.0		
Britain [c] (E)	3	3.1	30	12.8
Cuba	3	3.1		
USSR (E)	6	6.3	8	3.3
Morocco	1	1.0	4	1.7
Colombo	1	1.0		
Japan (E)	2	2.2	2	0.9
Korea	1	1.0		
Hungary	2	2.2		
E. Germany	1	1.0		
Egypt	1	1.0		
Iraq	2	2.2		
India	3	3.1		
(Kisenga) Congo	1	1.0	7	3.0
Poland	1	1.0	7	3.0
Czechoslovakia	3	3.1	6	2.6
Algeria	1	1.0		
Malaya	1	1.0		

Table 23 (Continued)

Countries	Tanjug Total Items	Tanjug % of Total	AP Total Items	AP % of Total
Turkey	2	2.2		
Spain	1	1.0	6	2.6
Austria	1	1.0	2	0.9
Belgium	3	3.1	1	0.3
China			9	3.8
Lebanon			1	0.3
Iran			2	0.9
Portugal			2	0.9
Denmark			3	1.2
Rumania			2	0.9
Yugoslavia			2	0.9
Belgium			1	0.3
Totals	96	100.0	235	100.0
Short news	-11			
	85			

Geographical Areas Covered by Agencies

Areas	Tanjug Total Items	Tanjug % of Total	AP Total Items	AP % of Total
Western Europe	25	26.0	118	50.3
Eastern Europe	16	16.7	25	10.6
Near East	9	9.4	5	2.1
Far East	18	18.8	29	12.3
North America	14	14.6	47	20.0
South America	8	8.3	0	0
Africa	6	6.2	11	4.7
Totals	96	100.0	235	100.0

[a] Internationaland: U.N., NATO, Manila conference, Free Trade Association conference
[b] Johnson trip: Domestic U.S. news
[c] Stocks: Domestic U.S. or British news (includes quotations)
(E) — Elite Nations

Europe and Vietnam dominate the news priorities of October 26, 1966, elite politics do not crowd out other topics of interest associated with the industrializing countries of the world. Table 23 indicates that the Associated Press gives the United States and three western European elite nations — Great Britain, West Germany, and France — nearly 42 percent of its total coverage while Tanjug devotes only approximately half, or 24 percent, to them. A survey of geographical areas based on country coverage also demonstrates the nonelite focus of the mixed news flow. Here it appears that while the commercial system concentrates over half of its reporting on the countries of western Europe, Tanjug concentrates only 25 percent of its items on this area and gives approximately equal coverage to other parts of the world. Thus the Far East, where the Vietnam war caused concern, eastern Europe, with common ideological ties, and North America rate about equal coverage, 18.8 percent, 16.7 percent, and 14.6 percent, respectively, of the total world report. Only Africa and South America, where emerging countries are struggling for independence, are somewhat less covered with 12.5 percent between them.

In general, Tanjug reporting of world events is much less elitist than that of the United States world service. It distributes its interest more equally among all geographical regions. It also covers a larger number of countries with different political systems and at different stages of economic development. The Associated Press, on the other hand, concentrates 70.3 percent of its total report on western Europe and the United States, leaving very little space for the industrializing world: 12.3 percent for the Far East, 10.6 percent for eastern Europe, and 6.8 percent for Africa and the Near East.

Table 23 also demonstrates Yugoslavia's interest in developing countries, a fact noted in Chapter 4. It includes thirteen more nations than the Associated Press in its daily report. A breakdown of coverage shows that the United States, UN and NATO headquarters, Vietnam, and the Soviet Union attract 38.6 percent of Tanjug's attention while another thirty-two countries command the remaining 61.4 percent of stories. Among them are ten countries, only three of which are elite nations. These are France, Britain, Germany, Brazil, Mexico, Bulgaria, Cuba, India, Czechoslovakia, and Belgium — all of them receive major coverage with three stories each. Another seven have two items — Yemen, Indonesia, Italy, Japan, Hungary, Iraq, and Turkey. The remaining group of fifteen has only a single report and are clearly nonelite. One-third of them are on the African continent — Senegal, Sudan, Morocco, Egypt, and Algeria. Another four are in Europe — East Germany, Poland, Spain, and Austria. Three are in the Far East—Burma, Korea, and Malaya; two, in Latin America — Colombia and Chile.

It is interesting to note in this connection that Tanjug's four selection emphases previously deduced from the morgue also affect daily foreign news production. The October 26, 1966, coverage of thirty-six countries confirms that (1) world power and trade partners, (2) states with historical friendship, enmity, or joint international policy ties, and (3) countries with a similar political structure attract Tanjug's foreign news attention, in that order. Only the Soviet Union is removed from its prominent position, ranking fourth instead of first as the morgue hints. This suggests that the reason for its disproportionately large number of entries in the organization memory may be a result of historical necessity rather than ideological preference. In the late 1940s and early 1950s, the Cominform break, Stalin's death, and the Communist party congresses provided information which was of vital interest to Yugoslavia's survival. Today the Soviet Union no longer presents as great a threat and thus takes its place among other elite countries.

It may be legitimately asked if one day's news output accurately reflects Tanjug's geographical coverage over time. Often single events, such as coups or disasters, propel countries into the limelight which otherwise do not gain international attention. Investigation of company records detailing the geographical content of news items, however, essentially confirms the conclusions reached on the basis of the October 26, 1966, sample. Here, too, the Soviet Union is removed from its top position. Table 24 ranks western Europe highest in news attention with 5,780 stories, Africa next with 4,102, Asia third with 3,987, and socialist countries with a similar political structure in fourth place with 3,456 reports.

The next two commercial news flow biases in favor of elite coverage of people as well as personification of interpretation will be treated together, since the latter stems from the former. According to Galtung and Ruge, a large western agency has a tendency to "present events as sentences where there is a subject, a named person, or collectivity consisting of a few persons, and the event is then seen as a consequence of the actions of this person. The alternative would be to present events as the outcome of social forces, as structural more than idiosyncratic outcomes of the society which produced them. In a structural analysis the names of the actors would disappear much as they do in sociological analysis."[22]

This point seems to echo the distinction made by Gerbner in his comparison of the *New York Times* and Hungarian coverage of the 1960 General Assembly meeting, where he found a clear distinction between what he called "procedural" versus "substantive" reporting. A content analysis of headline emphasis, direction, and the use of action words and names indicated that the *New*

Table 24
Items about Major World Regions in 1963
(from Tanjug Foreign Desk)

Month	Socialist Countries	Western Europe	Africa	Asia	North America	South America
1	281	666	391	395	261	87
2	311	482	316	319	189	96
3	278	562	428	373	191	131
4	315	439	426	381	239	145
5	268	396	421	326	207	79
6	342	511	355	324	210	70
7	375	472	284	269	175	56
8	304	334	218	345	180	71
9	234	457	227	313	216	95
10	218	514	404	290	190	73
11	269	440	325	360	243	105
12	261	507	307	292	206	145
Totals	3456	5780	4102	3987	2507	1153

SOURCE: Table 9, *Mesečni Bilten o Radu Agencije*, Godina III, Broj 13 (April 1964).

York Times preferred dynamic terms such as "buffer bloc" and modifiers like "coldly" to supply color to the "drama of highly personalized encounter and clash."[23] Gerbner found also that the *Times*'s greater "personification" was reflected in the use of thirty-six names in sixty lines. In contrast, the Hungarian paper heads were short on "hard news" content and long on declarations of intent. Their procedural verbs focused on progress toward aims and rarely dealt with people. Only three major headlines (one line in eight) named individuals.

What evidence is there of Tanjug's neglect of elite people in its coverage and of a more structural interpretation of world events? Table 25, which registers the number of items referring to specific people, indicates that about 30 percent of Associated Press ticker is people-oriented versus only 23 percent for Tanjug. A further breakdown of these items into elite and nonelite people indicates the far greater elite orientation of the commercial news flow. Here 79 percent of all items are about United States, British, French, or German citizens, while the remaining 21 percent refer to leaders in smaller European countries. Tanjug, in contrast, uses 60 percent of its people items to report on nonelite leaders such as the Honduran, Cuban, and Bolivian presidents, Cairo's Nasser, India's Ghandi, as well as the heads of state in Czechoslovakia, Algeria, and Iraq.

Both services, it appears, tend to stress the activities of governmental leaders over those of ordinary people, a bias already noted by Einar Östgaard. The same writer mentioned that all governments of the world are engaged in weighing the news in their own interests either by means of censorship or by flooding the news channels with a plethora of information releases. The lives of ordinary people enter the selection process of both systems only when something extraordinary happens to them. This indicates that there is some validity to Karl Rosengren's reformulation of one of John Galtung's hypotheses. Assuming that negative events tend to happen more to common than to elite people, one should test whether the lower the rank of the actor the stronger the tendency to overrepresent negative events and underrepresent positive ones.[24] This seems to be borne out by the Associated Press ticker, which mentions common people primarily when they engage in sport competition, strange behavior, or fall victim to accidents. They consequently reported soccer matches, drug smug-

Table 25
Items Referring to Elite and Nonelite People

	Tanjug		Associated Press	
	Numbers	Percent	Numbers	Percent
Total number of items	96	100	235	100
Total items about people	22	23	79	30
Elite	7	32	63	79
Nonelite	15	68	16	21

gling, the conversion of a typist to a belly dancer, and the foiled attempt of thirty Chinese students to lay a wreath on Stalin's tomb, not to overlook monkey bites and deaths by tidal waves. Tanjug, too, carries soccer scores and a report of the demise of six people in the Austrian Alps.

Tanjug's tendency not to "personify" the news and to stress a structural orientation is most easily demonstrated by comparing the two agencies' reporting of the Vietnamese war. This will be done by determining the number of people-oriented items and analyzing the different themes covered. Counting each paragraph with a caption as one item, Table 26 indicates that Tanjug has a total of twelve items dealing with Vietnam, whereas the Associated Press has forty-eight. Only three of Tanjug's items, or 25 percent of the total coverage, are about people, specifically Johnson's secret visit to Kam Ran Bay. They provide short descriptions of what the President did throughout the day.

The Associated Press, on the other hand, devoted twenty-one, or 70 percent of its items, to only two Johnson themes: his visit and conjectures about his whereabouts as he cut short a stay in Manila. A chase, as is well known, provides attention-getting headlines. Here was a major elite figure, already an attention-getting person, adding suspense to an otherwise dull foreign policy meeting. No wonder it was played hardest in the commercial service. While this kind of coverage sells papers, it does not necessarily provide informative

Table 26
Themes and Emphases in Vietnam Coverage

	Tanjug	AP
Number of items on Vietnam	12	48
Variety of themes discussed	7	5
Jointly discussed themes:		
1. Vietnam war roundup	3	6
2. Johnson visit to Vietnam	3	18
3. "Oriskany" aircraft carrier fire	1	4
Tanjug discussed themes:		
1. Economic effects of war	2	
2. North Vietnamese agricultural mission to socialist world	1	
3. Polish concern over China's reaction	1	
4. U.S. Communist party dismay at bombing of North Vietnam	1	
AP discussed themes:		
1. Conjecture about Johnson's whereabouts		19
2. South Vietnamese Assembly elections		1
Sources of Vietnam news items:		
1. Own government	0	5
2. Own staff	3	38
3. Foreign agencies	5	1
4. Foreign government	4	4

coverage or serious backgrounding of Vietnam war issues. Here the comparative theme analysis indicates that the Yugoslav reader acquires not only a more varied but a more "structural" explication of the issues involved.

The Tanjug item selection, in contrast to the Associated Press coverage, focuses on the economic and political implications of the war, as well as the attitudes of other communist countries toward the struggle. Four of its additional themes probe the economic effects of the war on the United States and Mexico, point to the need for agricultural help to North Vietnam, note Polish anguish at China's unwillingness to join the Soviet and eastern European nations in mapping a joint Vietnam stand, and outline objections raised within the United States to the administration's new bombing plan.

Can it be argued that the variety of sources affects the quality of interpretation? Table 26 records that the sources of Tanjug's Vietnam information are fairly evenly distributed. Its own correspondents supply three reports; foreign agencies like the Associated Press, Reuters, and TASS provide five, and foreign government spokesmen for the United States military and for the Saigon government contribute material for four others. In the Associated Press's case, their own reporters provide thirty-eight out of the forty-eight articles. The only foreign information sources are the New China Agency and the Saigon government. The conspicuous absence of reports from other European agencies like Agence France Presse and Reuters, with different commitments and interests in the Vietnamese conflict, can perhaps be explained by the fact that the European service does not wish to duplicate material that its customers already receive.

Though the question cannot be unequivocally answered, the least that can be said is that the Associated Press's heavy reliance on staff reports facilitates the emergence of a nationalistic bias, already noted in a UNESCO evaluation of news agencies twenty-two years ago.[25] Tanjug's more diversified datelines suggest that such a bias, contrary to expectations, is perhaps not as easily fostered in a small agency with limited resources which has to compete hard for its international clients.

Differences in reporting which result from the two countries' differing ideological commitments on Vietnam can be even more clearly illustrated by comparing the two agencies' war roundups, by checking on the use of evaluative modifiers, by references to material destruction, and by the way in which South Vietnamese as well as the National Liberation Front's (NLF) war casualties are treated. Tanjug's war-tally notes:

Item 21. News and Telegrams, Saigon

South Vietnamese freedom fighters yesterday shot down two American helicopters. One was downed when it attempted to land in Kucci, west of Saigon. The members of the crew were saved. The second helicopter was shot down about 150 kilometers northeast of Saigon in the sector of the American "Bird" operation. Two members of the crew were wounded. The French press announces that 15

Saigon soldiers were wounded in a mine explosion which hit their truck. The mine was planted in a road near the village of Gunlijem, in the province of Vin Bin, about 100 kilometers southwest of Saigon.

The Associated Press reports the same incident:

Item 132.135, Vietnam: War Roundup by Robert Tuckman
Saigon Oct. 26—U.S. air cavalrymen and supporting planes routed a company of Viet Cong in a two-hour battle on the coast 110 miles northeast of Saigon yesterday and reported 48 enemy killed and two captured.

Casualties among the cavalrymen were reported light, but a U.S. H 13 observation helicopter was shot down during the engagement and its two crew members were wounded, a U.S. spokesman said.

A second helicopter — a troop transport — was knocked down by ground fire in another engagement 36 miles northwest of Saigon, but the spokesman said there were no casualties among the crew or troops aboard.

A comparison of the two reports, using such categories as use of evaluative modifiers, reference to material destruction, and mention of South Vietnamese as well as NLF casualties, elicits specific insights into the impact of the Yugoslav and American Vietnamese stands. The Tanjug report reflects Yugoslavia's identification with the NLF's independence struggle by referring to them as "South Vietnamese freedom fighters." In such a context, victories are emphasized and defeats minimized. Guerilla accomplishments, such as the downing of two United States helicopters and the successful mining of roads, are played up. The cost in terms of lives extracted in fighting a militarily superior enemy is not mentioned.

The American report uses no evaluative modifiers. It in turn emphasizes military organization and superiority. Three stylistic devices accomplish this task. United States troops are referred to as "U.S. cavalrymen," the enemy is described as "a company of Viet Cong," and enemy casualties are given in figures, though United States losses are merely described as "light." The downed helicopters, potential symbols of defeat, are presented as equipment losses and thus made congruent with the image of military superiority. This report in its turn leaves out the truck-mining incident. Both reports are "objective" in the sense of describing events which have happened. Both of them are not complete, however, leaving out certain vignettes. The differences between them are by no means as gross as apologists for the American news system would have us believe.

The cumulative evidence indeed substantiates that the socialist service tends not to personalize its news coverage, paying only one-quarter of its attention to President Johnson's mysterious disappearance and activities. Moreover, it also appears that Tanjug's Vietnam coverage is richer than that of the Associated Press, in spite of the fact that both agencies devote approximately the same amount of their total report (12 percent versus 15 percent) to this topic. It covers a greater number of themes, seven versus five, and was culled from more variegated sources. The choice of these themes, in turn, demonstrates an orientation which stresses economic and political interrelationships rather than personalities to explain the unfolding of events.

The third and final aspect of the news flow to be investigated is the modality in which world events tend to be reported. A number of researchers, among them Östgaard, have drawn attention to the superfluity of negative events in the western newsstream. Galtung and Ruge postulate that negative events tend to be preferred over positive ones for a number of reasons: negative events unfold faster than positive ones and thus better fit into the twenty-four-hour reporting cycle. Moreover, they are more unambiguous and consonant with the West's relatively pessimistic world pre-images. They are also rarer and therefore more unexpected than positive news.[26] Following these researchers, all items are classified from a neutral rather than a personal standpoint as taken by the actors or other groups. Reports were divided into "negative," "positive," or "neutral" where these categories refer to content in which something is being torn down, destroyed, or disrupted, or something is being constructed, built-up, or put together. The neutral class, in turn, contains those items which do not fit into either of the two other classifications. Such an enumeration provides a rough indication of the differing item mix in the two international newsstreams.

Table 27, which investigates distribution of negative presentation among the original fourteen categories, indicates a systematic preference for the negative modality in all categories of commercial reporting. The highest percentages of negative items are, however, found in the six "soft news" categories: human interest, religion, disasters, social measures, culture, and crime. Tanjug, as

Table 27
Mode of Presentation of News Categories
(in rounded percentages)

Categories	Tanjug % of Total	Negative	Positive	Neutral	Associated Press % of Total	Negative	Positive	Neutral
War	13	58	17	25	19	48	32	20
Foreign rel.	23	33	22	45	14	69	10	21
Economics	14	10	60	30	12		7	93
Politics	17	38	19	43	11	60	10	30
Sports	10			100	10			100
Educ., sci., tech.	11		81	19	6	7	85	8
Human interest					5	100		
Religion					5			100
Defense & NATO	1			100	4	55		45
Judicial and UN	4	25	25	50	3	12	13	75
Disasters	3	100			3	100		
Misc. Correct.					2			100
Social measures	3		66	33	2		100	
Culture	1				2	75	25	
Crime					2	100		

noted earlier, does not cover most of these. Greater negativism, however, is also evident in the four most important "hard news" categories which constitute approximately 67 percent of all Tanjug and 56 percent of Associated Press items. Here, except in the war category where Tanjug leads with 58 percent of all negative items, the commercial service presents 69 percent and 60 percent, respectively, of its foreign relations and political information in largely negative terms.

It is often claimed that the content of the mixed and autocratic newsstreams does not have a purely "informative" character, that it is collected and organized for a purpose. The very generality of this statement makes it misleading. It obscures the fact that all information is collected purposefully, since it must satisfy some recipient. As already noted, in Yugoslavia it must interest the public as well as government agencies, whereas in the United States it must speak to the audience as well as the advertisers who finance the media.

Another example of differing news values arising out of the context into which a report is placed rather than from the way in which it is described, is given by Tanjug and the Associated Press's coverage of the Manila conference.[27] This clearly indicates the hidden normative assumption made by an advertising financed news system that purely informative writing is somehow more "objective." Such a system must appeal to the largest possible audience. This can be accomplished only by keeping content and writing so bland as not to offend the majority of readers or listeners. "Blandness" and "objectivity" are, however, not necessarily the same thing. A more unbiased way of interpreting objectivity would be in terms of inclusiveness of presentation and straight reportorial style, which will be used here.

A comparison of Tanjug and Associated Press texts clarifies the point that both agencies are objective in that they select some overlapping facts and present them in a straight reportorial style. Beyond this, however, they attach different meanings to these facts. The differences stem from the already discussed differing world pictures into which facts have to "fit" in Yugoslavia and the United States. In its coverage and interpretation of Manila, Tanjug gives a total of four reports. One describes the Japanese position as analyzed by KYODO. The other three, from Tanjug's own foreign correspondents, analyze government and press responses in Britain, France, and the United States. Tokyo sets the general tone for the Manila interpretation, while the other stories add minor points and reinforce the negative evaluation of what was achieved at the conference.

Item 23. Disappointment

According to the KYODO news agency, disappointment was voiced in the inner circles of the Japanese Foreign Ministry about the fact that the Manila Conference of seven nations fighting with the United States in Vietnam did not succeed in providing a formula for the peaceful settlement of the Vietnamese problem.

The disappointment stems from the fact that the only proposal for a peaceful solution is the one citing that foreign troops will withdraw from South Vietnam if North Vietnam pulls back its soldiers and stops its infiltration.

The Manila meeting also did not, according to informed Japanese diplomatic circles, give any guarantees against further escalation of the war. The general impression is, as reported by the Japanese agency, that the seven countries are ready to continue the war.

From London a Tanjug staffer adds,

Item 45. Vietnam

President Johnson's visit, according to British reports and commentaries, did not have the goal of searching for peace. . . . He intended instead to strengthen the position of his coalition partners who are under pressure at the moment. The Australians and New Zealanders are faced with parliamentary elections back home.

The Paris correspondent notes,

Item 91. Commentaries

Proclamations about "its readiness to explore all possibilities which lead to world peace," says the Paris press — are completely unconvincing. "The American government," says *Combat* — "always repeats this and at the same time sends new troops and bombs to Vietnam."

In New York, finally, the New York *Times* is quoted and the Tanjug reporter points out,

Item 95.

The United Nations Assembly states that the participants of the Manila conference completely ignored Tantov's proposal asking for a cessation of bombing in Vietnam. . . . The opinion prevails that the United States and its allies will extend their war efforts in the face of Westmoreland's appeal for new troops in the next twelve months.

The Associated Press's Manila news roundup interestingly enough makes the same negative estimates as Tanjug about the conference's effect on Vietnamese peace possibilities and western European reactions. A news analysis by William Ryan, however, adds an American foreign policy and humanitarian perspective for the meeting, which is not noted by Tanjug.

Item 160. Manila, October 26

` The Manila summit conference produced something for everybody and probably wholly satisfied nobody. One of the results is likely to have strong and lasting impact on this area. The United States deeply committed itself, as a Pacific Ocean power, to the future of the whole Asian area with all its dread problem of poverty, disease, illiteracy and hunger.

That appeared to be one of the things America's allies not only wanted to hear, but wanted to have set down unequivocally and irrevocably on paper. Perhaps the Vietnam peace drive has progressed a little bit farther toward communication with the communists in Hanoi.

The summit conference offered to withdraw foreign allied troops from South Vietnam within 6 months of the time that North Vietnam meets their conditions.

There was an element of challenge in this since it emphasized the U.S. rejection of a contention that it never intends to get out of Vietnam.

This proposal, however, fell far short of a proffered solution, a real peace formula, or a rock-bottom final offer to the communist side. It was vague with respect to the Viet Cong withdrawal to the North.

It made no mention of a Viet Cong role at a peace conference; in fact, it left the American hands untied in that respect and the whole question of the approach to negotiations is still wide open. There likely was substantial difference of opinion on whether the Viet Cong should be recognized as a political entity.

The impact of the conference's "goals of progress," the "declaration on peace and progress in Asia and the Pacific" and the final joint communique will suffer from a widespread attitude of skepticism and even cynicism with which the summit conference was regarded.

Many — not only in Asia — suspect that there is more than coincidence in the fact that four of the Allies at the meeting face elections in the near future: the United States, Australia and New Zealand in November, and South Korea next April. . . . Heavy emphasis was placed on the theme of Pacific region unity, but behind closed conference doors the tables may have been somewhat less harmonious than the public display of unanimity indicated.

Premier Ky had strongly indicated his regime did not want to be committed, in any offer to the North, to giving up its efforts to eliminate the Viet Cong as a political force in South Vietnam. He also appeared to seek assurance that U.S. protection would not be withdrawn until the communist threat was safely under control.

A simple theme count and analysis of the use of color words reveals that the Tanjug and Associated Press reports indeed differ in their degree of objectivity. Tanjug covers six themes and the Associated Press, nine, only four of which are overlapping and given the same interpretation. The total evaluation is, as expected, not the same, because Yugoslavia's and America's political sympathies are not identical. As an agency located in a small country fearful of a world war over which it has no control, Tanjug plays up the fact that Manila provided no guarantee against escalation and the extension of the war and ignored the United Nations request for a bombing cessation. The Associated Press, speaking for a country with immense military power and global strategy concerns, left these facts out. It focused instead on the American involvement in Asia, the problems of Pacific regional unity, and the as yet undecided issue of the future Viet Cong role in a peace conference.

Tanjug's report shows adequate style and is free from color words and the obvious propagandistic slogans so dear to Soviet journalists. Korionov, in a *Pravda* article included in the Associated Press ticker, has the following to say:

Item 112. The Farce Is Ended, the Aggression Continues
Under the cover of hypocritical phrases on peace in Manila another step has been taken along the road of continuing and escalating the colonial war of American imperialism in the area of Indochina.

The Manila gathering clearly mirrored the subterfuges the United States ruling quarters are resorting to in their vain efforts to avoid defeat in Vietnam, to strengthen their position in the international arena. . . .

News Flow Analysis

According to previous writers in the field, five variables seem to be particularly relevant for explaining differences in news patterns and mix. They are amount of hard news content, disproportionate emphasis on elite nations, disproportionate numbers of elite people, personification, and negativism. How do all of these apply to the different news flows analyzed in this chapter? Table 28 summarizes the major findings and registers the relative presence or absence of the selected variables without precise quantification, which must await additional empirical studies.

Though it is difficult as well as misleading to draw generalizations from material as complex as that presented here, several points stand out. These challenge many of the popular beliefs about the difference between autocratic, mixed, and commercial foreign news flows prevalent in the literature. They represent important conclusions and also serve as partial answers to the question asked at the outset: how do Tanjug and the Associated Press through selection, treatment, and emphasis help define significant foreign news realities for Yugoslav and American audiences?

In the area of selection, the comparative material reveals that hard news dominates all three international news flows, though not to the same degree. Theodore Kruglak reported in 1962 that almost 98 percent of the content of the TASS foreign ticker consists of three categories: politics, foreign relations, and economics. There is an utter void, he noted, in the coverage of culture, science, and education.[28] Both Tanjug and the Associated Press, in contrast, balance hard news against soft news content for their audiences. Hard news dominates foreign news outlooks all over the world because of continually rising collection and dissemination costs. To balance its budget and satisfy its varied customers, Tanjug focuses its soft news reporting primarily on two categories: education-science-technology (11.5 percent) and sports (11.5 percent), which are of interest to both industry and the media. The Yugoslav press and broadcast stations use their own correspondents to write the human interest stories increasingly preferred by Yugoslav audiences.

Table 28
Comparative Patterns of News Flow

	Percentage of Hard News	Emphasis on Elite Nations	Emphasis on Elite People	Personification	Neg.
Autocratic (TASS)	98	Yes	Yes	No	No
Mixed (TANJUG)	73	No	No	No	No
Commerical (AP)	63	Yes	Yes	Yes	Yes

Interestingly, this is almost the same amount of space that the Associated Press devotes to the above categories, adding, however, the human interest-religion complex not represented in Tanjug. The Associated Press wire for European customers is thus considerably closer in hard news orientation to that found in a socialist country like Yugoslavia than to its United States counterpart. This substantiates Einar Östgaard's hunch that a country's foreign news outflow is more hard-news oriented than its inflow.[29] While human interest stories are in third place with 14.2 percent of total wire copy in the Associated Press's American service, according to a recent study,[30] they occupy only seventh place on the European wire with 5.5 percent of all stories.

Another point to note is the matter of elite nation reporting which results in the commercial agency's disregard for large parts of the globe. Many have noted that the less developed nations break into the world news flow only on the occurrence of conflict and/or catastrophe. The comparative survey of countries presented here indicates that the United States commercial service is much more elite-oriented than Yugoslavia's. It concentrates two-thirds of its coverage on events in such nations as the United States, Great Britain, France, West Germany, the Soviet Union, and Japan. Tanjug, in contrast, gives less than one-third of its space to these countries, reporting instead on thirty nonelite nations, many of them located in the developing world.

A mixed system like Tanjug, moreover, covers the seven world regions much more equally than its commercial counterpart. In contrast to the Associated Press, which concentrates about 70 percent of all its stories on western Europe and the United States, Tanjug gives merely 44 percent to these areas. The remaining four world regions are covered almost equally. The Far East receives 18.8 percent of all stories, eastern Europe, 16.7 percent, and Africa and South America, 14.5 percent each. As national news agencies proliferate, Tanjug and similar small agencies may become valuable access channels for nonsensational news about the industrializing part of the world.

Galtung and Ruge have suggested that the commercial news flow's disproportionate emphasis on elite people and nations may be a function of the size and status of the country in which the agency is located. They, therefore, postulate that irrespective of other structural differences, the TASS autocratic and the Associated Press commercial flow might resemble each other. The data reported here provide only an indirect verification of this link between country size and elite outlook in that Tanjug, a national agency in a small nonelite country, does not reflect the same elite myopia as the global Associated Press. Similar evidence comes from Swedish sources, which find a wider scanning of the world and less emphasis on elite nations in the Swedish national news agency TT.[31]

A third difference between the mixed and commercial patterns of international news flow emerging from Table 27 has to do with the perspective from which events are explained. Here it was noted that the commercial news flow gave more play to elite people, and in its Vietnam coverage clearly demonstrated a strong tendency toward personification. This meant that of the forty-eight war items only three themes received 80 percent of the coverage. These had to do with President Johnson's visit and conjectures about his whereabouts, as well as the tragic *Oriskany* fire. The remaining seven items dealt with a war tally and South Vietnamese elections emphasizing "standings" of the two foes in the struggle. Tanjug, in contrast, devoted its coverage to a more structural explication of issues demonstrated by the fact that it covered more themes than the Associated Press and selected political and economic rather than human interest categories for major play. The same lack of personification is evident in the TASS services, according to Mark Hopkins, who commented that it tends to reproduce long official documents drafted by groups rather than pronouncements from individual statesmen.[32]

Finally, there is the question of negativism as a selection perspective in the two types of news flow. Here Table 27 indicates that the commercial flow is more negatively oriented than the mixed or autocratic flows, though negativism is found in these as well. The Associated Press and Tanjug content comparison indicated that 43 percent of all items were negative in the American service versus 31 percent in the Yugoslav. This negativism, it appeared, was particularly pronounced in the soft news categories, which may be one reason why the autocratic and mixed flows, which rarely report these, show less negativism. A prevalence of negative reporting in the commercial service's hard-news categories, however, indicates that it is more reasonable to assume that the western audience receives more negatively oriented news because of the economic and ideological needs of its system.

Much has been written about the varying definitions of "news" in autocratic, mixed, and commercial information systems, but few have attempted to empirically specify the values which underlie these definitions. In a system where the primary purpose is to sell material products, "news" will be defined as "that which changes from day to day." Its content, it was demonstrated, will tend to stress the negative, the short term, and the dramatic, and elite nations and individual actors will come to the fore as a means of making sense out of kaleidoscopically changing events. With this goes a characteristic commercial style of reporting, which Reston describes in the following terms: "We are pretty good at reporting 'happenings,' particularly if they are dramatic. We are fascinated by events, but not by the things that cause events. . . . We are not covering the news of the mind as we should. Here is where rebellion, revolution, and wars start. But we minimize the conflict of ideas and emphasize the conflict in the streets without relating the second to the first."[33]

Reporting which separates opinion from interpretation tends to stifle further inquiry into causes and makes copy noncontroversial by reporting the facts without context. The values of personification and perishability, which foster sales, tend to invade both information as well as entertainment content and to deprive United States audiences of insights into complex world happenings. The "search Johnson" approach to Vietnam is a clear example of commercial values dominating war reporting. As Harry Pross noted: "In the commercial system the prevailing political element is not control by the state, not even the alliance of state and capital. . . . It is commercial advertising."[34] The latter cultivates big business expectations rather than satisfy the survival needs of its citizens, who must alone make sense out of rapidly changing social conditions.

In mixed systems which are regulated by state laws and often financed by subscription from different audiences, the definition of "news" is usually pluralistically determined. Hence, it is much more difficult than in the commercial or state autocratic systems to force unified outlooks. In Yugoslavia, "news" tends to be defined in terms of ongoing processes which operate over long time periods. It is also less negative in its outlook. Two policy statements from Tanjug journalists clarify the differing news values underlying the selection process in this country. A Tanjug editor noted:

> Apart from events and what has just happened, Tanjug hopes to give information about social changes and movements here and abroad. We want to know about developments in economic integration, problems of developing countries, international workers' movements . . . problems of unemployment, strikes, different roads to socialism in Asia and Africa. These, in our opinion, are the topics which have not been covered [by the world agencies] or covered from a different point of view. According to our opinion these topics have been seen as black or white. . . . We have tried to give a more variegated shading, and are becoming more interesting for [agencies from] various regions.

In addition, the shift editor mentioned that though the service could make more money from the media if it included more disaster and human interest coverage, the agency council decided against it. Summing up his group's feelings he stated: "The event must have social importance (in order to be covered). We are not interested in the number of people killed in an automobile accident, but in the fact that the driver was drunk. Possibly the discovery that no one was killed is more important than anything else."

The previous analysis has already indicated how these perspectives lead to a broader world coverage, especially of under-developed countries, and a structural or process orientation emphasizing trends toward social change. Disasters and negative coverage are played down because they run counter to the educational role of the media in social self-government and do not interest two of Tanjug's three customers: the economic enterprises and government agencies. Thus, while a certain number of disasters are selected for the country's newspaper readers and radio listeners, these must not be allowed to overshadow occurrences of a political and international nature which are important to the government or trade developments which are essential to industry. While the buying patterns of John Doe determine "newsworthiness" in the United States, in Yugoslavia these are tempered by industry's economic interest and government's political needs.

The cumulative evidence suggests that what becomes "news" in any type of information system does not depend so much on psychological as on economic, political, and ideological factors. All of these are demonstrated in the previous pages. The analysis of Tanjug selection practices, for instance, indicated the impact of media consumption patterns on agency news production goals. The item mix of approximately 100 daily foreign items versus fifty domestic items reflects restricted press and broadcast space, as well as scarce transmission facilities for news distribution in this rapidly developing nation.

Governmental determination of "newsworthiness," moreover, is demonstrated by the agency's broad geographical selection focus and its emphasis on big power and trade partners, which reflect the Tito government's drive for a third-bloc diplomacy and the growing need for new export markets. Major candidates for nonalignment are found in Latin America, Africa, and the Far East, while Europe and North America provide the best trade partners. Both of these priorities are evident in the August 26, 1966, content, where activities are monitored in such third-bloc nations as India, Egypt, Indonesia, Burma, Algeria, and Mexico, all of which had presidential visits in the 1960s.[35] Trade priorities, on the other hand, require reporting of the Soviet Union, Italy, West Germany, Great Britain, and the United States, which were the five largest export markets, according to 1970 statistics, and provided approximately 60 percent of Yugoslavia's total export value.[36] Though it is difficult to establish governmental determination of newsworthiness from a single day's output, company records of yearly output indicate similar focuses. Here, too, a geographical focus of attention places Europe and North America first in magnitude, Africa, second, Asia, third, and Latin America, sixth.

The impact of ideology, finally, is demonstrated by the way in which the three filtering stages transformed global raw information into Yugoslav foreign "news." Processing not only reduces variety but imposes interpretative frameworks. The October 26, 1966, wire indicates that although Yugoslav foreign correspondents collected only a miniscule 17 percent of raw inputs, they provided thirty-nine items, or 41 percent, of all stories in the finished product. Another sixteen items (16 percent) were written by Tanjug special editors, digesting other incoming information, and the final forty-one items (43 percent) were stories translated and shortened from foreign agencies. In each case the interpretations of these stories mirror a conception of "newsworthiness" which does not stress perishability.

If economics, politics, and ideology are important factors in deciding the content and mix of different international news flows, is there any way of finding out how much diversity in content these variables account for? Also, do John Galtung and Mari Ruge's largely psychological news factors play any appreciable role in news determination? While the material presented here does not permit an answer to this question, Rosengren's predictive study of election coverage in Swedish, London, and East German newspapers provides some clues. In testing two of Galtung's psychological variables, "strength" and "cultural proximity," it turns out that these are best translated into an economic and a physical distance variable. The former measures export and import relations between the election and reporting country, while the latter indicates geographical proximity. Taken together, these variables explain between one-fourth and two-thirds of the variance in a newspaper's coverage of foreign parliamentary elections.[37] Of the two, however, the economic variable turns out to be by far the stronger. Physical distance adds merely another 2 to 4 percent to the total figure. The fact that geographical distance alone is a poor predictor of coverage is in agreement with earlier research which shows that subjective distance is a much better predictor of people's emotional involvement with another country than objective distance.[38]

Rosengren thus agrees that a theory of news values must be couched in economic, political, and ideological terms rather than be based on psychological variables. The values guiding news selection, it turns out, are not a result of a reporter's personal psychological idiosyncracies, but an integral part of the particular socioeconomic system in which he carries out his work. The Galtung news factors of frequency, intensity, meaningfulness, and consonance turn out to be intervening variables. They seem to confer an important aura of meaningfulness and coherence to brute economic and political facts, but they possess only small explanatory power of their own.[39]

With a socioeconomic theory of news values generally sketched out, attention turns to a closely connected question, that of the role of the mass media in nation-building. This evaluates whether the "alternative realities" presented by Yugoslavia's six republican networks tend to feed or undermine the common outlooks among the country's multicultural and multinational population.

---

1 Chaney, *Processes of Mass Communication,* p. 132.

2 Walter Lippman, *Public Opinion,* p. 312.

3 James D. Halloran, Philip Elliott, and Graham Murdock, *Demonstrations and Communication: A Case Study,* pp. 25-26.

4 George Gerbner, "Ideological Perspectives and Political Tendencies in News Reporting," pp. 508-509.

5 Siebert, Peterson, and Schramm, *Four Theories of the Press.*

6 John C. Merrill, "The Press and Social Responsibility," pp. 15-20; also Hamid Mowlana, "Toward a Theory of Communication Systems: A Developmental Approach," pp. 17-28.

7 Theodore Kruglak, *The Two Faces of Tass;* and Mark W. Hopkins, *Mass Media in the Soviet Union.*

8 Einar Östgaard, "Factors Influencing the Flow of News," pp. 39-63.

9 Galtung and Ruge, "The Structure of Foreign News," pp. 64-91.

10 Rosengren, "International News: Methods, Data and Theory."

11 George Gerbner, "Press Perspectives in World Communication: A Pilot Study," p. 313.

12 Maxwell E. McCombs and Donald Shaw, "The Agenda-Setting Function of Mass Media," pp. 176-187.

13 Karl Erik Rosengren, "International News: Intra and Extra Media Data," p. 101.

14 *Facts on File: World News Digest with Index,* pp. 401-430.

15 For a detailed discussion of the methodological implications of content analysis, consult

Klaus Krippendorff, "An Examination of Content Analysis: A Proposal for a General Framework and an Information Calculus for Message Analytic Situations," Chapters I and III.

16 International Press Institute, *The Flow of the News,* pp. 217-218. Abbreviated definitions of the fourteen categories are as follows:

War includes all stories about the Vietnam and other wars as military operations. Also stories of guerrilla actions elsewhere.

Politics is news with primary emphasis on the domestic policies of the country from which the news originates.

Foreign relations includes all political stories involving the relations of the country from which the news originates with one or more other countries.

Defense news is about a foreign country's defense and occupation forces or efforts to sustain these.

Economic news is about a foreign country's economic life.

Cultural news covers fine arts, and news of popular entertainment.

Education, science, and technology is news of scientific developments and education.

Judicial and legal news deals with interpretations by courts, civil suits, and the legal system.

Social measures are stories about welfare and other measures not primarily political.

Human Interest news includes a wide variety of features, oddities of nature and human temperament, celebrities, and so on. The categories of crime, disaster, sports, and religion are self-explanatory.

17 It was interesting to hear a top Tanjug executive remark in an editorial board meeting that the agency's account of the Congo crisis had been, in retrospect, disproportionately lengthy as a result of inflated foreign agency reports.

18 Gerbner, "Press Perspectives," p. 314.

19 Östgaard, "Factors Influencing the Flow of News," p. 46.

20 Galtung and Ruge, "The Structure of Foreign News," pp. 68-70.

21 International Press Institute, *The Flow of the News,* p. 214.

22 Galtung and Ruge, "The Structure of Foreign News," p. 68.

23 Gerbner, "Press Perspectives," p. 316.

24 Rosengren, "International News: Methods, Data and Theory," p. 100.

25 UNESCO, *News Agencies: Their Structure and Operation,* p. 200.

26 Galtung and Ruge, "The Structure of Foreign News," pp. 69-70.

27 *Tanjug Manila themes:*

1. No peace formula.
2. Troop withdrawal proposal.
3. No guarantees against escalation.
4. Allies face elections.
5. Peace not real goal of U.S.
6. Ignored request for bombing cessation.
7. War efforts will extend.

A.P. Manila themes:

1. No peace formula.
2. Troop withdrawal proposal.
3. Peace drive.
4. Allies face elections.
5. Peace not real goal of U.S.
6. American commitment to Asia.
7. Viet Cong role at peace conference.
8. Little progress for negotiations with Hanoi.
9. Pacific region unity.

28 Kruglak, *The Two Faces of TASS,* p. 125.

29 Östgaard, "Factors Influencing the Flow of News," p. 41.

30 Paul B. Snider, "Mr. Gates Revisited: A 1966 Version of the 1949 Case Study," p. 424.

31 Karl Erik Rosengren and Gunnel Rikarsson, "Middle East News in Sweden," p. 12.

32 Hopkins, *Mass Media in the Soviet Union,* p. 285.

33 James Reston, *The Artillery of the Press: Its Influence on American Foreign Policy,* pp. 83-84.

34 Harry Pross, "Radio and Television as Political Institutions: The Symbolic Approach," p. 9.

35 Auty, "Yugoslavia's International Relations," p. 190.

36 Federal Institute for Statistics, *Statistical Pocket Book for Yugoslavia 1972,* pp. 80-81.

37 Rosengren and Rikarsson, "Middle East News," p. 22.

38 Ulf Lundberg, *et al.* "Emotional Involvement and Subjective Distance: A Summary of Investigations," pp. 169-177.

39 Rosengren, "International News: Methods, Data and Theory," pp. 22-23.

CHAPTER 9

Ethnicity and Political Communication

To complete the analysis of how different kinds of events are made meaningful for the Yugoslav audience, this chapter will focus on the interpretation of national issues. In Yugoslavia these interpretations are colored by the country's ethnic diversity and by its striking differences in regional economic development. The country thus presents a unique opportunity for evaluating some of the theoretical claims about the role of the mass media in national economic development and in ameliorating ethnic strife.

To trace how and why the so-called "nationalities" problem has once again surfaced and how it affects political communication in contemporary Yugoslavia is a complex task. It requires, first of all, the coordination of the League of Communists' changing ethnicity stances with revisions in information policy. There is, moreover, need of a theory to explain the connection between politics, ethnicity, and the media in multinational societies. Finally, media behavior during a recent political crisis involving ethnic issues must be scrutinized in order to clarify the power distribution between communicators and politicians in the information field.

The History of "Nationalism"

A number of writers have noted that ethnic, religious, or nationalistic outlooks strongly influence the way in which political questions are conceived in multinational societies. The reasons for this are manifold. Common ethnic, racial, or religious stances provide the largest common denominator for dissent and thus a popular base for a variety of calls to greater "freedom" in economic and political decision-making.[1] Such stances are also potentially very dangerous because they may reflect a desire for separation. Thus they may alter the very boundaries of the existing nation-state.[2] Moreover, they often package social issues in such a way that compromise becomes impossible.

No wonder that Vladimir Bakarić, one of President Tito's principal lieutenants and elder party statesmen in Croatia, considered ethnicity one of the country's major unsolved problems in the late 1960s. He noted a few years ago that "Yugoslavia has two main problems — the economic reform and the nationalities question — and if the first cannot be solved, the second will immediately move to the fore as problem number one."[3] This prediction has come true in the wake of the country's steeply rising living costs and growing economic deficits during the past five years. Since the early 1970s hundreds of factories have been closed by wildcat strikes because of lack of cash to pay wages to their workers.[4] What Bakarić fails to note is that the mass media may have had something to do with the increased ethnic unrest characterizing his country since 1967. It remains to be seen what their role has been.

According to Ivo Lederer, Yugoslavia's history of nationalism after World War II can be divided into three periods, which roughly coincide with the communication periods mentioned earlier. During each, there were noticeable shifts in the relevance of ethnicity to communication policy. During the first, or "administrative period of socialism," which lasted until approximately 1951, ethnicity had very little importance and communication policy was centrally formulated, programmed, and distributed through the country's national news agency, Tanjug. People then were preoccupied with the larger task of rebuilding the war-ravaged country and with healing the hatred engendered by the widespread fratricidal killing of the Serbian and Croatian populations during the occupation. Long-standing ethnic and religious differences were further defused by creating national republics and by establishing a separate republic of Bosnia-Hercegovina which solved the thorny issue of whether Bosnians are Serbs or Croats. Unity was finally helped by the country's international isolation following the 1948 Cominform expulsion and by the fact that Slovenian and Croatian irredentism vanished with the return of Istria and the Zadar region from Italy. Moreover, President Tito, a Croat, and his partisan comrades enjoyed great popular esteem for ridding the country of foreign occupation.[5]

Beginning with the early 1950s and throughout the next ten years of the so-called "transition period," this calm began to be eroded and the "nationalities issue" once again came to the fore. Lederer mentions a series of economic and ideological causes contributing to this erosion. Among them are decentralization in agriculture and industry, an effort at uplifting the underdeveloped southern parts of the country by redistribution of central funds, the modification of a previously command economy, and an expansive global foreign policy.[6] Sveta Lukić adds a change in ideology to these socio-economic developments. The leadership in the face of local experience abandoned the Stalinist interpretation of "nationalism" which assumed that problems of ethnicity would automatically solve themselves with the demise of the capitalist system. Instead, the League of Communists realized that ethnicity was here to stay and that novel institutional forms would be necessary to curb its divisive force in Yugoslavia. Consequently two new constitutions, 1963 and 1974, were introduced to cement federalism.

As a result of this shift, Yugoslavia developed a decentralized communication system which is regionally organized within the country's six republics. These networks are run by personnel speaking three major languages, trained in different journalism schools, and belonging to separate professional organizations. Cohesion for this loosely federated system is supplied by the Yugoslav Radio Television Association and the League of Communists. The former functions as a clearinghouse for network extension and joint broadcast programming, while the latter ratifies the appointment of all top media executives.[7]

The increased tempo of industrialization accompanied by League fragmentation, however, launched Yugoslavia into another period characterized by sharply increased ethnic conflict during its third, or "decentralized," media period. Two major economic reforms, in 1965 and 1968, devalued the local currency and made it convertible. This increased the gulf between the "have" and "have-not" republics. Furthermore, important constitutional amendments between 1968 and 1971 strengthened republican autonomy and transformed the country from a federation into a confederation of states with equal rights.[8]

The renewed prominence of purely ethnic identifications in Yugoslavia during this period is graphically illustrated by a succession of occurrences with nationalistic overtones. There was first of all the 1967 Literary Manifesto signed by 100 Zagreb writers and intellectuals and presented to the local parliament. It requested that Croatian be recognized as a separate official language, though it is very similar to Serbian and mutually understandable. The gist of the declaration's argument, according to Fritz Hondius, was that a nation is entitled to have a language with a proper name. It also alleged "that the Serbian literary language" threatened to impose itself upon Yugoslavia as a "state language" owing to Serbia's preponderant position as the center of the federation, while Croatian was relegated to the position of a regional dialect.[9] A year later there was Macedonia's ethnic nation-building which culminated in the establishment of a separate Academy of Arts and Sciences using the Macedonian language. In 1967 there were also clashes with police in the streets of Priština in the autonomous province of Kosovo, where thousands of Albanians called for greater minority rights, more representation in the federal government, and possibly even a republic of their own.[10]

Then there were scandals in the Serbian Central Committee involving such prominent intellectuals as Dobrica Ćosić, the writer, and Jovan Marjanović, the historian, who criticized some of the constitutional amendments designed to delegate vast powers to the constituent republics. Both were forced out of the League of Communists after publicly voicing their concern over the effect of these anti-Serbian shifts in Yugoslav political life.[11] Finally, there was the re-emergence of increasingly nationalist feelings among some segments of the Croatian public, which exploded into the 1971 Zagreb student strike and precipitated a major political crisis. How these developments affected the content and functioning of the Croatian media will be the topic of a separate section at the end of this chapter.

For the present, it is important to note that ethnicity has waxed rather than waned in Yugoslavia's thirty-year postwar period. It has not only colored much of the country's politics during the 1960s and forced the League of Communists to re-evaluate its future role, but also sensitized the leadership to the great importance of the mass media in representing "alternative" political realities. As David Chaney notes, "these alternative views can either feed or nourish a dominant consensus, or they can operate as deviant refuges, private realities, corresponding to the multiple aims of a heterogeneous society."[12] To determine whether the country's six information systems contribute or thwart the development of a sense of unity in multinational Yugoslavia has become crucially important to a leadership facing such internal challenges as President Tito's succession, superpower pressures over Middle East oil resources, and Mediterranean naval priorities.

The Media, Modernization, and Political Change

The recent ethnic turbulence in Yugoslavia raises a question important to political scientists, communication analysts, and policymakers alike. It concerns the capacity of the mass media to integrate the conflicting outlooks of different populations in multinational states. What is known about the interrelationships between macro-societal and micro-individual changes in modernizing socialist societies and about the role of the mass media in this process?

Two kinds of theoretical models have been offered. The most prevalent asserts that modernization neutralizes and submerges ethnic, racial, religious, or tribal politics with their attendant conflict. It also asserts that the media contribute to this process on both the macro-societal and on the psychological levels. Supposedly the mass media aid not only in mobilizing people to accept and work for industrialization, but also encourage them to exchange parochial for universal value systems. Availability of mass media, urbanization, and economic development, it is argued, undercut the organizational bases of communal politics through the emergence of new kinds of socio-economic roles and associations, participated in by people with modern outlooks.[13]

A counter model based on empirical evidence from Nigeria and other modernizing societies asserts exactly the opposite. Modernization tends to aggravate ethnic conflict in nation-building, and the mass media tend to exacerbate this by reinforcing existing ethnic attitudes rather than inculcating new ones. The social and psychological dynamics involved in this process are described as follows: When people acquire new jobs and new life-styles, their wants and aspirations tend to change in the same direction. As a result, conflict increases. Everyone suddenly wants the same things, and yet the supply of resources is unable to keep up with these demands. Increased competitiveness, in turn, encourages the insecure urban newcomer to fall back on ethnic ties to make his way. Such behavior suggests that his value systems and outlook are not totally transformed and "modernized," but simply acquire new facets.[14]

Continued reliance on ethnicity raises three interrelated questions for politics and the mass media in Yugoslavia. First, in what ways has ethnicity affected media functioning and the political process? Second, what role have the Yugoslav press, radio, and television played in magnifying or reducing regional and/or federal perspectives in the selection, interpretation, and evaluation of socio-political issues? And finally, how important is it for the country's national unity to develop a population with a "Yugoslav" rather than a particular ethnic outlook? In answering these questions, this chapter will challenge the macro-societal theory that mobilized people submerge their ethnic conflict in the process of modernization. It also casts doubt on the claim that the media tend to foster a more "rational" or "universal" outlook. In fact, increased media use does not seem to lead to an automatic substitution of universal for particular value systems and social identities among the diverse people of contemporary Yugoslavia.

Many writers endeavoring to explain the persistence of ethnic politics in countries all over the world have followed Karl Deutsch and noted that societies which are divided by language, religion, or ethnicity also tend to be composed of groups which are segmented and compartmentalized at the local and national levels. In other words, multinational societies seem to be characterized by a more or less complete set of parallel institutions and subcultures. In a country with ethnic, religious, and cultural cleavages, such as Yugoslavia, this leads to each ethnic group having its own set of social institutions with its own values and norms structuring social life. Each of these subgroups will additionally be characterized by its own "complementarity of communication." This is defined as "the ability to communicate more effectively and over a wider range of subjects with your own members, than with outsiders."[15]

In such a setting the processes of modernization are traditionally assumed to aid in eradicating ethnic strife. How is this possible? According to Deutsch, modernization is sparked by a process of social mobilization which involves large parts of the population in a variety of changes. Among these are "changes of residence, of occupation, of social setting, of face to face association, of institutions, roles and ways of acting, of experiences and expectations, and finally of personal memories, habits, and needs, including the need for new patterns of group affiliations and new images of personal identity."[16] The degree of social mobilization is measurable by discovering what percentage of a population has undergone changes in residence, employment, media exposure, literacy, and per capita income over a period of time. The people available for new patterns of life, Deutsch argues, are those who have moved into cities, are exposed to the media, can read, travel, and have industrial jobs.

Once a majority of the population has been mobilized, as it has been in Yugoslavia during the past fifteen years, it is additionally hypothesized that the mass media aid in the process of political integration by fostering attitudinal consensus among different ethnic groups.[17] Both Daniel Lerner and Alex Inkeles believe that social mobilization creates the emergence of more rational values, which in turn lead to the evolution of a set of "universal" political norms transcending particularistic concerns.[18] When a person is mobilized, in other words, he is supposed to become less traditional. His value system will enlarge and he will be made more "mobile" by moving to the city, listening to radio broadcasts, and finding a new job in a modern factory. In general, industrial change, urbanization, and socio-economic development are supposed to bring about new societal and individual phenomena.

Though the interlinking hypotheses about social mobilization as a precondition for the development of modern attitudes may be correct, the role of the mass media in mobilization and in attitude change has traditionally been vastly overrated. Two arguments seriously challenge the claim that they are the causes of this dynamic. First of all, it is theoretically inadmissible to use indexes of media availability *alone* to prove that the mass media have, in fact, been used for modernization and nation-building purposes. Second, the results of Yugoslav attitudinal studies contradict the assertion that those more exposed to communication stimuli develop more "universal" outlooks and attitudinal consensus. Let us check these assertions against Yugoslav media content studies and attitudinal change data.

Most researchers following Deutsch have developed a media index which equates a population's media exposure with the audience size for radio, television, and the press. But how can the mere *existence* of technical communication channels prove that the message flow contains information about new ways of behaving, new personal identities, and new socio-political goals? Both Edward Douglass[19] and Theodore Schultz point out that only in countries where the media have carried modernizing economic, educational, and political content, do they contribute to the process of social mobilization mentioned by Deutsch. "Development opportunities are not created by the mass media but through research and development planning. . . . The proper role of the media is to make people aware of the development opportunities that exist."[20]

What evidence is there for asserting that the mass media carry modernizing information in Yugoslavia? Table 29 presents a very rough comparative survey of programming which indicates that all of the Yugoslav mass media feature a large amount of information and culture/education content. For radio and television, this amounted to an average of 50 percent and 68 percent, respectively, of all 1962 programming, while for the press it constituted 60 percent of newspaper space during Yugoslavia's initial period of rapid industrialization. Overall programming statistics, although indicating a trend, do not tell us much about the actual subject matters covered. Personal observation corroborates that

Yugoslav information programs, like the Canadian, typically emphasize local events. Beyond that, however, they cover such national issues as election news, the fiftieth anniversary of the League of Communists, and international trouble spots like Vietnam and the Middle East. Each day, time is devoted in both radio and television and on children's news programs to describing economic developments and to reporting on Yugoslav industry and labor.

Table 29 suggests that culture/information programming has recently decreased, providing in 1970 only 42 percent of all radio and 41 percent of all television content. In spite of these reductions, which are due to increased local autonomy over programming in the latest media period, it is evident that Titoist media ideology differs from both the United States and the Soviet Union. In the former entertainment predominates, while in the latter greater attention is paid to hard news and education. Yugoslavia stands somewhere in between. Such a content distribution indicates that in decentralized socialist Yugoslavia not only government plans but also audience preferences play a role in program decisions. This is the case because readers and listeners, not the state, support the media. It may be concluded that in socialist Yugoslavia mass media facilities contribute to macro-societal change by mobilizing the population and carrying content which provides information about social and psychological development opportunities.

If socially mobilizing media content is indeed available to Yugoslav readers and listeners, is there any evidence that this content has contributed to changes in individual outlooks by "modernizing" and "universalizing" Yugoslav beliefs and value systems? Yugoslav attitudinal data collected by the Belgrade Center for Public Opinion Research (Centar za Istraživanje Javnog Mnenja) may provide some clues. According to Lerner, "modernism" refers to the "infusion of a rationalist and positivist spirit," and "universalism" stands for patterns of identification transcending nationality, language, locale, family, and personal norms.

Table 29
Yugoslav Media Programming, 1962 and 1970
(in percentages of total space or air time)

		Information and Current Affairs	Culture and Education	(Music) and Entertainment	Advertising
Radio	1962	31	19	44	6
	1970	18	24	46	12
Television	1962	34	34	26	6
	1970	29	12	46	13
Press	1962	40	20	20	20
	1970	35	15	30	20

SOURCES: Radio: *JRT Yearbook, 1963*, pp. 64-65; *JRT Yearbook, 1970*, pp. 138. Television: *JRT Yearbook, 1963*, pp. 107-113; *JRT Yearbook, 1970*, p. 239. Press: 1962, personal content analysis of two months of *Politika;* 1970, personal content analysis of morning and evening papers.

Figure 7. Cross-National Comparison of Psychological Change Patterns

Slovenes:	.31	Slovenes:	.21
Serbs:	.30	Serbs:	.40
Croats:	.50	Croats:	.41
Macedonians:	.51	Macedonians:	.45

Mobilization ⟶ Modernism ⟶ Universalism

Slovenes:	.12
Serbs:	.25
Croats:	.29
Macedonians:	.46

Source: Garry K. Bertsch, "A Cross National Analysis of the Community-Building Process in Yugoslavia," *Comparative Political Studies* IV:IV (Jan., 1972), pp. 438-460.

If these correlations do hold, the Slovenes with the highest potential exposure to the mass media, according to Yugoslav press, radio, and television statistics, should also exhibit the most "modern" outlook and the most "universalist" set of values. Unfortunately this is not true. Using Guttman scaling to measure the interlinkages between social mobilization and the two attitudinal values, Garry Bertsch[21] found not only that the gamma correlations were relatively weak, but that they differ for the various ethnic groups as well. In spite of the fact that 66 percent of the Slovenes rank as "modern" on the scale, Figure 7 indicates that the mobilization-universalism connection is weaker for them than for any other nationality. The Slovenes, it turns out, although they live in the most developed part of Yugoslavia and have a more modern outlook on life, paradoxically cling to a strongly particularist value structure. Bertsch explains this discrepancy by noting that the interlinkages between macro-social and micro-psychological changes, though rooted in social mobilization, may not be totally determined by it.

In a later study,[22] Bertsch suggests that the differences in rates of change manifested by the different ethnic groups in Yugoslavia may be influenced by the regime's nation-building strategy as well as the group's degree of ethnic marginality. The very weak gamma coefficient for the Slovenes may thus be explained by the relative disadvantage of this small population vis-à-vis the other ethnic groups in Yugoslavia. Their lack of attitudinal change reflects a fear of losing their identity in the larger union of South Slav nations, and makes the Slovenes cling to their particularistic value orientation anchored in ethnicity, language, and religion.

Personal investigations strongly suggest that a third factor, media content, must be added to marginality and nation-building to explain variations in attitudes and outlooks among the major Yugoslav ethnic groups. If the media are carriers of ethnically colored content, they will also tend to support and reinforce particularistic outlooks. What is known about ethnicity and media content in contemporary Yugoslavia? Do the media tend to select and foster regional rather than national perspectives,·and if this is the case, how does this affect the outlooks of the various populations? Any one engaged in media research is aware that no unequivocal answers can be given to inquiries about the media's micro-psychological impact, but there are partial data which suggest that the media content of the six republics have a strong regional flavor.

Three kinds of evidence support the ethnic specificity of Yugoslav media content. It has already been noted that the media system in this multinational federated state is regionally subdivided and manned by ethnically distinct communicators who write and broadcast in separate languages. In a setting where politicians as well as media men and the audience are all members of subgroups characterized by Deutsch's "complementarity of communication," MacLean suggests, the criteria for content selection will tend to be regionally ethnic rather than national.[23] This is easily demonstrated. Television news production, for example, which before 1965 originated solely from the capital, is now decentralized and programmed in the republican cities of Zagreb, Ljubljana, Skopje, and Sarajevo. Interviews with editors elicited the fact that these programs contain 50 percent republican items and 50 percent national and international news. Newspapers, which are printed in distinctive languages and scripts, also tend to stress local news, as in the United States and Canada. Prime-time radio programming, popular satirical television shows, local travelogs, and widely acclaimed folk music reflect regional humor and music traditions as different as the kolo and the polka.

A second bit of evidence confirming the predominantly regional outlooks of the Yugoslav audience comes from a study of Croatian reading patterns. It reveals that though the Croats understand the dominant language, Serbo-Croatian, only 2 percent read a daily from Serbia or a news magazine like *CIK* or *NIN,* both published in Belgrade.[24] This contrasts sharply with comparable Canadian figures, where nearly four in ten, or 39 percent, of the population over age fifteen read a news magazine with content stressing national issues and perspectives.[25] The same compartmentalization is also found in the broadcast media, where transmitters are not strong enough to carry programming across republican boundaries and where retransmission of programs by ethnically different channels is the exception rather than the rule.

A third and final practice reinforcing ethnic perspectives is Yugoslavia's four-year job rotation system designed to combat government centralization and bureaucratization. As a result, politicians and governmental officials who used to remain in the federal capital must now return to their republican home bases to assume new assignments. With increased states' rights in the late 1960s, these politicians tend to use the media of their states to espouse locally popular solutions to political and economic issues.

All of this evidence documenting the predominantly republican focus of Yugoslav media content would be interesting but inconclusive if recent studies of the agenda-setting function of the media had not indicated a strong correlation between what the media select and feature and what an audience considers important. Several researchers summarize the impact of the press by noting that the press and broadcasting are not too successful in telling people what to think, but stunningly successful in telling them what to think *about*.[26]

Agenda setting has been done in several ways. Maxwell McCombs and Donald Shaw, for instance, compared the rank orders of the issues suggested by undecided voters in the 1968 United States presidential campaign with the rank orders of the same issues in the press. They found that "what the voters considered most important—Vietnam—was receiving heaviest play in the press and this match-up of voter choice and media emphasis was true generally for all major issues."[27] Berg, who studied audience responses to news agenda changes after President Nixon's price freeze, provided two further insights into the media's agenda-setting power. The *composite* picture of the world they create and that television news features reinforces the print media's selection, ordering, and evaluation.

Much research remains to be done, but in spite of this it can be plausibly argued that the Yugoslav media fulfill an agenda-setting function for their society. In this country's multinational setting, content is selected with ethnic priorities in mind; this tends to encourage regionalism and fosters hermetic points of view. Bertsch's attitudinal survey failed to take into account that such content would reinforce the particularist value stances of Slovenes, Macedonians, Croats, and Serbs which are anchored in language, ethnic, and religious differences.

Another way of interpreting this evidence is to point out that the essence of modernity may not lie in the transition from particularistic to universalistic outlooks, but in a people's ability to compartmentalize both kinds of value structures. How well different groups and individuals are able to do this is an empirical question. Judging by the Yugoslav data, both the less modern Macedonians and the more modern Slovenes rank highest of all nationalities on the "particularist" scale. This is understandable if one recalls that both of these groups are smaller than the dominant Serbs and Croats and must therefore guard more strongly those elements on which their differing culture is based.

Lerner's assertion that the media generally promote psychological change toward universalist outlooks must be modified. It is entirely too optimistic to believe that the media have the power to cause singlehandedly either social mobilization or attitude change. They must instead be viewed as intervening variables, as contributors to the processes of macro-societal or micro-psychological change if and only if two conditions are met: they actually carry "modernizing" types of content and they are not thwarted by such other interfering variables as ethnically specific content and ethnic marginality, both of which tend to slow down the "universalizing" process for given sub-populations.

Media in Crisis: A Case Study in Ethnic Control

The final interrelationships which require investigation and evaluation in the Yugoslav context are those among the mass media, social mobilization, ethnicity, and conflict. Do the processes of technological and economic development in multinational societies ultimately submerge ethnic strife, or is it an integral aspect of change during social mobilization? Until very recently empirical evidence seemed to settle this question in favor of the first interpretation. Studies in Nigeria, India, and other multinational states, however, are casting doubt on the dichotomous tradition-modernity models which have guided many of the earlier investigations. From the standpoint of conventional theory, it seems paradoxical that ethnicity has intensified rather than diminished political conflict and that this state of affairs has also affected the way in which a country's mass media are apt to behave.

Four hypotheses explaining the persistence of ethnic strife can, however, be advanced. Two of these involve social processes; two, psychological ones.

(1) In multinational societies, the competition engendered in social mobilization will tend to be defined in ethnic terms.

(2) The subordination of political institutions to the interests of particular communal groups tends to reinforce and politicize communal conflicts.

(3) Mobilization and competition lead to increased economic and ideological differentiation of ethnic categories and thus involve a multiplication of social identities.

(4) Social identities are situationally specific, which makes it possible for particularist as well as universal value orientations to exist side by side in people's outlooks.[28]

An investigation of these propositions will determine if they explain Yugoslav media behavior. The first section of this chapter adduced ample evidence that accelerated social change did engender social competition in Yugoslavia. Croats, Macedonians, Slovenes, and Albanians translated and publicized their grievances in ethnic terms throughout the 1960s and thus tended to politicize conflicts which often belonged to other spheres of life. Language and educational rights and other cultural matters led to lengthy debates and public outcries. It remains to investigate whether and how the media became subordinated to communal groups and then to trace whether ideological differentiation fosters a multiplicity of social identities rather than a Yugoslav outlook among the South Slavs.

Communal co-optation of the media was a crucial strategy in the initial success of the Croatian nationalist movement. The grave nature of this movement was exposed to public view on the afternoon of December 2, 1971, when Yugoslav radio stations interrupted their regular programs to broadcast a speech by President Tito at the twenty-first session of the League Presidium the previous day. In it a number of Croatia's top party officials, among them the chief executive Savka Dabčević-Kučar, were asked to resign. It was also announced that representatives Miko Tripalo and Pero Pirker had been removed from the collective presidency designed to carry on after President Tito's death and that they had lost their posts in the Executive Committee of the League of Communists as well. The grave charges advanced against these officials included the claim that they had pandered to nationalists and separatists organized around the Matica Hrvatska publishing house who were fomenting a "counter revolution." Close on the heels of this announcement followed a cleansing of the Croatian judicial and governmental system in which many politicians and intellectuals associated with the "nationalist cause" lost their jobs. Though the total number of resignations is not exactly known, it is thought to be in the hundreds.[29]

What are the facts which led up to these events and what was the role of the media in this ethnic crisis? In November, 1971, a large group of students led by Dražen Budiša, the newly elected "nationalist" president of the Zagreb Student Federation, closed down the university in support of their elected government representatives who were negotiating a more equitable foreign currency distribution for their republic. This precipitating event was, however, merely the visible top of a dramatic political struggle which had been forming since 1969 and was being carried on at three closely interrelated levels: within the Croatian party leadership itself; between parts of this leadership and other political forces, both party and nonparty, in the republic as a whole; and at the federal level between the Croatian spokesmen Savka Dabčević-Kučar, Miko Tripalo, Pero Pirker, and President Tito. On all of these levels, except the federal, media control was an essential ingredient to political success.

To cement their power, it turns out the Dapčević-Kučar group co-opted and used the mass media not only to gain control over the party apparatus by silencing the other faction in the leadership, but also to rouse the public to support their side by denying the opposition media space. An article by Erna Darossi-Bjelajac, a member of the Croatian Executive Committee opposed to the views of the Tripalo-Dapčević-Pirker faction, describes what went on. According to this informant, "nationalist forces took over Matica Hrvatska as their central institution and readjusted its cultural function to suit their political goals. . . . In expanding their organization and movement, the Matica particularly sought to win over public opinion, to which purpose an important role was played by their periodicals *Hrvatski Gospodarski Glasnik* and *Hrvatski Tjednik*. . . . [The *Hrvatski Tjednik*] played a special role in the period when the amendments to the Republican Constitution were under discussion, when it set forth an opposition platform on the subject of the statehood and the overall organization of the socialist Republic of Croatia."[30] The potent influence of this periodical in subsequent months can be easily assessed by the fact that its circulation grew to 100,000 within the short span of six months from March to August, 1971.

Other media which were co-opted included the major Croatian daily, *Vjes-nik,* and the influential weekly, *Vjesnik u Srijedu,* under the editorship of Džeba, who was also a member of the Croatian Central Committee on the side of the Dabčević group. He, it turns out, used his position as president of the Croatian Journalism Association to co-opt the airwaves of Zagreb's radio-television studio in addition to censoring opposition news out of his newspaper. A monopolistic position for nationalistic reporting in both print and broadcasting was thus assured and illustrates the silencing of other executive members who spoke out against the sessionist nationalist trends in their republic.[31]

The Tanjug chapter illustrated that though the Yugoslav media are organizationally autonomous, there are at least two ways in which party influence can be exerted: either through the newspaper's aktiv, which is entrusted with translating social goals into practice, or by influencing the chief editor directly. Both of these strategies, according to published reports, were used in the Croatian situation. A March, 1972, article entitled "Vjesnik was on the way to becoming the mouthpiece of the 'Croatian Mass Movement'" notes "the influence of the editorial group was strong enough to insert information and provide an unreliable picture of the political situation in Croatia. This led to the use of biased information serving the political needs and ambitions of a small group of high political functionaries. . . . Those who objected to this nationalism were able to speak out only sporadically and unsystematically. The editors who took part in using *Vjesnik* were not only manipulated, but they themselves manipulated other editors."[32] Examples of such bias were found in the elimination of speeches by two Croatian Central Committee members, Bilić and Vrhovec, who criticized "nationalistic trends" in Croatian politics at the twentieth session of the League of Communists, May 13 and 14, 1971. Their speeches received no mention in Croatia's *Vjesnik* but did get wide publicity two days later in Belgrade's weekly news magazine *NIN.*[33]

All of this evidence adds up to the conclusion that ethnicity facilitates the co-optation of the media, since these are organized along communal lines. As a consequence, and contrary to official pronouncements, the Yugoslav communicator is as yet a severely restricted watchdog of the people and cannot effectively fulfill the "scrutiny" function in the political communication process. The reasons for this, as has been seen, are both institutional and psychological. In multinational Yugoslavia, communication positions are staffed by the ethnic majority living in the particular republic. They write and broadcast in their distinctive languages and script. In addition, communicators and politicians come from the same social background, belong to their own regional League of Communists, and see each other at frequent board meetings.

Psychologically it becomes difficult for the communicator to disassociate himself from the majority views espoused by his governmental colleagues on the state level and to criticize their policies. He thus finds himself sometimes forcibly co-opted, but more often quietly seduced. Oskar Davičo, a writer, has described insightfully this psychological ambivalence by characterizing the position of the writer-journalist in contemporary Yugoslavia as that of a "faithless lover." Lukić adds that many communicators have actively participated in the creation of their country's socialist revolution and now find it difficult to seriously probe Yugoslavia's social problems.[34]

The final two hypotheses assert that mobilization and competition affect individual personality structures in multinational societies by differentiating social identities along ethnic lines so that both particularist and universal value orientations tend to exist side by side. These psychological predictions are also supported. A survey of political attitudes indicates that far from becoming generally modernized and attitudinally similar, Yugoslavs do, in fact, remain the possessors of a multiplicity of social identities. Only a small minority of people in Yugoslavia claim "Yugoslav" nationality rather than one based on ethnicity. These tend to belong to the dominant ethnic groups; 61 percent are from Serbia, Croatia-Slovenia, and Bosnia. They have, in addition, a high level of education (81 percent finished gymnasium or middle school), 85 percent are under forty-five years old, and 70 percent are communists.[35]

The majority of Yugoslavs, especially the Slovenes, Macedonians, and Albanians, are not only against political integration, but are attitudinally dissimilar from the other cultural groups as well. Social identities, it turns out, are situationally specific. This means that in Yugoslavia every actor in the political arena has a multiplicity of potential focuses of social solidarity. Some of these are situationally specific and include both ethnically particular and universal value systems. A Slovene may join his local writers' union in support of language rights, unite with Croat Catholics to urge the normalization of relations with the Vatican, and encourage his local labor union to legitimate the right to strike in a mismanaged factory. On the universal level he may support the social values of self-management, the equality of nations, and the need for federal regulation of foreign currency in a period of rapid economic growth.

Such evidence together with the previously noted differences in Yugoslavia's regional network content suggest that ethnic marginality and ethnic media programming are relatively permanent features of the Yugoslav setting. Both of these, if unchecked, tend to reinforce the competitiveness between groups. Consequently, the cumulative data support the contention that ethnic strife increases rather than decreases with social change in culturally heterogeneous societies. Such societies must therefore consciously dampen this strife through mutual agreements, as in the 1974 Constitution, or build in opportunities for beneficial cooperation.

Precisely this was the purpose of the 1972 reorganization of the League of Communists and the tightened control over the mass media. Recent personnel changes in both the Croatian and Serbian Central Committees re-emphasized federal League control over the republican communist parties to counterbalance the centripetal forces generated by increased republican autonomy. At the same time, legislation was introduced to give the Socialist Alliance greater control over media performance and content.[36] Opportunities for mutually beneficial media cooperation spring from financial and technological imperatives. These include the increasing cost of the jointly imported Eurovision services and the experience of working together in the cooperative Yugoslav Radio Television Association, where broadcast laws and satellite developments are planned and equipment purchases for all networks are coordinated.

Conclusions: Practical and Theoretical

Four major conclusions emerge from the assembled material on the saliency of ethnicity and its power to color the content and functioning of print and broadcast media in contemporary Yugoslavia. First of all, it appears that ethnicity is not a causal but an intervening variable in politics which tends to magnify the differences between competing groups during periods of rapid social change. Robert Melson and Howard Wolpe, as well as Maurice Pinard, concur with this assessment. All three note that in multinational societies with complete sets of parallel institutions, communal segmentation is neither a necessary nor a sufficient condition for communal conflict. It varies, instead, with the kinds and degrees of cultural, functional, communication, and normative integration found in a particular country at a particular point in time. In the Yugoslavia of the 1970s, communicative and functional integration were reinforced to counterbalance the erosion of cultural and normative integration resulting from economic development and decentralization.

Ethnicity, moreover, encourages politicians to see themselves as Montenegrins or Macedonians first and Yugoslavs second. With strong republican parties and rotation of jobs, these politicians must ultimately return to their home bases. Here they co-opt the media to espouse locally popular solutions to political and economic issues, which in turn reinforce their power base. Co-optation is facilitated by the fact that both politicians and communicators belong to the same ethnic group and are League members. A common social background, and other informal linkages through organization "aktivs" and publishers' councils, tend to confound the organizational distinctions between political and media hierarchies, making it difficult for communicators to "guard the guardians." Yet this is precisely what the constitution's information clause demands of them. With few exceptions, journalists are neither adequately trained nor legally protected to stand up to and question politicians. As a result, they tend to fulfill their channel roles by fitting in with the government of the day rather than by fulfilling their responsibility to the audience. Ethnocentricity creates a climate in which, as in a family, common issues are open to scrutiny, while selected other topics are not. At present it is easier for a Slovenian journalist to deplore wasteful economic investment in other republics while ignoring the financial drain of his own "political" factories.

Ethnicity coupled with a decentralized League organization make the interpretation of Yugoslavia's national events open to elite domination. Politicians, rather than market or audience needs, shape the media's picture of Yugoslav news. Because of the ethnic cleavages, political information content is furthermore oriented toward local rather than national themes. Such a conclusion is supported not only by content analyses, but by Mladen Zvonarević's study of elite access to Croatian newspapers as well. This study hypothesized that those who participate most in the mass media have potentially greater impact on public opinion formation than those who do not.[37] Participation in this study was defined as (1) writing articles or giving interviews, (2) actual mentions in the press, and (3) answering requests for interviews not in one's own field of specialization.

Though these indexes say little about the absolute degree of participation of various groups in the public communication process, they do describe *relative* participation. Table 30 demonstrates that three groups, intellectuals, mass organization (League) leaders, and legislators, have high participation indexes. The mass communicators with scores in the upper sixties are about medium, and the federal administrators and economic leaders are definitely low. Such evidence suggests once again that federal points of view and perspectives, as expressed by federal administrators, have a difficult time competing with the republican definition of political realities in multinational Yugoslavia.

In addition to being explicative, the Yugoslav data also help resolve the long-standing theoretical controversy about media contributions to modernization and nation-building. Contrary to conventional wisdom, discussion here indicates that the mass media are not the sole causes of either the macro-process of modernization nor the micro-process of attitude change involved in developing a more universal outlook. In Yugoslavia, the media carry content which makes people aware of economic development opportunities, but it was the government's development planning, not media information, which sparked

Table 30

Participation of Public Opinion Makers in Newspapers

(in percentage)

	1.	*2.*	*3.*	*4.*	*5.*
Total	75	50	54	60	
Legislators	68	69	62	66	H
Federal administrators	62	55	38	52	L
Mass organization leaders	79	55	67	67	H
Economic leaders	72	39	43	51	L
Mass communicators	79	41	44	55	L
Intellectuals	89	47	70	69	H

LEGEND: 1. Active collaboration in newspaper
        2. Mentioned in the newspaper
        3. Interview not in own field
        4. Average for all participation
        5. Classification of participation (high, medium, low)
SOURCE: Mladen Zvonarević, "The Relationship between Public Opinion Makers and Public Opinion," *Working Papers for the International Study of Opinion Makers*, III Columbia University, (1970), p. 3.

industrial growth. Moreover, the data point out that the media's capacity for inducing attitude change among the country's multinational population is severely limited by such social "givens" as ethnic subgroup size, culture, age, and educational attainment. Very few people claim "Yugoslav" nationality, indicating that there is a low sense of communality or psychological kinship in the country of the South Slavs.

Ivo Lederer agrees with this assessment, citing that multinational Yugoslavia has survived for fifty years in spite of major internal and economic strains. The precarious Yugoslav union not only endured but also prospered during the 1910s and 1930s, in spite of the centralized unitary hegemony of the Serbs and foreign pressures resulting from the world depression. Between 1941 and 1945 this unity was momentarily shattered by war and invasion, only to emerge once more in the wake of fratricidal fighting. As a federal system with equality of nationalities after World War II, other forces were set in motion. Decentralization and industrialization strained the national design, forcing the political apparat to seek new ways to balance the emergent power of alternate pressure groups in Yugoslavia's pluralistic society. Yet in spite of this it seems "the mosaic's outer frame and inner design are fundamentally secure."[38]

The mass media have reflected and contributed to this growing pluralism or democratization by giving each republic, whether populous or not, developed or under developed, rich or poor, a voice to express its own views on issues of national concern. The emerging opinion pluralism, with at least six different definitions of political realities, has at its best contributed to government through bargaining rather than through executive fiat. At worst it has encouraged a sense of regionalism with a tendency toward hermetic points of view. These could be potentially destructive of federal unity by undermining the search for and definition of mutually acceptable political alternatives. Like Canada's "two solitudes," the republican media may pay less attention to understanding each other's positions than to expressing the particularist points of view of their linguistic constituents. Yet by doing this, another study shows, they also may be indirectly strengthening the realization that confederation is essential.[39]

Yugoslavia's leadership seems to be aware of these dangers, and consequently the role of the republican media as alternative views or "deviant refuges" has been dampened in the crucial decade of the 1970s. New communications policies, it appears, will permit ethnic particularity to affect political communication only to the extent that it feeds and nourishes the minimal consensus necessary to keep the country a working unit.

---

1 Ghita Ionescu, *The Politics of the European Communist States,* p. 179.
2 Karl W. Deutsch, *Political Community and The North Atlantic Treaty Area.*
3 John C. Campbell, "Yugoslavia" in *The Communist States in Disarray, 1965-1971,* eds. Adam Bromks and Teresa Rakowska-Harmstone, p. 189.
4 Sterling, "Tito's New Balancing Act," p. 47.

5 Peter F. Sugar and Ivo J. Lederer, *Nationalism in Eastern Europe*, pp. 436-437.

6 *Ibid.*, p. 437.

7 Lukić, *Contemporary Yugoslav Literature*, p. 180.

8 "Constitutional Changes in Yugoslavia."

9 Hondius, *The Yugoslav Community of Nations*, p. 326.

10 Pavlowitch, *Yugoslavia*, pp. 336-337.

11 Paul Lendvai, in his *Eagles in Cobwebs'* notes on page 171: "The Trend toward identifying the republics with ethnic groups increased the Serbian malaise, since of all ethnic groups, the Serbs had the largest proportion living outside "their" republic. . . . For that reason, Serbian opinion was not keen on giving yet more power to the republics at the expense of the federation, and the Serbian Party Leadership was in an awkward situation trying to avoid being identified with either Yugoslav centralism or Serbian nationalism."

12 Chaney, *Processes of Mass Communication*, p. 4.

13 Daniel Lerner, *The Passing of Traditional Society*.

14 Robert Melson and Howard Wolpe, "Modernization and the Politics of Communalism: A Theoretical Perspective," pp. 1112-30.

15 Karl W. Deutsch, *Nationalism and Social Communication: An Inquiry into the Foundations of Nationality*, p. 91.

16 Deutsch, "Social Mobilization," p. 593.

17 Statistical references in Yugoslavia's *Statistički Godišnjak 1950-1971* document increases in standard of living, increased mobility of populations, and a rising number of citizens living in urban centers.

18 Alex Inkeles, "Making Men Modern: On the Causes and Consequences of Individual Change in Six Developing Countries," pp. 208-255.

19 Extensive empirical documentation of this point of view is found in Edward F. Douglass, "The Role of the Mass Media in National Development: A Reformulation with Particular Reference to Sierra Leone," p. 105ff.

20 Theodore W. Schultz, *Economic Crisis in World Agriculture*, p. 26.

21 Garry K. Bertsch, "A Cross National Analysis of the Community-Building Process in Yugoslavia," p. 443.

22 Garry K. Bertsch, "Molding the 'New Man' in Communist Societies: The Multi-National Czechoslovak, Soviet and Yugoslav Cases."

23 Bruce Westley and Malcolm S. MacLean Sr., "A Conceptual Model for Communication Research," p. 36.

24 Kolektiva Radio-Televizija Zagreb, *Naš studio*, p. 9.

25 Canada, *Report of the Special Senate Committee on Mass Media: Good, Bad or Simply Inevitable*, p. 13.

26 Bernard C. Cohen, *The Press and Foreign Policy*, p. 13.

27 Maxwell E. McCombs, Donald Shaw, and Eugene F. Shaw, "The News and Public Response: Three Studies of the Agenda-Setting Power of the Press," p. 2.

28 Melson and Wolpe, "Modernization," p. 1114.

29 James Feron, "Purge Goes Deep into Croatian Life."

30 Erna Darossi-Bjelajac, "Karakteristika i dimenzije idejnopolitičkih devijacija u savezu komunista Hrvatske," pp. 9-14.

31 Dennison I Rusinow, *Crisis in Croatia, Part II: Facilis Decensus Averno*, p. 15.

32 "Vjesnik Was on the Way to Becoming the Voice for the Croatian 'Mass Movement,' " pp. 3-4.

33 Rusinow, *Crisis in Croatia*, p. 15.

34 Lukić, *Contemporary Yugoslav Literature*, p. 164.

35 Bertsch, "Molding the 'New Man,' " p. 25.

36 Bulatović, "The Right to Information," p. 26.

37 Mladen Zvonarević, "The Relationship between Public Opinion Makers and Public Opinion," p. 3.

38 Sugar and Lederer, *Nationalism*, p. 438.

39 Arthur Siegel, "Canadian Newspaper Coverage of F.L.Q. Crisis: A Case Study of the Impact of the Press on Politics," especially the concluding chapter.

CHAPTER 10

The Audience: Readers, Listeners, and Viewers

Previous chapters have demonstrated not only that the main function of the media is social control through the dissemination of information and entertainment, but also that the press and broadcasting provide alternative conceptions of reality and thus cohesion for national subgroups with alternate visions. In Yugoslavia during the 1960s there was a delicate balance between these two social functions which is difficult to isolate and unravel. The recognition that mass communication content offers a variety of symbolic interpretations of social experience and has different meaning for different groups of people makes media content an indicator for distinguishing various audiences. Why do some people watch programs like "Mannix" and ignore documentaries, and what performances are preferred in different countries at different times? Both of these questions ultimately have to do with audience characteristics.

What is an audience? Traditionally audiences, which are the third link in the communication chain, have been studied in isolation against a backdrop of mass society theory. This approach has led both to a static definition of the audience and a one-directional conception of the mass communication process as moving primarily from the sender to the receiver. According to this view, mass audiences attending to the press and broadcasting are supposed to be very large, heterogeneous, and anonymous. As Herbert Blumer puts it: "The membership [of the mass audience] may come from all walks of life . . . [is] composed of anonymous individuals . . . [has] very little interaction or exchange of experience between its members . . . is very loosely organized and is not able to act with concertedness."[1]

However, recent research in the United States, Great Britain, and Scandinavia has indicated that communication is a social process in which the complex interrelationships between communicators, messages, audiences, and situations must be taken into account. Consequently, audiences cannot be studied without considering these factors. The following sections review the contributions of a symbolic and transactional communication theory to an understanding of audience membership and will use Yugoslav polls and content analyses to illuminate audience performance preferences and the question of media effects.

Characteristics of Audience Roles

A theory of communication as symbolic knowledge exchange assumes that meaning is attached to performances by the receiver rather than being an attribute of the "message" per se. It also rejects the notion that human behavior is merely predicated on dissonance reduction or pain avoidance. Instead, it notes that the actor has great flexibility in determining his perceptions, comprehension, and use of his environment, significant aspects of which derive their meaning from society at large.

Consequently this theory does not conceptualize audience behavior in simpleminded behaviorist terms. It does not assume that there is a linear cause and effect relationship between media content and the audience. Transactionalist symbolic theory instead alerts us to the fact that media performances are chosen or selected for various purposes. Audiences, in other words, do things with their environment, symbolic or otherwise, rather than being passively bombarded by its stimuli. It follows that contrary to previous assumptions, the audience need not be viewed as powerless. It may lack cohesion among its members, especially as compared to communicators, and the individual viewer or listener may be rarely known to the sender and thus fail to influence programming directly. Yet in spite of all this, audience members are part of primary groups like family, friends, and occupational circles, which help mold outlooks and screen attitudes, as well as determine media use patterns. Mass audiences, in other words, are neither passive receptors nor lacking in social organization.

But how can this audience membership be conceptualized? Considering that there is a multiplicity of contents, individuals, and settings in which people utilize media performances, most likely no single overall definition of the audience can be drawn. Consequently Chaney suggests that media audiences, when they persist, are more than "primary publics" or "mass publics." Instead they might be viewed as "social circles," varying along a continuum in which differences in internal characteristics, structural organization, and processes of group development constitute distinguishing marks.[2] Zora Kadushin has defined a social circle as a network of indirect interaction which exists through shared interests and is informal in the sense that it does not possess clear leaders, defined goals, or distinct membership criteria. He notes that different circles can be distinguished by their focus of activity, such as cultural, utilitarian, influential, or integrative, and by certain boundary-defining conditions.[3] Chaney concludes that audience rewards emerge from communication situations mediated by variations in media accessibility, the situation of reception, and the type of audience cohesion which is prevalent.[4]

Media accessibility is greater in local radio and cable television, for instance, because audience responses are not only easy to communicate by phoning in, but also are frequently immediately incorporated into a disc jockey's "patter" and format. The situation of reception, whether individual or group, also aids in predicting the kinds of meanings people are likely to attach to a performance. Here Herbert Gans found, for instance, that though Italian immigrants watch situation comedies like all other United States citizens, they reinterpret and reject the implications of the lack of fatherly authority in the home.[5]

Finally, the extent to which an audience views itself as an entity will also affect content production. A prime example of this close interrelationship can be found in magazine publishing. Here producers for mammoth audiences, like *Reader's Digest,* are less likely to innovate than the publishers of *Hot Rod* or *MS,* catering to special interest groups. Though both know their audiences well, heterogeneity in print and broadcast audiences seems to breed conservatism in content production.[6]

Twenty years ago, Elihu Katz and Paul Lazarsfeld conceptualized the flow of information between mass media organizations and the audience as a complex interrelationship in which exposure is dependent on at least three kinds of variables: economic resources which determine media networks and, therefore, availability; political considerations, like censorship, which may inhibit exposure; as well as social factors, like age, sex, and education, which give rise to differences in performance choices and media preferences.[7] Contemporary research has added a fourth set of variables having to do with the time of occurrence, degree of importance, and degree of anticipation of a reported event.[8]

With these theoretical points in mind, what do we know about Yugoslav audience characteristics and media use patterns? Yugoslav sectional data on the number and types of people attending to different kinds of programming illustrate both the close interrelationship between media availability and use as well as the predictable social differences among radio, television, and reading audiences. Table 31 summarizes 1968 media availability for each Yugoslav household in the six republics and shows that the country lags behind the rest of Europe. After a century of growth, Yugoslavia is still short of the UNESCO-recommended minimum of ten dailies for each 100 population, though broadcast facilities are closer to what would be expected in a middle-developed country.

Local researchers believe that the reason for this uneven diffusion of print and electronic media results from both economic and social factors. Inadequate newspaper distribution to the villages and the greater availability of television during the decade of the 1960s have inhibited press growth, as have cultural primitivism and the country's average illiteracy rate of 20 percent in the poorer republics.

Availability also affects use, namely, the daily listening, viewing, and reading habits of the population. While figures differ from republic to republic, a 1968 Belgrade Institute of Journalism opinion poll indicates that more Yugoslavs (75 percent) watch television daily than listen to radio (69 percent) or read the daily press (66 percent). Such figures are in stark contrast to statistics from highly developed Canada or the United States, where media diffusion is virtually total. In Canada 91 percent watch television daily, 89 percent listen to the radio, and 88 percent read newspapers.[9]

Table 31
Media Distribution by Republic and Household
(1 household : 4 people)

	Households per Radio	Households per TV	Households per Daily Press
Highly developed republics			
Slovenia	1.0	2.7	2.7
Middle-developed republics			
Croatia	1.3	3.1	4.7
Serbia (total)	1.6	3.7	1.5
Vojvodina	1.4	3.4	9.5
Kosovo	2.5	8.0	15.3
Less-developed republics			
Macedonia	1.5	3.4	6.7
Bosnia-Hercegovina	2.0	6.3	7.8
Montenegro	2.3	6.3	—
Yugoslavia	1.5	3.7	3.2

SOURCE: *Novinar i novinarstvo,* Godina 3-4 (1968), pp. 204-206.

Table 32 indicates the interrelationship between social variables and media preferences. Higher education and high occupation, coupled with an urban setting, apparently go hand in hand with greater media use. Consequently, the better educated are also the potentially better informed. Lower educational level is positively correlated with radio listening and negatively correlated with newspaper and television usage. Less reading is well known to be determined by educational level, but less television usage is not so correlated in highly developed countries. In Yugoslavia, however, ecomomic factors, such as the cost of receivers, and inadequate television coverage to the villages mitigate against rural television usage.

Another interesting point emerging from the data is that, contrary to statistics in the United States and Canada, membership in political and social organizations is positively connected with both increased press and television usage, though not with radio listening. Moreover, it appears that women in Yugoslavia use all the media less than men. This is a result both of lower educational levels and social conditions, which place a heavy housekeeping burden on women in rural locations where over 40 percent of the population still live.[10]

Table 32 provides evidence that age is negatively related to media usage, another finding which differs from North America. The generation under thirty utilizes all except the print media more than their elders. At least one-third of those over forty-five, it appears, make no regular use of broadcasting, and less than half of the older generation attends to print. The reasons for these age discrepancies are similar to those mentioned above, along with the fact that the less educated older population tends to live in rural areas.

The data in Tables 31 and 32 suggest three major differences of media systems at various levels of economic development which have also been noted

Table 32
Social Characteristics of Yugoslav Listeners, Viewers, and Readers
(in percentages)

	Radio Listeners		Television Viewers		Newspaper Readers	
	Regular	Infrequent or Never	Regular	Infrequent or Never	Regular	Infrequent or Never
Total	69	31	75	25	66	34
Education:						
Primary	64	36	45	55	46	54
Secondary	79	21	75	25	76	24
High school and above	74	26	86	14	91	9
Location:						
City	74	26	75	25	87	13
Village	36	64	15	85	15	85
Occupation:						
Farmers	29	71	9	91	9	91
Workers	68	32	38	62	37	63
Professional and academic	76	24	85	15	74	26
Sex:						
Male	48	52	67	33	70	30
Female	62	38	56	44	54	46
Membership in pol. and soc. organizations						
Yes	77	23	83	17	84	56
No	76	24	62	38	16	44
Age: Years						
Young (18-29)	78	22	82	18	64	33
Middle (30-44)	74	26	76	24	66	34
Old (45 and over)	69	31	65	45	53	47

SOURCES: General information: Jugoslovenski institut za novinarstvo, *Čitaoci, Slušaoci, Gledaoci* (Beograd, 1965). Occupational breakdown: Firdus Džinic, "Raširenost Političko-Informativnog Dejstva Radija, TV i Štampe u SFR Jugoslavije," Jugoslovenski institut za novinarstvo (Beograd, 1969). Age and television: Miroslav Djordjević, "New Year's Eve Shows on Radio and T.V. as Determinants of Audience Behavior," *Utilizacija Javnih Informacija*, Jugoslovenski institut za novinarstvo (Beograd, 1970).

by other researchers around the world. In developing countries, daily press saturation does not precede broadcast diffusion, as in western Europe and on the American continent. According to a 1971 study, every sixth home in Yugoslavia has a television set, though it may not have a newspaper. Many households acquire television before they install other modern necessities such as water or indoor toilets.[11] Furthermore, audiences in general utilize the media less in developing than in developed countries, mainly because they are not as readily available or as widely diffused.

A third difference suggested by the Yugoslav data relates to television viewing, which in Yugoslavia is inversely related to level of economic development. Television watching is most prevalent in the least developed republics of Macedonia and Montenegro, where 98 percent and 89 percent, respectively, own sets, while the average for the whole country is 77 percent. In Slovenia, on the other hand, only 67 percent of all television owners watch their screen daily. Scholars suggest that the medium's novelty has worn off in this northeastern republic which has an Italian standard of living. In the southern republics, on the other hand, this is not the case. Television studios are still being built and local program production is at most two years old. The majority of the highly educated Slovenes watch two hours or less daily, while 61 percent of the less educated Macedonian or Albanian viewers spend more than three hours daily with television.[12]

Media Content and Program Preferences

Conventionally, media content and an audience's program preferences are analyzed and dealt with as unrelated items in the process of mass communication. Taking account of the symbolic dimension of human communication, however, alerts us that meaning is not "in" the codified data supposedly being transferred between senders and receivers, but is something attached by the audience itself. The individual reader, listener, or viewer, in other words, is the creator of whatever significance a message has for him or herself in a particular situation. Choices and preferences for certain types of media content consequently tell us something about a country's varied audiences, their interests, and their beliefs.

If, for instance, it is found that many audience members generally prefer entertainment or fictional over realistic or informational content, this may give us both psychological and social clues about differences in audience types. According to Karl Rosengren, a preference for fictional content may indicate an audience with a high degree of media dependence and involvement.[13] On the social level such a preference may, on the other hand, point to a communication system in which certain types of content are more heavily "filtered" than others. Fictional content in such a situation is preferable precisely because it passes relatively unchanged through the dissemination network. Political information is more carefully screened to conform to the "official" point of view. As a result, audiences learn to disregard much of this content and to read between the lines. Solzhenitsyn gives a literary example of this selectivity in his *Cancer Ward,* where Krushchev's denunciation of Stalin and its implications for daily life are being evaluated by a minor security official. To understand what types of content Yugoslav readers, listeners, and viewers pay attention to and prefer, it is necessary to describe and differentiate that country's media programming from what is found on the American continent and in the Soviet Union.

Programming in Yugoslavia is strictly a regional matter, with each republic more or less "doing its own thing." This is in line with the new kind of grass-roots democracy based on the self-management principle introduced in the 1950s. In broadcasting, complete local autonomy is tempered by the economics of programming. Consequently, the radio stations, which have formed six networks, and the six television studios, supplement locally produced content with a common program to which everyone contributes. Only the press operates primarily on a single paper principle, covering mostly local and regional events. Yugoslavia has a handful of newspaper chains of less than ten papers and magazines located in the republican capitals. Among them are the *Borba* and *Politika* publishing houses, which bring out the only nationally distributed dailies. Two-thirds of the country's total circulation comes from weekly local papers and the factory press which cover economic and political questions from various points of view. There is, in other words, no hierarchical system of guided information transmission, as in the Soviet Union, where such national papers as *Pravda* and *Izvestia* structure the attention and discussion agendas for the whole nation. Yugoslavia's press, radio, and television raise a cacophony of voices reminiscent of western European rather than iron curtain media.

Radio is Yugoslavia's most prevalent medium. In 1970, Yugoslavia's six major radio stations broadcast a total of nineteen different schedules daily, while the 144 local stations are on the air for only two to three hours. The four largest republican stations in Zagreb, Ljubljana, Novi Sad, and Belgrade, which cover the most populous parts of the country, have a three-tiered program schedule similar to that of Great Britain's BBC. Skopje has two programs for Macedonia, and Radio Titograd in Montenegro and Radio Priština in Kosovo, with their smaller audiences, have only one each. The national capital is also experimenting with a purely entertainment-oriented metropolitan sender, Belgrade 202, and broadcasts a program for foreign countries as well.

According to Table 33, the first program everywhere is of a universal nature. It contains a mix of from two-thirds to approximately one-half music and the spoken word, depending on the republic. Belgrade's first program, probably because it covers national as well as local events, has the highest percentage of spoken versus musical content — 53 percent versus 47 percent. Such programming is similar to the Canadian Broadcasting Corporation's AM content, which is 60 percent music and 40 percent spoken. CBC's FM stations and private Canadian and United States outlets drastically reverse the percentages. Here there are approximately 79 percent music and 21 percent spoken information.[14]

The emphasis in Yugoslavia on current events and information strongly contrasts to United States programming. Table 33 indicates that the spoken program contains approximately 22 percent politico-informational content; 34 percent culture, education, and entertainment; and a remainder of 34 percent in advertising. Such a content division reflects that radio as the most prevalent medium must have a strong social service component. Yugoslav information programs typically emphasize republican events, but in 1970 they also covered such national issues as election news, the fiftieth anniversary of the League of Communists, international trouble spots like Vietnam and the Middle East, economic development in nonaligned nations, and reports on Yugoslavia's industry and labor.

Table 33
Comparative Survey of Radio Programming Content
(in percentages of total)

Broadcast Station		Music Total	Spoken Total	Information Current Affairs	Culture, Education, Entertainment	Advertising
Belgrade	I	53	47	32	34	34
	II	63	37	9	75	16
	III	68	32	15	79	6
Belgrade 202		83	17			
Foreign broadcast.		21	79			
Zagreb	I	67	33	54	32	14
	II	77	23	43	31	26
	III	72	28		96	4
Ljubljana	I	55	45	41	35	24
	II	81	19	60	40	
	III	78	21	69	31	
Sarajevo		60	40	41	38	21
Skopje	I	61	39	38	45	17
	II	75	25	42	54	3
Titograd		68	32	51	28	21
Novi Sad	I	58	42	56	26	18
	II	78	22	55	17	28
	III	70	30	39	61	
Priština		50	50	39	32	28
Average all first stations				44	34	22

SOURCE: *Jugoslovenski radiotelevizija godišnjak* (1970) p. 140.

Radio Novi Sad's first and second program represent a particularly interesting example of a station responding to ethnic needs. It broadcasts in five languages to the major populations of the autonomous province of Vojvodina, which is part of Serbia. In contrast to Quebec, where English and French services are separated, the same studios and wavelengths are used to acquaint audiences with ethnic writers and artists. Radio dramas utilize local humor and characters, serial discussions cover the world of science, while youth and children's programs further ethnic heritages. Education series finally are an hour long and designed to supplement regional school instruction in literature, language (English, French, German, and Russian), music, and history.

The second program, with the exception of Radio Belgrade, is usually lighter, often containing up to 80 percent popular or folk-style music. It is generally geared to a younger audience as well as to the housewife. In spite of its lighter content, a recent Serbian study indicates that the first program as well as local radio are more popular than the second. About 1,229,999 people listen to it, 258,000 to the second, and 480,000 to local radio.[15] Lower audience figures are probably a result of the polarization between beat and popular music listeners, who do not overlap.

A third program modeled on the BBC's "high-brow programming" was innovated as recently as 1965. It caters to a small urban audience of about 19 percent of all Yugoslav radio listeners, composed of governmental officials, professionals, artists, students, and engineers. Seventy-seven percent are between the ages of twenty-five and fifty, and more than 60 percent have a college education.[16] They tend to listen on the average of one hour weekly, concentrating on favorite programs. Among the most popular programs in this series are concerts, political discussions, cultural readings, and scientific presentations, produced from two to four hours nightly in the four major urban centers. Political panels on controversial and timely issues where government officials are questioned are also widely listened to and discussed. Ljubljana's schedule includes "Pages from Slovenian Prose and Poetry," "Film Library," "Literary Evening," "Living Thoughts," "Evening Art Talks," and original radio plays, all reflecting the very high cultural level of Radio III content.[17] It aims to keep listeners abreast of contemporary literary, musical, and social experiments both at home and abroad. In contrast to the United States, often otherwise unpublished or as yet untranslated works and music by local and international authors receive their premieres over the air in Yugoslavia.

Turning to Yugoslav television, it, too, is subdivided into six regional programs with strong ethnic orientations, originating in the republican capitals. Plans call for the creation of two additional studios in the autonomous provinces of Vojvodina and Kosovo to provide additional program diversification for the various national minorities. In addition, there is experimentation with color broadcasts in the second service. Interviews with Yugoslav Radio Television Association officials reveal that by 1980 Yugoslavia hopes to staff a third television channel. These developments which depend on republican rather than federal investments of many millions of dinars may be delayed because of the country's recent economic instability.[18]

In contrast to radio, where informational and political content overshadow entertainment and culture, television reverses priorities and devotes about 60 percent of its program to popular entertainment, sports, and ads. The latter are presented in a twenty-minute block during prime time. The exact breakdowns for 1969 were culture and entertainment, 35.4 percent, information and current events, 28.6 percent, education, 12.1 percent, sports, 10.1 percent, and commercials, 13.8 percent.[19] Where much of the program used to be jointly produced by three studios serving the Croatian and Serbian majorities, programming, as noted in Chapter 3, has become increasingly decentralized in the late 1960s and 1970s. This has resulted in much greater regional diversity, especially in news, humor, and musical productions, than was hitherto the rule. The majority of Yugoslavs watch television between two and three-and-a-half hours daily, about the same as audiences on the North American continent, whose average, according to a Temple University survey, is two hours and forty-seven minutes.[20] This is only a fraction more than the averages for radio listening.

A Belgrade study indicates that there seem to be few differences between radio listening patterns in developed and less developed countries. As in Canada and the United States, radio is listened to mostly as a background for other activities. In the morning, there is a peak between 4:00 A.M. and 8:00 A.M., when people get ready to go to work (starting time, 7:00 A.M.) and when there is no competition from television. After work, which ends about 2:00 P.M., there is another listening peak between 5:30 P.M. to 7:30 P.M., when the popular musical "Evening Review of Your Choice" is broadcast. In the evening, however, television comes into its own, with maximum Yugoslav viewing in prime time, between 7:00 P.M. to 11:00 P.M.

On weekends Belgrade's first program is most attended to between 2:00 P.M. to 8:00 P.M., with television competing in the time slot between 3:00 P.M. to 5:00 P.M. At this time sports events are broadcast, and from 9:00 P.M. to 11:00 P.M. there are light entertainment shows. All of these patterns are related to Yugoslav working habits and program content, and exhibit the typical displacement of radio by television for a variety of entertainment needs.[21]

Though the daily press is the oldest medium in Yugoslavia, its content is being discussed last for a variety of reasons. First of all, it is relatively badly diffused. There is only one copy of a daily paper for every 3.1 households in 1970 Yugoslavia, a figure which is only slightly less than that for television. With an average of thirteen people per paper, Yugoslavia places last in the roster of European countries which have one to two dailies per household. Only in Albania are there fewer newspapers than in Yugoslavia. In addition, Yugoslavia's total daily circulation of its twenty-five papers is around 1.6 million copies, where Canada's 116 dailies, serving a population of the same size, publish 4.7 million. In Japan, Great Britain, Canada, and the United States, the circulation of dailies is generally larger than the total number of households.

In addition, it has already been noted that the daily press has had only a very modest increase in the 1960s, from twenty-two to twenty-five papers. Most print growth, probably under the influence of economic prosperity and the television explosion, has been in weekly and monthly journals, which more than doubled from 350 to 759 in the ten years between 1959 and 1969. Total circulation of these periodicals at 4.4 million is also double that of the daily press.[22] It is no wonder that the daily press attracts numerically the smallest audience of all the mass media. Only 65.7 percent of all Yugoslavs read a daily paper regularly.

Among this group, not all read the same kind of content. A more detailed breakdown reveals that 35.8 percent look for news and information of all sorts; 23.5 percent for such entertainment features as ads, stories, comic strips, and pictures; 17.6 percent seek excitement in disasters and court reports; the remaining 13.5 percent and 9.6 percent, respectively, read their newspapers primarily for sports news and the literature and culture section.[23]

What explains this generally low interest in and utilization of political information content in contemporary Yugoslavia? A 1968 study of all the mass media indicates that 75 percent of all Yugoslavs are regular television viewers, 69 percent are regular radio listeners, and 66 percent are regular newspaper readers. Only 39 percent of all citizens read the daily political columns, 47 percent watch the news on television, and 61 percent listen to some newscast on radio.[24] As suggested earlier, one of the reasons for this lack of interest is the fact that political content is more highly screened in the Yugoslav system than economic and cultural matters. As a result, its content is more formal and less absorbing, often contradicting the audience's personal experiences. These logical incongruities between the official versions of political and economic reality have made a large part of the population uninterested in political content, preferring other types of expressive performances.

Audience research in all Yugoslav media has consequently recorded a strong preference for more entertaining content since the mid-1960s. In radio, for instance, the favorite shows are folk and light music hours based on written or phoned audience requests, or satirical programs, sports, and the half-hour of ads.[25] A comparison with earlier programming schedules indicates that since 1965, stations have increased their "folk" and "country" music shows, decreased the large number of generally unpopular serious music broadcasts, and encouraged authors to write or adapt more humorous plays or satires for radio. As a result, the amount of time spent on political information programming in the past decade shrank from 50 percent to an average of 44 percent on Radio I and 28 percent on the "light" Radio II. Interestingly, all of these requests for program changes came from city and country audiences alike, though the more educated tended to find popularized folk music less appealing. This provides strong confirmation for the view that political content is generally rated low.

The same conclusion can be drawn from changes in television programming where informational content declined 5 percent to 28.6 percent of the total between 1962 and 1969, while cultural shows went down by 18 percent in the same time. A 1971 survey inquiring "what do you like to watch most on television?" turned up the following preferences: On the average, 25 percent of all television owners chose films; 13 percent, documentary and informational programs; 12 percent, sports events; and 9 percent each, quiz and entertainment reviews and drama.[26] Does the content of Yugoslav television reflect these preferences? Definitely not, because Yugoslav editors must balance the doctrine of "giving the public what it wants" with such political functions as public affairs, education, and other goals. Consequently in 1969, films made up only about 18 percent, humor, music, and satirical shows, 7.7 percent each, and sports, 10 percent of the total television program. The rest went to public affairs, education, and advertising. Bowing to the popular request of 25 percent of all television viewers, feature films, however, are now shown more often, approximately three to four times a week, and serials and documentaries, twice. While most television programs are locally produced, Yugoslavia's 18 percent imports are feature films and serials from the United States.[27] Many of these are old westerns, like "Gunfight at Dodge City" and "Comanche." To escape the danger of "cultural imperialism" by the United States, more German, Swedish, and Canadian films are being imported to add to those coming from countries like Czechoslovakia, Hungary, and Poland.

The growing disinterest of audiences in public affairs has spurred all radio networks to make their programming more "immediate." In Zagreb, editors are updating their news programming by innovating "open lines" to encourage listener participation and by concentrating on reporting controversial issues in depth. They are also introducing shows like "Timely Conversations" which are based on listener ideas. Furthermore, they are enlarging the variety of themes discussed and exploring new ways of reporting by relating timely issues to everyday life.[28] Television is doing the same by "demystifying" politicians in panels and in live sessions with their constituents, a practice generally frowned upon in other eastern European countries. They are also garnering interest through heavier local public affairs programming, as mentioned in the previous chapter. It was shown that republican events dominate the daily television news roundups to the detriment of federal coverage. By the late 1970s, the second television channel will certainly reinforce the trend toward republican programming, taking the political and entertainment interests of the varied national audiences into account and laying the foundation for satellite communication in another decade.

Whether added entertainment content and informational program adaptations will satisfy audience preferences is a question which is difficult to answer. At present, it certainly seems to have given Yugoslav readers, listeners, and viewers a much greater content variety than exists anywhere else in eastern Europe. Furthermore, it indicates, as Ionescu has pointed out, that all communist systems must pay increased attention to public opinion in their program of ideological mobilization.[29] Certainly this is better accomplished through public persuasion than the heavy-handed terrorist tactics so prevalent in Stalinist Russia during the 1930s and 1940s. Yugoslavia's leaders, as has been noted, are well aware of these alternatives, and have solidly opted for persuasion mixed with entertainment to keep their audiences happy.

Audience Selections and Media Use

Just as audiences cannot be classified in one all-encompassing definition but are more accurately understood as differentially participating in the mass communication process, the very choices of particular types of media content help predict the media participation of different groups in society. Media use, it turns out, is not an isolated pattern of behavior but part of what is generally called "leisure time activity." Bennet Berger notes that most researchers have drawn the wrong conclusions from the dichotomy between work and leisure; they assume that leisure is without activity. In fact, he observes, all time is filled with some kind of action. Activity is part of work as well as leisure. The crucial distinction between these two concepts lies somewhere else: namely, in the realization that leisure time is primarily constrained by ethical considerations while work is constrained by expediency.[30] Different types of leisure patterns constitute different normative styles of living rather than indiscriminate ways of filling "free" time. A study of leisure patterns, among them media use, may tell something about the life-styles of different audience groups.

These insights have led media uses and gratification studies to view the audience as an active participant in the communication process, "bending" information to their needs rather than being overpowered by the media. Many of these have been designed to probe, add to, and refine Lasswell's classic fourfold typology which posits surveillance of the environment, correlation of society, transmission of the social heritage, and entertainment as the major social functions of mass communication.[31] What do varying Yugoslav audiences think about media performances, and how do they use what they select? Do they prefer one medium over another and for what purposes? And how do these uses and preferences differ from those made by audiences in highly developed countries?

Answers to all of these questions are still sketchy in socialist Yugoslavia, where the media are audience-financed as well as vitally important to the League of Communists' socialization program. As a result, audience and public opinion research which originated in the late 1950s has been concentrated on two issues: program preferences as well as political and social opinions helpful to decision makers.

Five important social science institutes in the more developed northeastern republics concentrate on opinion polling; in addition, the research departments of the six broadcast networks do media analyses. Among these are the Institute of Social Science (Institut Društvenih Nauka) in Belgrade (1956), which emphasizes history and social relations, as well as demographic and elite research. Then there is the Federal Center for Public Opinion Research (Institut Društvenih Nauka, Odeljenje za Masovne Komunikacije i Javno Mnenje), a branch of the same institute which has done Gallup-type polling on timely social issues since 1964. The Institute of Journalism (Institut za Novinarstvo) has also engaged in various types of mass communication research since 1960, as have the Croatian Institute for Public Opinion in Zagreb (Institut za Javno Mnenje S.R. Hrvatskoj) and the Center for Public Opinion and Mass Communications Research in Ljubljana.

Since the late 1960s these institutes have kept the government informed on public opinion about current social and political issues. They also chart responses to major new pieces of legislation, such as the electoral reforms of 1968 and the new press law of 1971; moreover, they tell the League of Communists how various groups of people, like students and workers, feel about its activities, and try to explain crises like those in housing and nonsocialized agriculture.

While more detailed uses and gratification research is still lacking, some basic information on the Yugoslav audience's media preferences and their ability to satisfy various social and personal needs is available. Yugoslav data from a stratified sample of 5,675 respondents representing 4.2 million television homes indicates that the Yugoslavs, like people around the globe, in 1971 preferred television to both radio and the press. Their reasons for this preference are different from those in the developed countries. Two-thirds of all Yugoslavs, in contrast to North Americans, believe that television is the "speediest" and the most complete medium when it comes to "backgrounding."[32] Such a belief is a result of Yugoslavia's insufficiently diffused print media and the relatively low quality of much local radio programming in the villages. Local researchers believe that their compatriots' confidence in television as an information medium will be eroded as soon as the media network becomes more developed. This author's opinion differs from this assessment. The Federal League of Communists' desire to develop a more uniform national information policy in the 1970s will probably utilize television as a major component in this strategy.

The same survey also shows that television is used primarily for information and entertainment and relatively little for education. This dual use is substantiated not only by audience interviews but also by information about the number of viewers a particular show attracts and by program preferences. The informational use of television in Yugoslavia is substantiated by the fact that "TV Dnevnik" (TV Daily) draws the largest audience, followed by quiz, film, drama, and humorous programs. When it comes to preferences, however, informational content, as previously noted, does not rate as high. It falls into seventh place after such entertaining content as film, popular music, humor, sports, and drama.[33] Blumler explains this discrepancy by noting that audiences may view informational content in order to keep in touch with their environment. Yet this may not be their most preferred programming.[34]

Another question for which Yugoslav data are available has to do with people's estimations of whether or not the needs served by the media can be satisfied in other ways. Information indicating that there are a variety of ways of gaining knowledge of the world, strengthening status and knowledge of self, having contacts with friends, and experiencing one's culture and tradition raise grave doubts about the still popular view that the mass media have unlimited capacity to be "all things to all men." In fact, this power is severely limited by interpersonal contacts between friends, public lectures, religious holidays, and so on.

Two studies substantiate this point: the first investigates the use of leisure time among Zagreb high school students, while the second comments on media nonuse among nearly one-third of the country's total population. A 1968 Institut za Društvena Istraživanja survey of fourteen- to eighteen-year-old boys and girls indicates that the two to five hours of free time enjoyed daily by the majority of these young people was primarily taken up with nonmedia-related activities. These included sports, hobbies, housework, and spending time visiting with friends in cafes, dancing, and walking, going to meetings, and sleeping. The remaining time was divided as follows: 20 percent was devoted to print media for information purposes, while another 20 percent was devoted to being entertained by television, radio, and records.[35]

The substantial level of media nonuse in Croatia, which adds further confirming evidence that the media are not able to satisfy all of our human needs, is documented in Table 34. A large group of people can do without radio (17 percent), daily newspapers (26 percent), and television (39 percent). Who are they? Closer investigation reveals that illiteracy (12 percent in Croatia) limits newspaper reading, while lack of reception facilities inhibits the use of televi-

Table 34
Circulation of Mass Media in Croatia
(in audience percentages)

	Regularly	Sometimes	Never
Daily newspapers	21	53	26
Radio	25	58	17
Television	21	40	39

SOURCE: Mladen Zvonarević, "The Relationship between Public Opinion Makers and Public Opinion," unpublished paper, University of Zagreb, 1969, pp. 5-6.

sion. Finally, but most important, rural areas have highly developed networks through which oral information is transmitted. These are based on the church and zadruga (cooperative) system, as well as the concept of factory self-management and village self-government. All of these offer opportunities for exchanges of opinion and are a strong part of Yugoslavia's contemporary rural life-style.

An Israeli study by Elihu Katz and others, which for the first time attempts to develop a comprehensive typology of media uses and gratifications, may help place Yugoslavia's scanty data into perspective.[36] The authors organized a list of thirty-five possible needs into a three-part typology, differentiating between institutional, self-growth, and self-gratification needs as reproduced in Table 35. Each of these clusters was then tested as to whether they could be satisfied by the media or through other forms of contact.

This representative survey of 1,500 Israeli adults found that people all over the world, not only the Yugoslavs, use the media first and foremost for information and education. Eighty-seven percent of the sample consider the media's ability to strengthen understanding of society, the state, and world very important, and 77 percent believe their educational functions to be crucial. As to providing varied experience, such as strengthening gratification and also self-understanding, 77 percent of the Israelis found this also an important function of the media.

The Katz survey provides an ordering of other types of media gratifications as well.[37] Among these are the media's ability to entertain; to provide a topic of conversation in nonvital encounters with other people; a central component in

Table 35
Classification of Media-Related Needs

A. Mode	B. Connection	C. Referent
1. To strengthen	1. Information, knowledge, understanding (cognitive)	1. Self
		2. Family
2. To weaken	2. Gratification, emotional experience (affective)	3. Friends
3. To acquire	3. Credibility, confidence, stability, status (integration)	4. State, society
	4. Contact (integration)	5. Tradition, culture
	5. Escape (nonintegration)	6. World
		7. Others, negative reference groups

SOURCE: Elihu Katz, *et al.* "On the Use of the Mass Media for Important Things," *American Sociological Review*, 38; 2 (April 1973), p.166.

personal identity and reality rituals; a mythical way of explaining the unexplainable; and finally, a compensation for other and more direct forms of human interaction. The Israeli data show that the "mythical" functions which Katz considers as "being in a festive mood" and getting "closer to Jewish tradition" are third in order of importance, according to 70 percent of the sample. Both of these are best satisfied by television and books. The media's importance in providing personal identity and reality rituals are fourth down the list. Sixty-three percent of the sample claim that the media "order my day" while the same percentage believes that they are important for providing topics of conversation with friends, family, and strangers. Newspapers are again most favored. Entertainment and escape functions so strongly stressed in the United States commercial system are not nearly as important according to this study. They come in fifth place, an evaluation supported by the Yugoslav data. Sixty-one percent of the Israelis believe that cinema helps them release tension and be entertained, but only 16 percent mention that the media, especially television and books, are important for "killing time" or "escaping from reality."

In conclusion, Yugoslav and Israeli data suggest that the media are most successful in fulfilling socio-political and integrative needs as well as those associated with overcoming distance. They are not nearly as useful in gratifying personal ones. Friends and face-to-face contacts are the main support for confidence and security and the best outlet for tension, as well as a great source for learning.[38] Yugoslav studies raise, but do not answer, the question about differences in media use in developing and highly developed countries. Here variations in time spent with television in the various republics and lack of media utilization in Yugoslavia's rural areas suggest that the media are integrated into both the urban and the rural life-styles, but to different degrees and in different ways.[39] Furthermore, what these differences exactly are no one knows at present. Such variation does not seem to be present in highly developed countries where the urban/rural life-styles are more similar and homogenized.[40] While some progress has been made, future studies need to probe much more deeply into the relationship between content categories and various audience types, both in Yugoslavia and abroad, since these seem to be considerably more complex than originally assumed.

Media Uses and Effects

In concluding this chapter, it may be useful to summarize and elaborate on the theoretical advantages of a contextual analysis of the audience. Three of these advantages are particularly important. First, it appears that such an analysis alerts us to the impossibility of searching for a general definition of the "mass" audience, because the latter makes many and variegated uses of media performances. Second, it stresses that the process of mass communication is not an isolated human experience, but an adjunct to the social communication network of which each person is a part. Finally, and most important, it provides a new framework for media effects research which has previously been restricted to a simpleminded cause-effect model.

Previous sections have elaborated that, according to a transactionalist symbolic theory of communication, audiences attending to radio or television performances or reading the daily press are neither passive receptors nor do they lack social cohesion as mass society theory claims. Since there are a multiplicity of contents, individuals, and settings in which people utilize media fare, audiences, when they persist, will have to be differentiated in other ways. Berger suggests that these criteria are largely cultural, because leisure-time activities are determined by ethical and aesthetic rather than by expediency decisions. Different types of leisure and media use thus constitute normative patterns of living which are largely learned from family, friends, and co-workers. Life-styles, in other words, constitute coherent ways of behaving and thus provide a means for partially predicting how a particular group will *use,* and what meanings it will attach to, media offerings.

Audiences, it was suggested, vary according to internal characteristics, structural organization, and processes of group development. The audience for ''All in the Family'' seems to attract people with quite distinctive characteristics; nonprejudiced persons enjoy the show as satire and prejudiced ones because it ''tells it like it is.''[41] The audience for this show, moreover, attracts family groups whose focus of interest seems to be primarily integrative. Specialty magazines, like *One* and *Mattachine Review,* on the other hand, tend to satisfy a utilitarian function by bringing together existing subgroups lacking intercommunication links. Homosexual magazines, according to James Carey, turn locally based, decentralized, tenuously connected subcultures into a highly identifiable group, and link it to the larger society by providing a common ideology and an explanation of acceptable behavior. Specialty media thus bring together groups which were formerly dependent on face-to-face contact and link them over large geographical distances into audiences. A successful television series may also create entirely new publics by providing collective symbols which transcend time, space, and culture. Carey notes: ''By going public, that is by publishing, they nationalise a culture, create a national speech community, a standardised body of symbols, and a characteristic expressive style.''[42]

An interactive theory of the audience has a second theoretical advantage in that it draws attention to the fact that mass communication use is an adjunct to the social communication network of which we are all a part. The basic dynamic of mass communication thus inheres in the social and personal uses to which programs are put. It suggests that the morning news or the *Atlantic Monthly* may serve many functions. They may be used as a way of informing ourselves about international and cultural events; or as a source of conversation with friends or acquaintances. Finally, they may serve as a status symbol, identifying us as belonging to a particular group in society.[43] Such a socio-psychological interpretation must, however, be balanced by considerations of what media content is "available" at any particular point in time in a particular country. The Yugoslav data showed conclusively that availability is determined by economic and political considerations which shape both the dissemination network as well as the way in which knowledge about our human environment is coded.

Karl Rosengren notes that one use for the media is to function as an alternative for social interaction. Media performances can thus become supplements, complements, or substitutes for social interaction, depending on a person's psychological capabilities, social setting, and motives for turning to the mass media. Katz's work indicates, however, that the concept of "social interaction" may be too general a term for an adequate analysis of needs which can be satisfied by the media. He proposes a three-fold use typology based on self-identity, self-growth, and gratification, as well as needs springing from such institutions as politics, the family, religion, and education.

In addition, the Yugoslav studies and the Israeli data clarify those areas where the media are particularly successful substitutes for human interaction. Here the cumulative evidence points to the fact that the mass media are definitely not all powerful. They are largely limited to satisfying socio-politically related needs.[44] On the cognitive level, the media, especially print, help strengthen knowledge, information, and understanding, and on the integrative self-identity level, they strengthen confidence and stability. The media also help overcome distance, as previously mentioned, and are thus most influential in molding our view of faraway places and unknown people. They are much less able to satisfy affective needs where face-to-face contacts, primarily with friends, are most salient. For self-gratification, emotional experience, and such integrative needs as stability, credibility, confidence, status, and contact, we turn first and foremost to people. Only when people are not available, or the individual is psychologically incapacitated, may the media enter the picture as substitutes. Here more work along the lines pioneered by Rosengren in Sweden needs to be done.

Third, and most important, an interactive and symbolic theory of communication and the audience provides a new framework for the study of media effects. This simple-minded behavioral model assumed that the characteristics of both content and source alone cause changes in the attitudes or behavior of the audience. Communication viewed as an independent variable or stimulus has various weaknesses. It underestimates the role of the audience in determining media uses and effects. It also assumes that audiences like isotopes remain constant in the mass communication process. Finally, it believes that "meaning" is somehow transmitted where in fact only coded data are exchanged and "meaning" is attached by the receiver depending on his or her goals or purposes in attending to the content.

A symbolic perspective indicates that communication behavior is more fruitfully studied as a dependent variable. Though many of these interrelationships are as yet impossible to unravel, some connections are beginning to emerge. In order to understand human behavior, researchers must specify its social origins, the processes by which it is learned, and how it is maintained.[45] To do this, five types of variables seem most relevant: (1) age or position in the life-cycle of the receiver; (2) social structural constraints which affect learning; (3) the agent or source of the influence; (4) the learning process involved in socialization; and (5) the communication behavior to be explained.

Though the author does not completely share the conception that communication can best be studied in terms of various *fixed* stages of learning, a socialization perspective is indeed useful in that it takes into account more variables. Our approach to social relations as an ongoing adaptive process in which congruence and accuracy of symbolic understanding are central to behavior, emphasizes both the flexibility of human communication as well as its cultural base. In spite of these reservations, the material assembled in this chapter, both from audience studies in Yugoslavia and other parts of the world, can conveniently be summarized in terms of the above-mentioned variables.

Table 32 illustrates that media use is influenced quite differently in Yugoslavia by age or position in life-cycle than on the North American continent. Here the older group watches and reads less than the two younger generations, though United States data suggests that both of these activities increase with age.[46] Much of this variance, in the country of the South Slavs, was reinforced by such structural constraints as social status and can be measured by a combination of education and occupational characteristics. These influence which medium is utilized more extensively and for what purposes. The same table shows that print is more prevalent among the better educated and the professional, or white-collar, groups than others, though they in general tended to use all of the media more.

Agents or sources of influence, namely, available media programming, were seen to be related to audience preferences. It became apparent that news and public affairs programming was less preferred and less utilized by Yugoslav audiences in both print and electronic presentations than entertainment, in spite of its availability. Though the audiences for informative or more reality related programming are smaller all over the world, the sharp drop in Yugoslav interest was an indication of more stringent filtering of the political information content in that country. This may be a case of what Chaney would call a lack of "social accessibility" of certain types of performance. The drop in audience interest came about not as a result of the absence of certain decoding skills, but because of discrepancies between perceived political realities in Yugoslavia and their descriptions in the media.

Finally, the learning processes involved in socialization are still relatively little understood, and what is known pertains largely to the United States.

Doubtlessly the situation in Yugoslavia is quite different. In general, however, learning emerges from the social interaction between a child and significant others and is later in life influenced by one's circle of friends and co-workers. An audience's ability to recognize the symbols of certain roles and statuses which guide proper interaction is widely affected by the norms and values learned from others. Much research remains to be done about how these conceptions are developed and how they are related to other group values. In the United States, Jack McLeod and Garrett O'Keefe's study of family communication patterns and media use has made a suggestive beginning, using multivariate analysis. In general, it appears that adolescents from "protective" homes are higher television users than those from other types of families. Yet young people from "pluralistic" backgrounds are at one and the same time least interested in television per se, but watch a greater proportion of news and public affairs, a correlation which has not yet been successfully explained.[47]

In Yugoslavia, the study of adolescent leisure-time utilization, though not conceptualized in terms of family authority patterns, provides evidence of differences in leisure patterns between boys and girls, as well as between those with farming, working, or professional family backgrounds. Favorite activities showed girls more interested in pop music, dancing, and outings with friends than boys, who favored sports, exhibits, and newspaper reading. Family backgrounds were clearly influential in theater attendance, organizational membership, and museum attendance, all of which were more prevalent among children from professional families. Dancing was most favored by those from working families, while attendance in cafes is a universal pastime in Yugoslavia for *all* adolescents.

Media use was generally ranked low as a favorite leisure-time activity, far behind dancing, outings, and sports, which were selected by 13 percent, 10 percent, and 5 percent of all students. Television viewing, radio listening, records, and reading attracted only 2 percent of young people's votes and were relatively evenly distributed across family type.[48] It is fair to say that much more research needs to be done about the antecedents of communication behavior before a realistic picture can emerge. In general, it is argued here that learning viewed as interaction between people, rather than as mere modeling or reinforcement, will provide a better understanding of the way in which human communication behavior becomes transferred and utilized.

In conclusion, it may be noted that the earlier tradition of effects studies seems to be merging with the uses and gratification approach in the latest research. This shift counterbalances the historical overemphasis on the power of the media to *do* things *to* people, with a more balanced view which investigates what people *do with* coded or symbolic knowledge about their condition and environment. In attempting a synthesis, new and more careful distinctions will have to be made among needs, gratifications, contents, and expectations. Certainly, as Rosengren and Halloran argue, it must be expected that mass media uses will vary with amount of consumption, type of motive for seeking out this alternative, and degrees of dependence and involvement.[49] However, in addition to these factors, the symbolic dimensions of performances must also be considered. Here it appeared that "legitimacy" is determined partly by what is physically available and partly by the conventions which social subgroups bring to the mass media material they utilize. The reason for this lies in the often-mentioned fact that media content is more than neutral food for thought. It selects, values, and legitimizes what any given audience at a particular place and time considers to be "real."

---

1 Herbert Blumer, "Collective Behavior," pp. 185-186.

2 Chaney, *Processes of Mass Communication,* pp. 15-16.

3 Z. C. Kadushin, "Power, Influence and Social Circles: A New Methodology for Studying Opinion-Makers," pp. 685-699.

4 Chaney, *Processes of Mass Communication,* p. 52.

5 Herbert J. Gans, *The Urban Villagers: Groups and Class in the Life of Italian-Americans,* pp. 181-196.

6 Dennis McQuail, "Uncertainty about the Audience and the Organization of Mass Communications," pp. 77-81.

7 Elihu Katz and Paul Lazarsfeld, *Personal Influence,* p. 21.

8 Karl Erik Rosengren, "News Diffusion: An Overview," p. 1.

9 Canada, *Report of the Special Senate Committee on Mass Media,* p. 11.

10 Dennison Rusinow, "Population Review 1970: Yugoslavia," p. 3.

11 Igor Leandrov, "Oblici ponašanja, stavovi i preferencije televizikih gledalaca u Jugoslaviji," p. 2.

12 *Ibid.,* pp. 5-6.

13 Karl Erik Rosengren and Gwen Windahl, "Mass Media Consumption as a Functional Alternative," pp. 166-194.

14 Canadian Broadcasting Corporation, *Annual Report, 1969-1970,* p. 53.

15 Igor Leandrov, "Istrazivanje dnevni barometar u RT Beograd," p. 5.

16 Miroslav Djordjevic, *Mesto i uloga trećeg programa radio-Beograd u sistem u difuzije kulturnih vrednosti,* pp. 6, 9, 12, 13.

17 *Yugoslavia Radio-Television Yearbook 1970,* p. 169.

18 Ivko Pustišek, "Materijalni i finansijski uslovi radija i televizija Jugoslavije," p. 15.

19 *Yugoslavia Radio-Television Yearbook 1970,* p. 239.

20 Leonard LoSciuto, *A National Inventory of Television Viewing Behavior,* p. 35.

21 Igor Leandrov, "Oblici ponašanja," p. 5.

22 Zivorad Stoković, "Tiraz jugoslovenskih dnevnih i većih nedeljnih listova u 1970 godini," pp. 179-181.

23 Jugoslovenski institut za novinarstvo, *Masovna komunikacija u jugoslaviji,* pp. 25, 96.

24 Firdus Džinić, "Rasinrenost političko-informativnog dejstva radija, TV i štampe u SFR Jugoslaviji."

25 Prvosalav S. Plavčić, *Odnos Beogradjana prema programima Radio Beograd,* p. 34.

26 Leandrov, "Oblici ponašanja," p. 10.

27 Tapio Varis, "Global Traffic in Television," p. 104.

28 Krešo Baumštark, "Opažanja o programu radija," p. 68.

29 Ionescu, *The Politics of the European Communist States,* pp. 169-180.

30 Bennet Berger, "The Sociology of Leisure."

31 H. D. Lasswell, "The Structure and Function of Communication in Society."

32 Leandrov, "Oblici ponašanja," p. 6.

33 *Ibid.,* p. 13.

34 Jay G. Blumler, "Audience Roles in Political Communication: Some Reflections on Their Structure, Antecedents and Consequences," p. 7.

35 Pavle Novosel, "How the Young Spend Their Free Time?," p. 14.

36 Elihu Katz, Michael Gurevitch, and Hadassah Haas, "On the Use of the Mass Media for Important Things," pp. 164-181.

37 Dennis McQuail, Jay G. Blumler and J. R. Brown, "The Television Audience: A Revised Perspective," pp. 177-179.

38 Katz, Gurevitch, and Haas, "On the Use of the Mass Media," pp. 177-179.

39 Joel Halpern, *A Serbian Village*.

40 Gerald F. Kline, "Media Time Budgeting as a Function of Demographics and Life Style," pp. 211-221.

41 Neil Vidmar and Milton Roheach, "Archie Bunker's Bigotry: A Study in Selective Perception and Exposure," p. 37.

42 James W. Carey, "The Communication Revolution and the Professional Communicator," p. 26.

43 Lee Thayer, "On the Mass Media and Mass Communication: Notes toward a Theory."

44 Alex S. Edelstein, *The Uses of Communication in Decision-Making, a Comparative Study of Yugoslavia and the United States*.

45 Jack M. McLeod and Garrett J. O'Keefe Jr., "The Socialization Perspective and Communication Behavior."

46 M. Samuelson, R. F. Carter, and W. L. Ruggles, "Education, Available Time and Use of the Mass Media," pp. 491-496.

47 McLeod and O'Keefe, Jr., "The Socialization Perspective," p. 151.

48 Novosel, "How the Young Spend Their Free Time," pp. 65-66.

49 Halloran, *The Effects of Television*, pp. 9-68.

Epilogue

To summarize a study as complex and diversified as this one is virtually impossible. How to recapitulate Yugoslavia's movement from a central to a regional media organization in the past thirty years? How to explain the changeover from an overtly political to a professional management in newspapers, radio stations, and the national news agency? How to sketch the changes in media content resulting from the substitution of audience for government financing? How, in addition, to highlight the essential characteristics of the country's journalism corps and the changing role of the audience? Instead of recapitulating what has already been said, this epilogue will discuss a few of the study's most important findings.

To begin with, the book has argued that the party is not monolithic and that the interrelationship between various party groups, the press, and the people is not simple. Political scientists like Ghita Ionescu[1] and Gordon Skilling[2] have documented the existence of at least four groups with power to articulate their opinions and to check the apparat in policy making. In descending order of influence, these are official bureaucracies such as the military, security, and economic managers. Their proximity to the leadership helps them articulate their opinions. Then there are the legislative, judicial, mass media, and cultural organizations. These include the intellectuals who are also strong contributors to public opinion formation. Last in order of influence come the workers and peasants who have bargaining power only as producers.

Since the media function as platforms and articulators of those who are able to speak out, Yugoslavia's liberalized media organization and content in the 1960s reflected a new balance between institutional order and freedom. Earlier on, as has been seen, national government and party bureaucracies ran the media through a variety of censorship procedures and content was primarily defined in terms of official political goals. A decade later professionalized mass communicators increasingly became the spokesmen for a variety of groups, often introducing conflicting points of view into Yugoslavia's political communication stream. A similar plurality emerged in economics and culture where administrators and technocrats as well as writers and university professors expressed their frequently dissident views. Yugoslavia consequently became the single most interesting example of socialist democracy in action.

The introduction at this writing of yet another media reorganization highlights another important finding. Under the surface of kaleidoscopic change and adaptation the political power over the media has remained virtually static throughout the past thirty years. It has shifted merely from the national to local party hierarchies and back again. Instead of solving the incongruities between the democratic self-management principles and party needs, new organizational forms were in fact devised *not* to affect the power base. While it is beyond the scope of this epilogue to fully evaluate the proposed 1975 setup, its aims will be scrutinized in relation to the new groups who will have access to decision making.

What is touted as the right to public access through the ''delegate system'' turns out to be a subtle means for neutralizing the crystallization and expression of public opinion. According to the new statutes, public representation will take three forms. There is to be increased representation through parity on publishers' councils, which are to be converted into two-chamber bodies. In addition there are to be two new supervisory bodies in the media, the ''joint editorial councils'' and the ''local information councils.'' The former are to have about ten to fifteen ''public'' members and to provide critical appraisal of media output; the latter are to function as intermediaries between broadcasters and their audiences. Mijalko Todorović claims ''the essential change introduced by the delegate system lies in the fact that decision-making in the broader socio-political communities is no longer exercised by some kind of general political representatives but through a type of political institution which ensures that interests formed in the base of the society are directly represented in the centers of political power.''[3]

Closer scrutiny reveals that the ''delegates'' on the new councils represent other organized groups, such as trade unions; the local administration; and factory, educational, and cultural groups. Still excluded from participation are private individuals of all sorts, as well as rank-and-file workers who are the backbone of Yugoslavia's self-management system. Federal statistics indicate that since the 1960s the already small representation of workers in public life has further declined. In 1963 there were 5.5 percent workers in the Federal Assembly as compared to .6 percent (five representatives) six years later. The same trend is visible in republican and regional assemblies, where participation dropped from 7.5 percent to 1.3 percent. Only in communal assemblies has representation of workers remained virtually stable at the 14 percent level between 1963 and 1969.[4]

This state of affairs corroborates that most reorganizations of public and media bodies have not involved the redistribution of political power. A Yugoslav commentator notes with regret: "It is not the associated workers who decide the existential issues of their own state, but it is the other way round — the state decides about these issues. . . . Only when associated workers will have been offered a chance to spell out what they really want from their 'state,' how much of their 'state' they need, and what 'state' they desire, will it be possible to remove the discrepancy between words and deeds and to carry out reforms."[5]

All over the world the media serve as a channel between the governors and the governed, transmitting information and values through which social and political courses of action become defined. They also help integrate conflicting needs and formulate critical outlooks which serve as a check on government. Performance of these roles requires a balancing of economic necessities against normative demands.

The major difference between Yugoslavia and the United States our study shows is that the balancing of media roles is primarily determined by political ideology in the former and by market values in the latter. In Yugoslavia's political communication system, social integration is assumed to be the prerogative of government and party councils whose norms dominate the articulation of public opinion. In the United States, it is generally accepted that the balancing is left to chance or to the interplay of various governmental groupings and market pressures. The upshot is that the Yugoslav press and broadcasting must tone down sensationalism and the reporting of "soft" news in the name of social responsibility. American chains and networks on the other hand are not guided by a conception of what is "good" for "John Q. Public" but what sells.

Still another finding of this study is that the clash between the dictates of self-management and the demands of the one-party state lead to severe contradictions in the role of the audience and of journalists in Yugoslavia's communication system. Though the media through their publishers and other councils are to be responsive to audience inputs, it appears that opinion pluralism is more evident in the cultural and economic than the political realms. Throughout the 1960s the Yugoslav audience which finances newspapers and broadcast stations has pushed for and received more entertaining content by buying papers and periodicals with a lighter content mix. Yet in the 1970s such audience preferences have once again been deemed frivolous, and "soft" news production has come under increased scrutiny and criticism. What balance will ultimately be struck between information and entertainment and how this will affect the financial survival of Yugoslavia's media is still an open question in need of a solution.

For journalists the contradictions arising from combining the articulation of party values with responsible reporting to the audience have meant a precarious balance between their advocate and public roles. It was frequently noted how difficult it is to be a critic in a situation where criticism must be "constructive." Since the leadership has reverted to a democratic-centralist style of rule without the right of minority dissent, the communicator must oscillate between justifying the top and expressing the base. Our data show that in peaceful times the public is better served than in times of national crisis. During the latter both publishers' councils and party colleagues urge the communicator to become a spokesman for the local party outlook in order to protect his precarious social status.

What about the future? Here as in so many past instances President Tito seems to be an accurate barometer of his country's mood. At eighty-four this last of the surviving wartime leaders is retiring from the world stage. Yugoslavia under his leadership has turned from a country with revolutionary zeal and a unique vision for the humanization of socialism into a country satisfied with its existing governmental system and preoccupied with its substantial standard of living. Precisely this economic success is what troubles both the leadership and some intellectuals, but for exactly opposite reasons. Yugoslavia's headlong rush toward affluence, which tripled real incomes during the past fifteen years, is exacerbating economic imbalances within the country and dampening people's zeal for such socialist goals as greater income, regional equalization, and enterprise equalization. In 1972, therefore, President Tito severely criticized his party's flabbiness and reverted to measures which have saddened his Western admirers.[6] Among these are purges of the ranks, some recentralization of power in the party's national hierarchy, a muting of the press, stricter economic controls, and stern warnings against Western "intellectual poisons."

Some Yugoslav students, intellectuals, economic administrators, and artists, on the other hand, are troubled because the potentialities of their country's unique participatory principles have never been truly tested. Self-management, they claim, was not allowed to evolve out of its factory setting and penetrate the society as a whole. By equating self-management with market values alone, they argue, and failing to apply them to the political realm, these principles seem to have become obsolete before maturing into a viable and humanistic social system. According to one observer, "the reason . . . is not that normative systems do not agree with actual processes in our worker organizations, nor is it that they do not determine social activity as a whole, but rather that they motivate this activity less and less."[7] As a result Yugoslavia in the mid-1970s has moved out of the political and ideological limelight where its maverick actions used to garner respect and admiration.

The country's immediate future is further darkened by a number of other debilitating pressures which, added to its inability to take the leap into political democratization, are causing grave concern. Among these are Yugoslavia's precarious political existence vis-à-vis the Soviet Union and the potential internal strife engendered by the succession and nationalities problems. As long ago as December, 1971, C. L. Sulzberger noted that "there is every probability that when the aging Marshal Tito dies, Moscow will use every trick short of outright intervention to try and either disintegrate Yugoslavia or bring it under Kremlin influence, something that has not been the case for twenty-three years."[8] The reason for this pressure lies in the Soviet's desire to eradicate once and for all the independent-of-Moscow regimes in Rumania and Albania which together with Yugoslavia have provided leaks in the Warsaw Pact military and COMECON economic alliance systems.

Frequent Yugoslav and United States press reports testify to the continued seriousness of this threat and indicate that Sulzberger's predictions were not pure fabrication. As recently as November, 1975, *Politika,* a Belgrade paper, announced that nine more persons had been arrested for pro-Soviet activities which subverted the local order. The article continued that since 1974 as many as 200 "Cominformists" may have been arrested, and the *New York Times* notes that those who came to public trial received long sentences.[9]

Another area of concern is the potential succession crisis smoldering just below the surface of Yugoslav politics in spite of President Tito's 1970 creation of a twenty-two-man collective presidency. This group, which is to take over after his death, will be divided into an executive of eight, made up of the republics' chief executives and the heads of the two autonomous provinces, plus a larger group of fourteen, and will be elected for five years. The succession crisis has two potential foci, one having to do with the group's ability to rule and the other concerning the seeming lack of qualified younger party chiefs growing up in the shadow of President Tito.

Yugoslav sources claim that effective collective rule will be determined by the leaders' personality and their relationship to the Federal Assembly. If they fail, the army, Yugoslavia's only centralized agency, will probably take over, and it is difficult to be optimistic about the implications of such a step for the continuation of self-managed socialism. The inability of younger leaders to flex their political muscles under the watchful eyes of the aging president may in turn prove detrimental to the stability of the country in the post-Tito era. It is well known that the resignations of such important functionaries as Marko Nikesić and Mirko Trepavać have inhibited the appearance of bright new personalities on Yugoslavia's political stage.

The final area of concern has historic roots and cuts across all matters Yugoslav. It has to do with the waxing and waning of the nationalities question. Though great strides have been made and successive constitutions have given the republics increasing autonomy over their own affairs, nationalism continues to cause strife. It permeates every facet of Yugoslav existence from the sublime to the ridiculous. It is a crucial element in national security planning, Soviet infiltration, the succession question, economic policies, tourism, education, media organization, and programming, not to mention the inability to choose a "representative" Yugoslav novel to submit for an international competition. How to cope with this virulent infection is of major concern to statesmen not only in the developing but also the developed worlds. Britain, Belgium, and

Canada join Yugoslavia, Lebanon, Nigeria, and others in trying to formulate adequate legislation which will make it possible for different races to live and work together peacefully. Up to now the progress has been slow and painful and in many instances less than spectacular. The reason may lie in the fact that contrary to Schopenhauer who said "the cheapest sort of pride is national pride,"[10] many people still view their national identification as of fundamental importance.

To chart a course for future communication research in Yugoslavia during the twilight 1970s is difficult if not impossible. Irrespective of what happens on the world stage, much remains to be done to clarify the working of Yugoslavia's maverick media. The early history, contemporary organization, and functioning of the country's self-managed media units are well covered by Yugoslav research. Less is known about the role of film and publishing, both of which merit greater attention since they were in the forefront of the 1950s campaign abrogating "socialist realism" in culture.

Regulation and control of the media, both formal and informal, are also relatively well understood, but there is a lack of studies of the relationship between media pesonnel and economic elites. How exactly have filtering practices changed in the past twenty years? How do large industries like Inex or General Export affect the information collection and distribution of Tanjug as well as the journalistic access to and coverage of economic issues in the firms' municipalities? It is known that the country's information flow contains at least three different streams, political, economic, and cultural. But it is not known exactly what these flows contain or how they differ from republic to republic.

Quite a bit has been written about the role of the national news agency in selecting and channeling international news to the Yugoslav media and about Tanjug's attempt to create a news product for third world distribution which will avoid some of the geographical and political biases of Anglo-Saxon reporting.[11] But much still remains to be done in the analysis of world news flows connecting countries with different cultures and political systems.

Though Yugoslav research institutes often survey questions of political and cultural concern, they lack funds to undertake investigations concerning journalists or audience members. The socio-political and demographic aspects of these two groups have been analyzed by the Yugoslav Journalists' Association, the Institute of Journalism, and the RTV audience bureaus. But it is not known whether Yugoslav journalists perform their jobs in ways different from their colleagues elsewhere or what they think about their professional responsibilities to themselves and to their audiences. Studies of women in the profession, their assignments, and their promotions are also lacking.

A number of investigations have documented regional variations in Yugoslav media availability, but less is known about differences in media utilization patterns throughout the country. Additional topics of interest are comparisons of audience roles in socialist and capitalist countries,[12] typologies explaining media utilization and the relationships between content preferences and political ideology. The questions of whether entertaining content is universally preferred and how much space or time should be devoted to it are still hotly debated. We are also in need of comparative data on socialization patterns to explain differences in Yugoslav and North American audience perceptions of the world.

Still another area of inquiry in need of research concerns public access to media organizations. Cable legislation in the United States favors an "access" model where groups are responsible for program ideas, production, and promotion. Canada, on the other hand, has opted for what Vernone Sparkes calls a "facilitator" approach, which places the cable caster in charge of developing community programming on the public channel.[13] Yugoslavia's new "delegate system" has not come to grips with this question and favors neither approach.

A final area of future research must deal with technological communication innovations and their impact on society. Who will control and have access to cable when it comes to Yugoslavia? How will regional networks be affected by satellite communication? What about the balance between local, regional, and federal cable networks in the country's multi-ethnic republics? These and similar questions need answers to permit future planning.

Summing up Yugoslavia's experiment in media self-management, the outside observer cannot but feel both elated and sad. This ambivalence results from the realization that though self-management has great potential for the press and broadcasting, this potential has been only partially explored. There is no doubt that the contemporary Yugoslav media are much more responsible to their varied audiences than is usual in other socialist systems. Yet, in spite of this, Yugoslav regulatory changes have up to now failed to integrate community groups into media governance. Entertainment and relaxing content are more available in Yugoslavia than in Poland or Hungary, but media professionals still view themselves as the rightful custodians of public knowledge, rather than as facilitators of public debate.

Furthermore, the dual trends of more stringent political information filtering and increased attacks on students, intellectuals, and artists are causing widespread concern at home and abroad. Both of these reinforce the disconcerting use of self-management principles to subvert cultural freedom of expression through self-censorship. Why ban Dušan Makavejev's film *WR: Or the Mystery of the Organism* which spoofs Soviet, United States, and Yugoslav ideologies?[14] Why close the Belgrade, Zagreb, and Ljubljana student papers in 1974 and a year later insist on the administrative removal of Marxist faculty from Belgrade university?[15]

Taken together these events raise questions about the degree of social criticism which will be permissible in Yugoslavia in the future. Whether a pluralistic balance will be maintained or not is impossible to predict at this time. All that can be said is that all those who favor the Yugoslav experiment in democratic socialism hope for its survival.

1 Ionescu, *European Communist States*, p. 155ff.

2 Gordon H. Skilling, "Group Conflict and Political Change," in Chalmers Johnson, *Change in Communist Systems*, (Palo Alto: Stanford University Press, 1970), pp. 215-234.

3 Mijalko Todorović, *Report on the Final Draft of the Constitution of the Socialist Federal Republic of Yugoslavia* (Ljubljana: Dopisna Delavska Univerza, 1974), p. 34.

4 Djordje Tozi and D. Petrović, "Political Relations and Composition of Assemblies and Socio-Political Communities," *Socialism*, XII:3 (1969), p. 1591.

5 Antun Zvan, "Ecstasy and Hangover of a Revolution," *Praxis* (Zagreb), VIII:3/4 (Fall/Winter, 1971), p. 484.

6 Sterling, "Balancing Act," p. 43.

7 Vjelko Rus, "Selfmanagement Egalitarianism and Social Differentiation," *Praxis* (Zagreb) VII:1/2, (Spring/Summer, 1970), p. 251.

8 C. L. Sulzberger, "Old Clouds in the East," *New York Times*, December 3, 1971.

9 Malcolm Browne, "Yugoslavs Seize Pro-Soviet Group," *New York Times*, November 23, 1975.

10 Arthur Schopenhauer, *Philosophy of Arthur Schopenhauer* (New York: Tudor Publishing Co., 1946), p. 52.

11 Malcolm Browne, "Yugoslavs Build World News Unit," *New York Times*, January 25, 1976.

12 Jay Blumer, "Audience Roles in Political Communication: Some Reflections on Their Structure, Antecedents, and Consequences," paper presented at the International Political Science Association Convention, Montreal, August 12-25, 1973, pp. 5-6

13 Vernone Sparkes, "Community Cable Casting in the United States and Canada: Different Approaches to a Common Objective," *Journal of Broadcasting* (Fall, 1976), forthcoming.

14 Pavlovitch, *Yugoslavia*, pp. 350-352.

15 Yugoslav Embassy, Washington, "On the Ideological and Moral Fitness of Professors and Teaching Staff at Belgrade University," *Telos*, XVIII (Winter, 1973/74), pp. 156-158. See also the response by Praxis Philosophen, "Auf dem Rückweg zum Stalinismus?," *Süddeutsche Zeitung*, Nr. 22, Sonntag 26/27 (January, 1974).

Code of Yugoslav Journalism

*Adopted at the VI Congress in 1965
and Amended at the Tenth Assembly
of the Yugoslav Journalists' Association
in 1969*

Taking as the point of departure the Constitution and laws on the position in society, function and freedom of the press, radio, and television, and considering the role of journalism in the Yugoslav socialist society, taking into account the publicness of work of state bodies and organs of social self-government, organizations, and bearers of public functions and competences, the Sixth Congress of the Yugoslav Journalists' Association has adopted a code determining the moral, political, and professional standards of journalism.

1. *General Principles*

Role, Function, and Status of Journalists

A journalist is a socio-political worker who, by carrying out his activity publicly, through the written or spoken word, cartoon, photograph, and film, takes part in the construction and development of the socialist society and strives for the fulfillment of the rights of the working people to self-government and for the establishment of humane relations among people. He is thus contributing to the development of socialist consciousness and to the forming of the socialist public opinion on all social phenomena and on concrete policies in various walks of life.

Acting in keeping with his socialist conscience and being aware of his own obligations and responsibilities toward the socialist public, a journalist should give correct information and interpret developments and phenomena truthfully and comprehensively.

In his polemics with and criticism of different views and attitudes, a journalist respects the equality of all people and their views.

A journalist struggles against bureaucratic, monopolistic, chauvinist, nationalist, and anti–self-governing tendencies and against all phenomena which hamper the development of socialist democracy. He likewise struggles for socialist and humane relations among people, for the all-round respect of man's freedom and dignity, and for the comprehensive respect of freedom, dignity, and equality of all our peoples and nationalities.

A journalist prevents misinformation of the public, combatting the introduction and maintenance among the public of all that is false, fabricated, and unverified.

The Journalist within the System of Information

A journalist is bound to preserve the social and professional reputation of his profession.

A journalist analyzes social processes, phenomena, and contradictions, and, with the help of objective realizations, forms his own views and attitudes and informs the public of them. As a committed socio-political worker he conveys, encourages, and sets in motion broad-based exchanges of views in the society and makes his contribution to the activity of socialist forces in the constant transformation of our society on the basis of socialist social self-government.

The aim of a journalist is to make mass information media an open platform accessible to all working people in the country. It is the social and professional obligation of a journalist comprehensively and objectively to inform the working people of social phenomena, needs, and relations so as to enable them to carry out their self-governing function as successfully as possible.

A journalist cooperates with sources of information, sees to their expansion and to increasing information and improving its quality.

A journalist respects embargo and all other agreed upon conditions for making information public and keeps secret the data obtained for his personal information exclusively.

A journalist departs from the fact that all information services are fully responsible before the society for the data given to a journalist for the purpose of being released.

He informs the public about the work of representative and other self-governing bodies, socio-political organizations, and public forums conveying without bias the expressed opinions and views.

In adopting his own views, a journalist relies on basic and generally accepted socialist principles and standards.

A journalist and his editorial board rectify on their own initiative any information released and later proved to be incorrect.

2. Moral-Political and Professional Obligations of a Journalist

A journalist is bound to endeavor on every occasion to give the public correct and objective information.

A journalist shall rather not release news than publish inaccurate and unreliable facts. A journalist bears in mind that any damage caused in this way can never be undone by any subsequent explanation or denial, regardless of the way in which this may be done.

Professional Integrity

A journalist is not obliged to reveal the source of information if the person who gives such information does not wish him to do so.

A journalist enjoys full integrity in his editorial board.

A journalist adheres to the principle that the following activities are incompatible with his professional morality: plagiarism; the collecting or mediating in the collecting of advertisements or texts of such a character; part-time and other relations with organizations through which objective information may be directly or indirectly jeopardized; damaging the reputation of his profession.

In his working organization a journalist combats all phenomena of unfair competitive relations toward other working organizations engaged in public information.

Respect of Man's Personality and Dignity

The respect of man's personality and dignity is an essential moral principle of our society which pledges a journalist to treat man, his actions and characteristics with full responsibility.

This principle presumes the special obligation of journalists to respect the right of individuals to private life which cannot be made public without the consent of the person in question.

The respect of man's personality and dignity comes to expression, among other things, through the journalists' approach in dealing in public with delicate themes, with a developed feeling for what is ethical. Such themes include: sexual excesses and perversions, prostitution, juvenile delinquency, maladjustment, suicide, and attempted suicide.

Articles on the above subjects should be deprived of any vulgarity, exaggeration, mockery, humiliation, provocation, and the like.

Any presentation of moral deformities or criminal acts or habits as normal occurrences in human society and therefore as acceptable phenomena is alien to a journalist.

A journalist exercises special responsibility and caution in publishing articles about elemental disasters, traffic, and other accidents, especially in publishing the names of persons.

A journalist approaches with exceptional caution the publication of reports on serious diseases of individuals and the actions of persons with physical or mental deficiencies.

A journalist deliberately avoids the public identification of persons by giving their names, initials, photographs, or films when this is not of essential importance for his information or when indicated by discretion. The public identification of persons who represent a permanent and direct danger to others is not contrary to journalists' ethics.

In headlines or otherwise, a journalist does not accentuate the race, nationality, profession, or religion of the persons about whom he writes, especially those arrested, accused, or sentenced, if this is not of exceptional significance for the case in point.

A journalist and his editorial board refrain from publishing statements, indictments, and accusations intended to cause scandal, serve as a means of extortion, or cause damage to a person's reputation.

A journalist does not prejudice court decisions by supporting one side only, nor does he make public statements and written documents submitted in court by one side only. A journalist avoids the public identification of persons suspected of crimes, arrested, or called to appear in court, during proceedings preceding formal indictment. The public identification of the victims of rape or other criminal offences is not permissible under any circumstances.

3. *Relations among Journalists*

A journalist is bound to strengthen professional solidarity and relations of comradeship in his working organization.

It is alien to him: — to misinform other journalists while on professional assignment; — to present another journalist in a bad light in order to improve his own position or to gain higher salary, if this causes material or moral damage to the former; — to prevent another journalist from publishing his articles or hinder him in doing so for reasons of personal intolerance; — to distort the meaning and substance of the text written by another journalist by arbitrarily making changes in it.

Any important change in a text is made together with the author. The author has the right to withdraw his signature from the text if he considers that the correctness of his information has become questionable through editing or that essential changes have been made without justification.

4. *Final Provisions*

Criteria and standards of this code are binding for all members of the Yugoslav Journalists' Association.

Editorial boards shall adhere to the criteria and standards of the code even if texts written by authors who are not members of the Yugoslav Journalists' Association are in question.

A journalist who acts in the spirit of this code enjoys the full support of his editorial board and professional organization. A journalist especially enjoys this support in the following cases: if he cannot carry out his task properly because the competent organs or sources of information have failed to supply him with the necessary data; if he has trouble for having published material the veracity of which has been checked and the release of which is not in contradiction with the law; or if he is deprived of information the publication of which is not in explicit contradiction with the law.

A journalist applies the criteria and standards of this code by applying them consistently in his everyday work and by expressing his views in his working organization, in journalists' actives, in sections, or elsewhere, on the contents and the factual aspect of the texts written by other journalists if the principles of truthfulness and objectivity are violated by such texts, thus damaging the social reputation of journalists.

The editorial board applies the standards and criteria of this code in the following ways: by making public the opinions of citizens about the contents and factual aspect of the texts written by its own members or by journalists from other working organizations, if the principles of truthfulness and objectiveness are violated in this way, thus damaging the reputation of journalists and public information media; by taking first-degree proceedings against the violation of professional ethics in accordance with normative regulations of the working organization.

Actives and sections of journalists' organizations apply the standards and criteria of this code by publicly considering the violation of professional ethics at their meetings and advising editorial boards and the courts of honor of professional organizations to initiate the necessary proceedings.

Forums and organs of the journalists' organizations apply the standards and criteria of this code by proposing, on a suggested or their own initiative, that proceedings be initiated in the working organization, actives, sections, or in the courts of honor.

The courts of honor of the journalists' organizations initiate on a suggested or on their own initiative, proceedings for the protection of the standards and criteria of this code, in keeping with the statutes of the Republican journalists' associations and the statute of the Yugoslav Journalists' Association.

Accepting the text of this code as the minimum of ethical standards, working organizations in the information domain and the Republican journalists' associations can further elaborate and amend individual parts of the code by their own documents.

Content of the Three Geographical Foreign Policy Registers (1964)

Country	Total Items Listed	Country	Total Items Listed
Europe			
1. Albania	82	19. German	
2. Austria	78	Democratic	
3. Balkans	21	Republic	72
4. Belgium	44	20. Germany	177
5. Benelux	8	21. Norway	38
6. Berlin	27	22. Poland	99
7. Bulgaria	92	23. Portugal	28
8. Czechoslovakia	98	24. Rumania	99
9. Denmark	35	25. San Marino,	
10. Europe	35	Monaco, etc.	5
11. Finland	36	26. Scandinavia	21
12. France	227	27. Russia	450
13. Greece	92	28. Spain	24
14. Holland	39	29. Switzerland	31
15. Iceland	11	30. Sweden	35
16. Italy	209	31. Vatican	24
17. Luxembourg	13	32. Great Britain	229
18. Hungary	120		
The Americas			
1. United States	262	6. Chile	30
2. Canada	34	7. Dominican	
3. Argentina	33	Republic	7
4. Bolivia	9	8. Equador	8
5. Brazil	39	9. Guatemala	7

Country	Total Items Listed
10. Haiti	7
11. Honduras	7
12. Columbia	7
13. Costa Rica	7
14. Cuba	67
15. Mexico	30
16. Nicaragua	7
17. Panama	10
18. Paraguay	9
19. Peru	11

Asia, Africa, and Oceania

Country	Total Items Listed
1. Africa	38
2. Algeria	116
3. Arab League	20
4. Australia	16
5. Afghanistan	10
6. Burma	41
7. Ceylon	11
8. Egypt	166
9. Ethiopia	43
10. Philippines	8
11. Taiwan (Formosa)	23
12. India	140
13. Indonesia	50
14. Iran	32
15. Iraq	40
16. Near East	22
17. Far East	37
18. Southeast Asia	31
19. Israel	53
20. Japan	114
21. Yemen	27
22. Jordan	16
23. Union of South Africa	17
24. Cambodia	16
25. Kuomintang	15
26. China	138
27. North Korea	39

Country	Total Items Listed
20. Salvador	8
21. Uruguay	8
22. Venezuela	7
23. Latin America	34
24. Panamerican Union (OAS)	16
25. Puerto Rico	1
26. Jamaica	5
27. Trinidad	6

Country	Total Items Listed
28. South Korea	76
29. Laos	45
30. Liban	28
31. Liberia	9
32. Libya	11
33. Morocco	31
34. Mongolia	14
35. Nepal	9
36. New Zealand	9
37. Oman	10
38. Pakistan	58
39. Saudi Arabia	28
40. Siam (Thailand)	13
41. Syria	54
42. Sudan	26
43. Tangiers	10
44. Turkey	117
45. Tunis	59
46. South Vietnam	17
47. North Vietnam	31
48. Ghana	25
49. Guinea	12
50. Malaysian Federation	8
51. Cyprus	54
52. Cameroon	7
53. Togo	7
54. Mali	13

Country	Total Items Listed	Country	Total Items Listed
55. Congo (Leopoldville)	60	66. Senegal	8
56. Madagascar	5	67. Nigeria	9
57. Somalia	7	68. Mauritania	7
58. Dahomey	8	69. Sierra Leone	8
59. Niger	7	70. Kuwait	13
60. Upper Volta	7	71. Tanganyika	11
61. Ubala Slonovace	6	72. Samoa	6
62. Chad	7	73. Rwanda	7
63. Central African Republic	7	74. Burundi	5
64. Gabon	7	75. Uganda	5
65. Brazzaville (Congo)	7	76. Kenya	7
		77. Zanzibar	10
		78. Malavia	8
		79. Zambique	8

Overlapping Subject Matter in Tanjug and Associated Press

	Number	Inches	Content	Source
T	92	6.5	Atlas-Centaur rocket launch	Foreign agencies
AP	176/197/19	14.0	Atlas-Centaur rocket launch	Cape Kennedy
T	21/119	5.5	South Viet. freedom fighters down 2 U.S. helicopters/U.S. military confirms downing	U.S. Military Command
AP	132/135	7.5	Vietnam: War roundup	Tuckman
T	216	3	Floods in Salerno	AP
AP	183/335	2/3.5	Floods in Salerno, Adriatic damage, night lead: weather	
T	211	6	U.S. Gov't studying Polish-Czech nuclear inspection proposal	Washington
AP	307		Erhard's reaction to nuclear inspection	Bonn
T	23	4.5	Japanese Foreign Ministry disappointment with Manila	KYODO
AP	201/203/ 206/207	15.0	Manila reaction roundup	Tokyo
T	29/36	10.75	Luna 12 enters moon orbit	TASS
AP	315	3.5	Luna 12 less than 100 miles moon, says British scientist	England

APPENDIX 3 *(Continued)*

Number	Inches	Content	Source
T 35	2.75	33 Americans killed in aircraft carrier fire	U.S. Military Command
AP 133/134/ 139/146	11.5	Oriskany fire	U.S. Military
T 102	2.5	Further details on Oriskany	AP
AP 220/222	7.0	Further details on Oriskany (43 killed)	U.S. Military
T 68	2.25	Emergency visit: Johnson at Kam Ran Bay	For. agencies
AP 219/223 /228	9.5	Johnson visits troops after strong Westmoreland urging	Gulick (en route)
T 45	10.5	British reactions to Manila	correspondent London
AP 207	6	British officials welcome evidence of unity	Tokyo
T 91	5.25	French press feels Manila added nothing new	correspondent Paris
AP —	—	France not covered in AP Manila reaction roundup	—
T 5/138	3.4	Japanese-U.S. communications satellite in Pacific/satellite launched	KYODO
AP 176/97	3.5	Atlas-Centaur rocket launching: Communications satellite for Pacific	Cape Kennedy
T 111	5.0	Details of Johnson's secret visit to Kam Ran Bay; emphasis on jet fighter protection during flight	Reuter
AP 217/221 /208/209 /242	17.25	Johnson gives medals, strict security (no mention of airplane cover as in Reuter)	Kam Ran Bay Base
T 61	2.3	Mobutu new President of Congo	AFP Codel
AP 163/165 /166/169 /170/234	22.5	Mobutu President, Mulamba head of defense in spite of army opposition	correspondent

APPENDIX 3 *(Continued)*

Number	Inches	Content	Source
T 95	12.23	U.S. press roundup on Manila: comment that it solved no problems and made no UN-asked assurances	N.Y. correspondent
AP 224/233	11.50	Manila reaction "Izvestia" — leaves out withdrawal	Moscow
T 97	8.5	37th Congress of Italian socialist trade unions in Rome (split with Social Democrats)	Rome correspondent
AP 149/150	9.5	Cooperation between socialist and Christian trade unions in European conference of free trade unions	Brussels
T 81	14.25	International conference on earthquakes	Skopje correspondent
AP 311	3.5	International conference on earthquakes	Belgium
T 101	5.0	W. German communique on Spanish Common Market entry	Reuter
AP 180	4.00	W. Germany supports Spanish Common Market entry	Bonn
T 109	5.25	Representation of China in UNESCO (French opposition stressed)	Reuter
AP 250	6.00	Changing votes played up (French opposition not mentioned)	Paris
T 110	1.5	Announcement of NATO headquarters move to Brussels (no interpretation)	AP
AP 252/253 (215/216 /289)	2.5 (15.0)	NATO move, De Gaulle's position	Broening, Paris

APPENDIX 3 *(Continued)*

	Number	Inches	Content	Source
T	93	9.00	Great power willingness to cooperate on spread of nuclear weapons; UAR reaction as speaker for underdeveloped group	N.Y. correspondent
AP	299	5.25	Guarantees for non-nuclear powers	UN
T	123	10.0	Socialist countries supporting Afro-Asian countries against South African political domination of Southwest Africa	TASS
AP	273/274 /281/282 /309	23.5	South African stand against Goldberg's adjournment proposal to discuss American-British compromise	UN
T	103	2.0	Bulgarian-Portuguese soccer tie in Plovdir	Sofia
AP	283/285 /295	7.0	Bulgarian-Portuguese soccer tie	Sofia
T	122	2.5	Poland wins European Soccer Cup of national champions 3 to 1 against England	AP
AP	238/239 /243	6.25	Details as above	AP Budapest
T	131	11.5	World Club soccer final: Spain-Uruguay	AP
AP	184/185	8.75	Direct transcript	Moya Madrid
T	137	2.00	Abstract of AP	AP
AP	325/337	7.25	Danish-Israeli match in Copenhagen	Copenhagen

Totals	Items	Percent of Total	Inches
T	30	31.3	215.70
AP	69	29.4	247.00

Bibliography

Books

Adizes, Ichak. *Industrial Democracy Yugoslav Style: The Effect of Decentralization on Organizational Behavior*. New York: The Free Press, 1971.

Akin, J., *et al. Language Behavior*. The Hague: Mouton, 1970.

Albig, William. *Modern Public Opinion*. New York: McGraw Hill Book Co., Inc., 1956.

Applebaum, Richard. *Theories of Social Change*. Chicago: Parkham Publishing Co., 1970.

Arnim, Gustav Adolf von. *Eine Strukturanalyse der Presse der Volksrepublik Jugoslawien, 1945-1963*. Münster: Arbeiten aus dem Institut für Publizistik, Universität Münster, 1968.

Auty, Phyllis. "Yugoslavia's International Relations (1945-65)." in *Contemporary Yugoslavia: Twenty Years of Socialist Experiment*. Wayne S. Vucinich, ed. Berkeley: University of California Press, 1969.

Bauer, Raymond A. "The Audience," in *Handbook of Communication*. Ithiel de Sola Pool, Wilbur Schramm, Frederick W. Frey, Nathan Maccoby, Edwin B. Parker, eds. Chicago: Rand McNally Publishing Co., 1973.

Berger, Bennet. "The Sociology of Leisure," in *Work and Leisure: A Contemporary Social Problem*. O. E. Smigel, ed. New Haven, Conn.: College and University Press, 1963.

Berger, Peter, and Thomas Luckmann. *The Social Construction of Reality: A Treatise in the Sociology of Knowledge*. Garden City, N.Y.: Doubleday Co., Inc. (Anchor Ed.), 1967.

Bjelica, Mihailo. *200 godina jugoslovenske štampe*. Beograd: Jugoslovenski institut za novinarstvo, 1968.

Blau, Peter M. *Exchange and Power in Social Life*. New York: John Wiley, 1964.

Blumer, Herbert. "Collective Behavior," in *Principles of Sociology*. A. Lee, ed. New York: Barnes and Noble, 1946.

———. *Symbolic Interactionism: Perspective and Method*. Englewood Cliffs, N.J.: Prentice Hall, Inc., 1969.

Blumler, Jay, and John Madge. *Citizenship and Television*. London: Political and Economic Planning, n.d.

Bogosavljević, Milutin. *The Economy of Yugoslavia*. Beograd: Jugoslavija, 1961.

Brown, Charles H. *News Editing and Display*. New York: Harper and Bros., 1952.

Brozović, Dalibor. *Standardni jezik*. Zagreb: Matica Hrvatska, 1970.

Buzek, Antony. *How the Communist Press Works*. New York: Frederick A. Praeger, 1964.

Cadwallader, Melvyn L. "The Cybernetic Analysis of Change in Complex Social Organizations," in *Communication and Culture*. Alfred G. Smith, ed. New York: Holt, Rinehart, and Winston, 1966.

Campbell, John C. "Yugoslavia," in *The Communist States in Disarray 1965-1971*. Adam Bromks and Teresa Rakowska-Harmstone, eds. Minneapolis: University of Minnesota Press, 1972.

Canada. *Report of the Special Senate Committee on Mass Media: Good, Bad or Simply Inevitable*. Vol. III. Ottawa: Queen's Printer for Canada, 1971.

Canadian Broadcasting Corporation. *Annual Report, 1969-1970*. Ottawa: Queen's Printer for Canada, 1970.

Carey, James W. "The Communication Revolution and the Professional Communicator," in *The Sociology of Mass Media Communicators*. Paul Halmos, ed. The Sociological Review Monograph No. 15. Hanley, Stoke-on-Trent: J. H. Brooks, Ltd., 1969.

Chaney, David. *Processes of Mass Communication*. New York: Macmillan Co., 1972.

Cohen, Bernard C. *The Press and Foreign Policy*. Princeton, N.J.: Princeton University Press, 1963.

Crawford, J. T. "Yugoslavia's New Economic Strategy: A Progress Report," in *Developments in Countries of Eastern Europe: A Compendium of Papers*. Submitted to the Subcommittee on Foreign Economic Policy of the Joint Economic Committee, 91st Congress of the United States, 2nd sess. Washington, D.C.: U.S. Government Printing Office, 1970.

Deakin, F. W. D. *The Embattled Mountain*. London: Oxford University Press, 1971.

Denitch, Bogdan. "Mobility and Recruitment of Yugoslav Leadership: The Role of the League of Communists." Vol. III. *Working Papers for the International Study of Opinion Makers*. New York: Columbia University, 1970.

Deutsch, Karl W. *Nationalism and Social Communication: An Inquiry into the Foundations of Nationality*. 2nd ed. Cambridge: Massachusetts Institute of Technology Press, 1966.

_____. *Political Community and the North Atlantic Treaty Area*. Princeton, N.J.: Princeton University Press, 1957.

Djilas, Milovan. *Razmišljanja o raznim pitanjima*. Beograd: Kultura, 1951.

Djordjevic, Miroslav. *Mesto i uloga trećeg programa radio-Beograd u sistemu difuzije kulturnih vrednosti*. Beograd: Jugoslovenski institut za novinarstvo, 1969.

Dragović, Vuk. *Srpska štampa izmedju dva rata*. Beograd: Srpska Akademija Nauka, Knjiga 8, Istoriski institut, 1956.

Edelstein, Alex S. *The Uses of Communication in Decision Making, a Comparative Study of Yugoslavia and the United States*. New York: Praeger Publishers, 1974.

Elliott, Philip. *The Sociology of the Professions*. London: Macmillan, Ltd., 1972.

Emery, Edwin, Phillip H. Ault, and Warren Agee. *Introduction to Mass Communications*. 2nd ed. New York: Dodd, Mead, and Co., Inc., 1965.

Emery, Walter. *Five European Broadcasting Systems*. Journalism Monographs, No. 1. Austin, Texas: Association for Education in Journalism, 1966.

Epstein, Edward. *News from Nowhere*. New York: Random House, 1973.

Facts on File: World News Digest with Index. XXVI: 1356-1358 (Oct. 20-Nov. 9, 1966), 401-430.

Federal Institute for Statistics. *Statistical Pocket Book for Yugoslavia, 1972*. Belgrade: Federal Institute for Statistics, 1972.

Federation of Yugoslav Journalists. *Izveštaj o radu*. Beograd: Federation of Yugoslav Journalists, 1969.

Gans, Herbert. *The Urban Villagers: Groups and Class in the Life of Italian-Americans*. New York: The Free Press, 1962.

Ginić, Ivanka. *Migracije stanovništva Jugoslavije*. Belgrade: Center for Demographic Research in the Institute for Social Science, 1971.

Hachten, William. *Muffled Drums: The News Media in Africa*. Ames: Iowa State University Press, 1971.

Halloran, James. *The Effects of Television*. London: Panther Books, 1970.

———, Philip Elliott, and Graham Murdock. *Demonstrations and Communication: A Case Study*. Harmondsworth: Penguin Books, Ltd., 1970.

Halmos, Paul. *The Sociology of Mass Media Communicators*. The Sociological Review Monograph No. 15. Hanley, Stoke-on-Trent: J. H. Brooks, Ltd., 1969.

Halpern, Joel. *A Serbian Village*. New York: Harper Colophon Books, 1967.

Hatt, Paul, and C. C. North. "Prestige Ranking of Occupations," in *Man, Work and Society: A Reader in the Sociology of Occupations*. Sigmund Nosov and William Form, eds. New York: Basic Books, 1962.

Hermann, Charles F. "International Crisis as a Situation Variable," in *International Politics and Foreign Policy*. James R. Rosenau, ed. New York: The Free Press, 1969.

Hoffman, George W., and Fred W. Neal. *Yugoslavia and the New Communism*. New York: Twentieth Century Fund, 1962.

Hondius, Fritz W. *The Yugoslav Community of Nations*. The Hague: Mouton and Co., 1968.

Hopkins, Mark W. *Mass Media in the Soviet Union*. New York: Pegasus, 1970.

Horvat, Branko. *An Essay on Yugoslav Society*. White Plains, N.Y.: International Arts and Sciences Press, Inc., 1969.

Horvat, Josip. *Povijest novinstva Hrvatske*. Zagreb: Stvarnost, 1962.

International Press Institute. *The Flow of the News*. Zürich: International Press Institute, 1953.

———. *The Press in Authoritarian Countries*. Zürich: International Press Institute, 1959.

Ionescu, Ghita. *The Politics of the European Communist States*. New York: Frederick A. Praeger, Inc., 1967.

Johnson, Chalmers. *Change in Communist Systems*. Stanford, Calif.: Stanford University Press, 1970.

Johnstone, John W., Edward J. Slawski, and William W. Bowman. *The News People: A Sociological Portrait of American Journalists and Their Work*. Urbana: University of Illinois Press, 1976.

Jugoslovenski radiotelevizija godišnjak 1971-72. Beograd: Prosveta, 1972.

Jugoslovenski institut za novinarstvo. *Masovna komunikacija u jugoslaviji: slušaoci, gledaoći, i čitaoci*. Beograd: Institut za novinarstvo, 1965.

———. *Štampa, radio, televizija, film, u Jugoslaviji, 1964*. Beograd: Jugoslovenski institut za novinarstvo, 1964.

———. *Tematka struktura sadržaja jugoslovenskih listova*. Beograd: Institut za novinarstvo, 1968.

Katz, Elihu, and Paul Lazarsfeld. *Personal Influence*. New York: The Free Press, 1955.

Kimball, Penn. "Journalism: Art, Craft, or Profession?," in *The Professions in America*. Kenneth S. Lynn, ed. Cambridge: Riverside Press, 1965.

Ko je ko u Jugoslaviji. Beograd: "Sedme Sile," Novinsko-Izdavačkog Preduzeća, 1957.

Kolaja, Jiri. *Workers' Councils: The Yugoslav Experience*. New York: Frederick A. Praeger, Inc., 1965.

Kolektiva Radio-Televizija Zagreb. *Naš studio*. Zagreb: Radio-Televizija Zagreb, 1970.

Kruglak, Theodore. *The Foreign Correspondents*. Geneva: Libraire E. Droz, 1955.

_____. *The Two Faces of TASS*. Minneapolis: University of Minnesota Press, 1962.

Lakatoš, J. *Hrvatska štampa: 1791-1911*. Beograd: n.p., 1911.

Landecker, Werner S. "Types of Integration and Their Measurement," in *The Language of Social Research*. Paul F. Lazarsfeld and Morris Rosenberg, eds. Glencoe, Ill.: The Free Press, 1955.

Lapajne, Ivo. *Razvojne smeri slovenskega novinarstva*. Ljubljana: n.p., 1937.

Lasswell, H. D. "The Structure and Function of Communication in Society," in *The Communication of Ideas*. L. Bryson, ed. New York: Harper and Bros., 1948.

Lendvai, Paul. *Eagles in Cobwebs: Nationalism and Communism in the Balkans*. Garden City, N.Y.: Doubleday and Co., Inc., 1969.

Lenin, Vladimir Ilich. *Collected Works*. I. Moscow: Foreign Languages Publishing House, 1960.

Lerner, Daniel. *The Passing of Traditional Society*. New York: The Free Press, 1958.

Lin, Nan. *The Study of Human Communication*. Indianapolis: Bobbs-Merrill Co., Inc., 1973.

Lippmann, Walter. *Public Opinion*. New York: Macmillan Co., 1922.

Litterer, Joseph A. *The Analysis of Organizations*. New York: John Wiley and Sons, Inc., 1965.

LoSciuto, Leonard. *A National Inventory of Television Viewing Behavior*. Philadelphia: Institute for Survey Research, Temple University, 1971.

Lukić, Sveta. *Contemporary Yugoslav Literature: A Socio-Political Approach*. Gertrude Joch Robinson, ed. Urbana: University of Illinois Press, 1972.

Macesich, George. *Yugoslavia: The Theory and Practice of Development Planning*. Charlottesville: The University Press of Virginia, 1964.

_____. "Major Trends in the Post War Economy of Yugoslavia," in *Contemporary Yugoslavia: Twenty Years of Socialist Experiment*. Wayne S. Vucinich, ed. Berkeley: University of California Press, 1969.

MacLean, Fitzroy. *Tito: The Man Who Defied Hitler and Stalin*. New York: Ballantine Books, Inc., 1957.

Marković Radivoje. "The Development of Radio and Television in Yugoslavia: From August 1904 to the Present Day," *Yugoslav Radio-Television Yearbook 1970*. Belgrade: Provesta, 1970.

Matejko, Aleksander. "Newspaper Staff as a Social System," in *Media Sociology*. Jeremy Tunstall, ed. Urbana: University of Illinois Press, 1970.

McLeod, Jack M., and Garrett J. O'Keefe, Jr. "The Socialization Perspective and Communication Behavior," in *Current Perspectives in Mass Communication Research*. F. Gerald Kline and Phillip J. Tichnor, eds. Beverly Hills, Calif.: Sage Publications, 1972.

McLin, John. *Eurovision*. American Universities Field Staff, Reports Service, West Europe Series, IV:II (1969).

McQuail, Dennis. "Uncertainty about the Audience and the Organization of Mass Communications," in *The Sociology of Mass Media Communicators*. Paul Halmos, ed. The Sociological Review Monograph No. 15. Hanley, Stoke-on-Trent: J. H. Brooks, Ltd., 1969.

_____, Jay G. Blumler, and J. R. Brown. "The Television Audience: A Revised Perspective," in *Sociology of Mass Communications*. Dennis McQuail, ed. Harmondsworth: Penguin Books, Inc., 1972.

Mead, George Herbert. *The Philosophy of the Act*. Chicago: University of Chicago Press, 1938.

Merrill, John C. "The Press and Social Responsibility," in *International Communication*. Heinz-Dietrich Fischer and John Merrill, eds. New York: Hastings House, 1970.

Moore, Wilbert E. *Social Change*. Englewood Cliffs, N.J.: Prentice-Hall, Inc., 1963.

National Bank of Yugoslavia. *Statistički bilten*. No. 11, Belgrade: National Bank of Yugoslavia, 1964.

Nešović, Slobodan. *Inostranstvo i nova jugoslavija 1941-1945*. Beograd: Prosveta, 1964.

_____. *Prvo i drugo zasjedanje AVNOJA*. Zagreb: Stvarnost, 1963.

The Network Project. *Office of Telecommunications Policy: Notebook Number Four*. New York: Columbia University Press, 1973.

The Newspaper Fund. *1971 Supplement: Where They Want to Work, an Employment Report of Journalism Graduates*. Princeton, N.J.: The Newspaper Fund, 1972.

Oreć, Mate. "Application of International Principles on Freedom of Information in Yugoslavia," in *Mass Media and International Understanding*. France Vreg, ed. Ljubljana: Department of Journalism at the School of Sociology, Political Science, and Journalism in Ljubljana, 1969.

Paris, Edmund. *Genocide in Satellite Croatia, 1941-1945*. Chicago: The American Institute for Balkan Affairs, 1961.

Pavlowitch, Stevan K. *Yugoslavia*. London: Ernest Benn, Ltd., 1971.

Pejanović, Dejan. *Štampa Bosne i Hercegovine, 1850–1941*. Sarajevo: Svjetlost, 1949.

Pejovich, Svetozar. *The Market-Planned Economy of Yugoslavia*. Minneapolis: University of Minnesota Press, 1966.

Plavčič, Prvosalav S. *Odnos Beogradjana prema programima Radio Beograd*. Beograd: Audience Research Department, Radio Beograd, 1970.

Pribićević, Svetozar. *Diktatura kralja Aleksandra*. Beograd: Prosveta, 1953.

Pye, Lucian W. *Communications and Political Development*. Princeton, N.J.: Princeton University Press, 1963.

Reston, James. *The Artillery of the Press: Its Influence on American Foreign Policy*. Published for Council of Foreign Relations. New York: Harper and Row, 1966-67.

Richman, Barry M. *Soviet Management*. Englewood Cliffs, N.J.: Prentice-Hall, Inc., 1955.

Robinson, Gertrude Joch. "Twenty-Five Years of 'Gate Keeper' Research: A Critical Review and Evaluation," translated into German in *Gesellschaftliche Kommunikation und Information*. Jörg Auferman, H. Bohrmann, and R. Sülzer, eds. Frankfurt: Athenäum Verlag, 1974.

Rosengren, Karl Erik, and Gwen Windahl. "Mass Media Consumption as a Functional Alternative," in *Sociology of Mass Communication*. Dennis McQuail, ed. Harmondsworth: Penguin Books, Inc., 1972.

Roshco, Bernard. *Newsmaking*. Chicago: University of Chicago Press, 1975.

Rosten, Leo. *The Washington Correspondents*. New York: Harcourt, Brace, and Co., 1937.

Ruesch, Juergen, and Gregory Bateson. *Communication: The Social Matrix of Psychiatry*. New York: Norton, 1968.

Rusinow, Dennison I. *Crisis in Croatia, Part II: Facilis Decensus Averno*. American Universities Field Staff, Reports Service, Southeast Europe Series, XIX:V (Sept., 1972).

_____. *A Note on Yugoslavia: 1972*. American Universities Field Staff, Reports

Service, Southeast Europe Series, XIX:III (July, 1972).

_____. *Population Review 1970: Yugoslavia*. American Universities Field Staff, Reports Service, Southeast Europe Series, XVII:I (Nov., 1970).

_____. *Some Aspects of Migration and Urbanization in Yugoslavia*. American Universities Field Staff, Reports Service, Southeast Europe Series, XIX:II (Dec., 1971).

Schramm, Wilbur. *Mass Media and National Development*. Stanford, Calif.: Stanford University Press, 1964.

Schultz, Theodore W. *Economic Crisis in World Agriculture*. Ann Arbor: University of Michigan Press, 1965.

Siebert, Fred, Theodore Peterson, and Wilbur Schramm. *Four Theories of the Press*. Urbana: University of Illinois Press, 1956.

Skerlić, Jovan. *Istorijski pregled sprske štampe, 1791-1911*. Beograd: Prosveta, 1911.

Skilling, Gordon H. "Group Conflict and Political Change," in *Change in Communist Systems*. Stanford, Calif.: Stanford University Press, 1970.

Smelser, Neil J. "Notes on the Methodology of Comparative Analysis of Economic Activity," in *Social Science Information* (UNESCO), VI:II-III (April-June, 1967), 7-21.

Socijalistička Federativna Republika Jugoslavija. *Statistički Godišnjak SFRJ, 1969*. Godina XVI. Beograd: Savezni zavod za statistiku, 1969.

_____. *Statistički Godišnjak SFRJ, 1971*. Godina VIII. Beograd: Savezni zavod za statistiku, 1971.

_____. *Statistički Godišnjak SFRJ, 1972*. Godina IX. Beograd: Savezni zavod za statistiku, 1972.

_____. *Statistički Godišnjak SFRJ, 1975*. Godina XII. Beograd: Savezni zavod za statistiku, 1975.

Sovietskaya Pechat. No. 9, 1962. Moscow.

Stockholm Journalists. *Stockholms journalister: A Report by Journalist forenings utredning om foretagsdemokrati*. Malmo: 1971.

Stojanovic, Svetozar. *Kritik und Zukunft des Sozialismus*. München: Carl Hauser Verlag, 1970.

Sugar, Peter F., and Ivo J. Lederer. *Nationalism in Eastern Europe*. Seattle: University of Washington Press, 1969.

Tadić, Jorjo. "Ten Years of Yugoslav Historiography, 1945-1955," in *Enciklopedija jugoslavije*. Zagreb: Leksikografski Závod, 1955.

Thayer, Lee. *Communication and Communication Systems*. Homewood, Ill.: Richard Irwin, 1968.

_____. "Communication — Sine qua non of the Behavioral Sciences," in *Vistas in Science*. E. D. Arm, ed. New Mexico: New Mexico University Press, 1968.

_____. "On Theory Building in Communication: II. Some Persistent Obstacles," in *Language Behavior*. J. Akin, ed. The Hague: Mouton and Co., 1970.

Tito, Josip Broz, Edward Kardelj, and Stane Dolanc. *Ideological and Political Offensive of the League of Communists in Yugoslavia*. Belgrade: Kultura, 1972.

Tunstall, Jeremy. *Journalists at Work — Specialist Correspondents: Their News Organizations, News Sources, and Competitor-Colleagues*. London: Constable and Co., Ltd., 1971.

_____. *Media Sociology: A Reader*. Urbana: University of Illinois Press, 1970.

UNESCO. *Basic Facts and Figures*. Paris: UNESCO Publication Center, 1962.

_____. *Mass Media in the Developing Countries*. Reports and Papers on Mass Communication, No. 33. New York: UNESCO Publication Center, 1961.

_____. *News Agencies: Their Structure and Operation*. Paris: UNESCO Publication Center, 1953.

_____. *Statistical Yearbook, 1965*. New York: UNESCO Publication Center, 1966.

_____. *World Communications, Press, Radio, Television, Film*. 2nd ed. Paris: UNESCO Publication Center, 1967.

U.S. Bureau of the Census. *Statistical Abstract of the United States*. 92nd ed. Washington, D.C.: U.S. Government Printing Office, 1971.

U.S. Department of Commerce. *Statistical Abstract, 1971*. Washington, D.C.: Department of Labor, Bureau of Labor Statistics, 1971.

Vatoveć, Fran. *The Development of the Slovene and Yugoslav Periodical Journalism*. Ljubljana: Visoka škola za politične veze, 1968.

Vojno Istorijski Institut. *Bibliografija izdanja u Narodno Oslobodilačkom Ratu, 1941-1945*. Beograd: Vojno istorijski institut, 1964.

Vucinich, Wayne S. *Contemporary Yugoslavia: Twenty Years of Socialist Experiment*. Berkeley: University of California Press, 1969.

Vuksan, D. D. *Pregled štampe u Crnoj Gori, 1834-1934*. Cetinje: Obod, 1934.

White, Llewellyn, and Robert Leigh. *People Speaking to Peoples*. Chicago: University of Chicago Press, 1946.

Whorf, Benjamin Lee. *Language, Thought, and Reality*. Cambridge: Massachusetts Institute of Technology Press, 1956.

Wildenmann, Rudolph. *Fernsehen in Deutschland: Gesellschaftspolitische Aufgaben und Wirkungen eines Mediums*. Mainz: Hase und Kochler Verlag, 1967.

Yugoslav Institute of Journalism. *Press, Radio, Television, Film in Yugoslavia, 1961*. Belgrade: Yugoslav Institute of Journalism, 1961.

_____. *Press, Radio, and Television in Yugoslavia, 1969*. Belgrade: Yugoslav Institute of Journalism, 1969.

Yugoslavia Radio-Television Yearbook 1962. Belgrade: Prosveta, 1962.

Yugoslavia Radio-Television Yearbook 1970. Belgrade: Prosveta, 1970.

Zaninovich, George. *The Development of Socialist Yugoslavia*. Baltimore: The Johns Hopkins Press, 1968.

_____. "The Yugoslav Variation on Marx," in *Contemporary Yugoslavia: Twenty Years of Socialist Experiment*. Wayne S. Vucinich, ed. Berkeley: University of California Press, 1969.

Zvonarević, Mladen. "The Relationship between Public Opinion Makers and Public Opinion," Vol. III. *Working Papers for the International Study of Opinion Makers*. New York: Columbia University, 1970.

Articles

Ančić. Zagorka. "Population Changes in Yugoslavia." *Yugoslav Survey* (Belgrade) XII:III (Aug. 1971): 1-8.

Anderson, Raymond. "A New Political Orthodoxy Is Asserting Itself in Liberal Yugoslavia." *New York Times*, Jan. 2, 1973.

Ashmore, Harry S. "Broadcasting and the First Amendment: Report on a Center Conference." *The Center Magazine* (A Publication of the Center for the Study of Democratic Institutions), VI:III (May-June 1973): 19-66.

Avramović, Miodrag. "The Press and the Socio-Economic Reform in Yugoslavia." Paper presented at the UNESCO Conference on Mass Media and International Understanding, Ljubljana, Yugoslavia, Sept., 1968.

Barton, Allan H. "Determinants of Leadership Attitudes in a Socialist Society." *Working Papers for the International Study of Opinion Makers*. Columbia University, 1970.

Bass, Abraham Z. "The Internal Flow of the News at United Nations Radio: Refining the 'Gate Keeper' and Intermediary Communication Concepts." Paper presented to the AEJ Convention, Lawrence, Kansas, Aug. 21, 1968.

Baumštark, Krešo. "Opažanja o programu radija." *Naš Studio* (Zagreb) XXV (1970): 67-71.

Begović, Bruno. "Podaci o tiražu jugoslovenskih i nedelnjih listove u 1964 godini." *Novinar i novinarstvo* Godina 1, Broj 2 (June 1965): 173-175.

Berg, Elizabeth. "Women in German Broadcasting." *EBU Review* XXVI:IV (1975): 19-20.

Bertsch, Garry K. "A Cross National Analysis of the Community-Building Process in Yugoslavia." *Comparative Political Studies* IV:IV (Jan. 1972): 438-460.

——. "Molding the 'New Man' in Communist Societies: The Multi-National Czechoslovak, Soviet and Yugoslav Cases." Paper presented at the National Convention of AAASS, Dallas, Texas, March, 1972.

Binder, David. "President Tito's New 35 Member Presidium." *New York Times,* Oct. 6, 1966.

Blumler, Jay G. "Audience Roles in Political Communication: Some Reflections on Their Structure, Antecedents and Consequences." Paper presented at the International Political Science Association, Montreal, Aug. 19-25, 1973.

Bogart, Leo. "The Overseas Newsman: A 1967 Profile Study." *Journalism Quarterly* XXXXV:II (Summer 1968): 293-306.

Bowman, William Winslow. "Distaff Journalists: Women as a Minority Group in the News Media." Ph.D. dissertation. Chicago: University of Illinois Circle Campus, 1974.

Breed, Warren. "Social Control in the Newsroom: A Functional Analysis." *Social Forces* XXXIII (1955): 326-336.

Browne, Malcolm. "Yugoslavs Seize Pro-Soviet Group." *New York Times,* Nov. 23, 1975.

——. "Yugoslavs Build World News Unit," *New York Times,* Jan. 25, 1976.

Bryan, Carter R. "The Press System of Yugoslavia: Communism with a Difference." *Journalism Quarterly* XLIII:II (Summer 1966): 291-299.

Bulatović, Vukoje. "The Right to Information." *Nedelne informativne novine* (Belgrade), Jan. 14, 1973.

Chomsky, Noam, and Robert S. Cohen. "The Repression at Belgrade University." *The New York Review of Books,* Feb. 7, 1974, pp. 23-33.

"Constitutional Changes in Yugoslavia." *Yugoslav Survey* X:III (August 1969): 1-29.

The Constitution of the Socialist Federal Republic of Yugoslavia. Secretariat of Information of the Federal Executive Council, Belgrade, 1963.

Cutlip, Scott. "Content and Flow of A.P. News — From Trunks to TTS to Reader." *Journalism Quarterly* XXXI (Fall 1954): 434-436.

Daniel, Clifton. "Coverage of Bay of Pigs Buildup." *New York Times,* June 2, 1966.

Darnton, Robert. "Writing News and Telling Stories." *Daedalus* CIV:I (1975), 175-193.

Darossi-Bjelajac, Erna. "Karakteristika i dimenzije idejnopolitičkih devijacija u savezu komunista Hrvatske." *Naše teme* (Zagreb) (Jan. 1972), 9-14.

Day, Lawrence J. "The Latin American Journalist: A Tentative Profile." Paper presented at the Association for Education in Journalism, Iowa City, Iowa, Aug., 1966.

Dečermić, Bogdan. "Spotlight on Publishing." *Review,* V (May 1968): 21-28.

Deutsch, Karl W. "On Communication Models in the Social Sciences." *Public Opinion Quarterly* XVI (Summer 1952): 356-380.

——. "Social Mobilization and Political Development." *American Political Science Review* LV (Sept. 1961): 582-603.

Dill, William. "Environment as an Influence on Management Autonomy." *Administration Science Quarterly* II (March 1958): 409-443.

Djilas, Milovan. "The Storm in Eastern Europe." *The New Leader,* Nov. 19, 1956.

Donohew, Lewis. "Newspaper Gatekeepers and Forces in the News Channel." *Public Opinion Quarterly* XXXI (Spring 1967): 61-68.

Douglass, Edward F. "The Role of the Mass Media in National Development: A Reformulation with Particular Reference to Sierra Leone." Ph.D. dissertation. Urbana: University of Illinois, 1971.

Dunn, W. N. "Ideology and Organization in Socialist Yugoslavia: Modernization and Obsolescence of Praxis." Paper presented at the American Association for the Advancement of Slavic Studies Convention, Dallas, Texas, 1972.

Džinić, Firdus. "Rašinrenost političko-informativnog dejstva radija, TV i štampe u SFR Jugoslaviji." Paper presented at simpozijium Korišćenje Javnih Informacija, Jugoslovenski institut za novinarstvo, Beograd, Dec., 1969.

Eder, Richard. "Mihajlov is Given New 4½ Year Term by Belgrade Court." *New York Times,* April 20, 1967.

Epstein, Cynthia F. "Encountering the Male Establishment: Sex-Status Limits on Women's Careers in the Professions." *American Journal of Sociology* CXXV:II (May 1970): 965-982.

Fagan, Richard. "Mass Media Growth: A Comparison of Communist and Other Countries." *Journalism Quarterly* XLI:III (Fall 1964): 563-568.

Federation of Yugoslav Journalists. *Bulletin.* No. 1., Belgrade: Federation of Yugoslav Journalists, July, 1964.

_____. *Bulletin.* No. 3., Belgrade: Federation of Yugoslav Journalists, Dec. 1969.

Feron, James. "Party Tightening Ordered by Tito." *New York Times,* Jan. 30, 1972.

_____. "Purge Goes Deep into Croatian Life." *New York Times,* Feb. 7, 1972.

Filosofija. XV:III-IV. Beograd: Srpsko Filosofsko Društvo, 1969.

Galtung, John, and Mari Holmboe Ruge. "The Structure of Foreign News: The Presentation of the Congo, Cuba, and Cyprus Crises in Four Newspapers," *Journal of Peace Research* (Oslo), II (Spring 1965): 64-91.

Gardner, Mary. "Journalism Education in Guatemala." Paper presented to The Association for Education in Journalism, Washington, D.C., Aug. 1970.

Gerbner, George. "Ideological Perspectives and Political Tendencies in News Reporting." *Journalism Quarterly* XLI (Autumn 1964): 495-509.

_____. "Institutional Pressures upon Mass Communicators." *The Sociological Review Monograph* XIII (Jan. 1969): 205-248.

_____. "Press Perspectives in World Communication: A Pilot Study." *Journalism Quarterly* XXXVIII (Summer 1961): 313-322.

Gieber, Walter. "Across the Desk: A Study of Sixteen Telegraph Editors." *Journalism Quarterly* XXXIII (Fall 1956): 423-432.

_____. "How the 'Gatekeepers' View Local Civil Liberty News." *Journalism Quarterly* XXXVII (Spring 1960): 199-205.

_____, and Walter Johnson. "The 'City Hall' Beat: A Study of Reporter and Source Roles." *Journalism Quarterly* XXXVIII:II (Summer 1961): 289-297.

Gluščević, Manojlo. "Neki indikatori mišljenja i ponašanja komunikatora testiranih na fenomenu društvene kritike." Paper presented at the symposium Korišćenje Javnih Informacija, Jugoslovenski institut za novinarstvo, Beograd, Dec., 1962.

Goy, E. D. "The Serbian and Croatian Novel since 1948." *Slavic and East European Review* XXXX (Spring 1961): 58-84.

"Grafički prikaz tiraža dnevnih listova." *Naša štampa* (Beograd) XX: 178 (Oct. 1970): 15.

Grossman, Gregory. "Economic Reforms: A Balance Sheet." *Problems of Communism* XV:VI (Nov.-Dec. 1966): 43-55.

Haug, Marie R. "Social and Cultural Pluralism as a Concept in Social System Analysis." *The American Journal of Sociology* LXXIII (Spring 1967): 294-305.

Howe, Russell W. "Reporting from Africa: A Correspondent's View." *Journalism Quarterly* XLIII:II (Summer 1966): 314-318.

Inkeles, Alex. "Making Men Modern: On the Causes and Consequences of Individual Change in Six Developing Countries." *American Journal of Sociology* LXXV (Sept. 1969): 208-255.

Janssen, Richard F. "Workers in Control: Yugoslavia's System of Letting Employees Manage Business Works Surprisingly Well." *Wall Street Journal,* Oct. 8, 1975, p. 36.

Kadushin, Z. C. "Power, Influence and Social Circles: A New Methodology for Studying Opinion-Makers." *American Sociological Review* XXXIII:V (Oct. 1968): 685-699.

Katz, Elihu, Michael Gurevitch, and Hadassah Hass. "On the Use of the Mass Media for Important Things." *American Sociological Review* XXXVIII (April 1973): 164-181.

Kautsky, John. "Communism and the Comparative Study of Development." *Slavic Review* XXVI:I (March 1967): 13-17.

Kempers, Frans. "Freedom of Information and Criticism in Yugoslavia." *Gazette* (The Hague), XIII:IV (1967): 317-336.

————. "Freedom of Information and Criticism in Yugoslavia." *Gazette* XIII:I (Jan. 1967): 3-21.

Kline, Gerald F. "Media Time Budgeting as a Function of Demographics and Life Style." *Journalism Quarterly* XLVIII:II (Summer 1971): 211-221.

Krippendorf, Klaus. "An Examination of Content Analysis: A Proposal for a General Framework and an Information Calculus for Message Analytic Situations." Ph.D. dissertation. Urbana: University of Illinois, 1966.

Kruglak, Theodore E. "Agerpress, the Rumanian National News Agency." *Journalism Quarterly* XXXV (Summer 1958): 343-347.

"The Latest Changes (1971) in the Constitution of the Socialist Federal Republic of Yugoslavia." *Yugoslav Survey* XII:IV (Nov. 1971): 1-36.

Leandrov, Igor. "Istraživanje dnevni barometar u RT Beograd." *Naša štampa* (Beograd) XX:198 (Jan. 1971): 5.

————. "Mass Communication in Yugoslavia." Paper presented at the UNESCO conference on Mass Media and International Understanding. Ljubljana, Yugoslavia, Sept., 1968.

————. "Oblici ponašanja, stavovi i preferencije televizikih gledalaca u Jugoslaviji." Audience Research Department, Radio Belgrade, 1971.

Lubin, Joann. "Discrimination against Women in the Newsroom." Master's thesis. Stanford: Stanford University, 1971.

Lukač, Sergije. "Novinarstvo na fakultetu političkih nauka u Beogradu." *Naša štampa* (Beograd) XX:178 (March 1970): 7.

————. "Professionalac Danas-Sutra." *Naša štampa* (Beograd) XX:178 (Aug.-Sept. 1970), 9.

Lundberg, Ulf, *et al.* "Emotional Involvement and Subjective Distance: A Summary of Investigations." *The Journal of Social Psychology* LXXXVII (1972): 169-177.

Marjanovich, Steven. "The History of the Yugoslav Press and Printing." *Training of Journalists* (Quarterly Review of the International Center for Higher Education in Journalism, University of Strasbourg) No. 16 (March 1963): 28-35.

Marković, Radivoje. "The Development of Radio and Television in Yugoslavia: From August, 1904, to the Present Day." *Yugoslav Radio-Television Yearbook 1970* (Belgrade: Prosveta, 1970), pp. 123-125.

"Marxismus: Baldachin für Heilige." *Der Spiegel* Nr. 10 (March 1970): 169-174.

Marzolf, Marion. "Daring to Go Ahead: The Modern Woman Journalist in Western Europe." Paper presented at the University of Michigan, Ann Arbor, 1972.

McCombs, Maxwell E., and Donald Shaw. "The Agenda-Setting Function of Mass Media." *The Public Opinion Quarterly*, XXXVI:II (Summer 1972): 176-187.

McCombs, Maxwell E., Donald Shaw, and Eugene F. Shaw. "The News and Public Response: Three Studies of the Agenda-Setting Power of the Press." Paper presented at AEJ Conference, Southern Illinois University, Carbondale, Aug., 1972.

McNelly, John T. "Intermediary Communicators in the International Flow of News." *Journalism Quarterly* XXXVI (Winter 1959): 23-26.

Melson, Robert, and Howard Wolpe. "Modernization and the Politics of Communalism: A Theoretical Perspective." *The American Political Science Review* LXIV (December 1970): 1112-1130.

Merčun, Milan. "TV Ljubljana u februaru eksperimentalni program u boji." *Naša štampa* (Beograd) XX:182 (Jan. 1971): 1.

Mihailovich, Vasa D. "Yugoslav Literature since World War II." *The Literary Review* XI (Winter 1967-68): 149-161.

――――. "Serbian Fiction 1965." *Books Abroad* XXXX (Summer 1966): 281-283.

Mowlana, Hamid. "Toward a Theory of Communication Systems: A Developmental Approach." *Gazette* XVII (1970): 17-28.

Nayman, Oguz B. "Professional Orientations of Journalists: An Introduction to Communicator Analysis Studies." *Gazette* XIX:IV (1975): 195-212.

Nixon, Raymond B. "Freedom in the World's Press: A Fresh Appraisal with New Data." *Journalism Quarterly* XXXXII (Winter 1965): 3-14, 118-119.

Novosel, Pavle. "How the Young Spend Their Free Time." Paper presented at the Institut za društvena istraživanja svenčilista u Zagrebu, Zagreb, 1968.

Osolnik, Bogdan. "On the Principles and Mechanisms of Information in Yugoslavia and the Social Role of the Media." Address to an international journalist group, Belgrade, Oct., 1963.

――――. "Sredstva informisanja kao integralni elemenat samoupravnja i neposredne demokratije u Jugolaviji." Paper presented at the I.A.M.C.R. Congress, Herceg-novi, Yugoslavia, Sept., 1966.

Östgard, Einar. "Factors Influencing the Flow of News." *Journal of Peace Research* (Oslo) II (1965): 39-63.

Peterson, Paul V. "Journalism Enrollment Tops 31,000 for 145 Schools." *Journalism Quarterly* XLVI:IV (Winter 1969): 893-895.

Pinard, Maurice. "Communal Segmentation and National Integration." Unpublished manuscript, McGill University, Montreal, 1973.

"Political Action Cannot Be Substituted for Administrative Action." *Naša štampa* XX:182 (Sept.-Oct. 1971): 1.

The Praxis Philosophers. "Auf dem Rückweg zum Stalinismus?" *Süddeutsche Zeitung*, Nr. 22 (January 26, 1974), 1.

"President Tito's Interview with Representatives of the Federation of Yugoslav Journalists." *Bulletin*, Belgrade: Federation of Yugoslav Journalists, 1969, 4-6.

"The Press as an Integral Component of Our Self-Governing Society." *Borba* XXVII (June 1972): 6-7.

Pross, Harry. "Radio and Television as Political Institutions: The Symbolic Approach." Paper presented at the International Political Science Association IX World

Congress, Montreal, Canada, Aug., 1973.

Pustišek, Ivko. "Materijalni i finansijski uslovi radija i televizije Jugoslavije." Paper presented at simposijum Korišcenje Javnih Informacija, sponsored by the Jugoslovenski institut za novinarstvo, Novi Sad, 1969.

———. "Radio i televizija u Jugoslaviji: snažno sredstvo informisanja." *Naša štampa* XX:178 (Aug.-Sept. 1970): 10-11.

Robinson, Gertrude Joch. "Communicator Studies: The State of the Art." Paper presented at international seminar on "Professionalization and Mass Communication." University of Iowa, Iowa City, Nov., 1975.

———. "Foreign News Selection Is Non-Linear in Yugoslavia's Tanjug Agency." *Journalism Quarterly* XXXXVII (Summer 1970): 340-351.

———. "The New Jugoslav Writer: A Socio-Political Portrait." *Mosaic* VI:IV (Fall 1973): 185-197.

———. "Tanjug: Yugoslavia's Multi-Faceted National News Agency." Ph.D. dissertation, University of Illinois, Urbana, 1968.

———. "Women Journalists in Canadian Dailies: A Social and Professional Minority Profile." Paper presented at Association for Education in Journalism convention. Ottawa, Aug., 1975.

———. "Writers as Fighters: The Effect of the Cultural 'Thaw' on Yugoslavia's Mass Media." Paper presented at the Association for Education in Journalism convention, Washington, D.C., Aug., 1970.

Rosengren, Karl Erik. "International News: Intra and Extra Media Data." *Acta Sociologica* XIII:II (1970): 96-109.

———. "International News: Methods, Data and Theory." *Journal of Peace Research* (Oslo) XI (1974).

———. "News Diffusion: An Overview." *Journalism Quarterly* (1976), forthcoming.

———, and Gunnel Rikarsson. "Middle East News in Sweden." *Gazette* XX:2 (1974) 99-116.

———, and Gwen Windahl. "Mass Media Consumption as a Functional Alternative," in *Sociology of Mass Communications*. Dennis McQuail, ed. Harmondsworth: Penguin Books, Inc., 1972.

Rus, Vjelko. "Self-Management Egalitarianism and Social Differentiation." *Praxis* (Zagreb), VII:1/2 (Spring-Summer 1970): 251.

Samuelson, M., R. F. Carter, and W. L. Ruggles. "Education, Available Time and Use of the Mass Media." *Journalism Quarterly* XL:IV (Autumn 1963): 491-496.

Schwarzlose, Richard. "The American Wire Services: A Study of Their Development as a Social Institution." Ph.D. dissertation. Urbana: University of Illinois, 1965.

Setinč, Frank. "About the Dilemmas of the Role of the Journalist in Changing Public Opinion." *Novinar i novinarstvo* (Beograd: Jugoslovenski institut za novinarstvo), II-III (Sept. 1966): 3-11.

Sherman, Charles, and John Ruby. "The Eurovision News Exchange." *Journalism Quarterly* CI:III (Autumn 1974): 478-485.

Siegel, Arthur. "Canadian Newspaper Coverage of F.L.Q. Crisis: A Case Study of the Impact of the Press on Politics." Ph.D. dissertation. Montreal: McGill University, 1974.

Sigelman, Lee. "Reporting the News: An Organizational Analysis." *American Journal of Sociology* CXXVII:IV (Jan. 1972): 660-679.

Singelmann, Peter. "Exchange as Symbolic Interaction: Convergences between Two Theoretical Perspectives." *American Sociological Review* XXXVII:IV (August 1972): 414-424.

"Situation Report." *Time*, XCIX:XII, March 20, 1972.

Smelser, Neil J. "Notes on the Methodology of Comparative Analysis of Economic Activity." *Social Science Information* (UNESCO), II:III (April-June 1967): 7-21.

Snider, Paul B. "Mr. Gates Revisited: A 1966 Version of the 1949 Case Study." *Journalism Quarterly* XLIV:III (Fall 1967): 419-427.

Šoškić, Budislav. "Ideological-Political Platforms of Activity of the League of Communists of Yugoslavia: Current Questions Concerning the Social Position and Role of the Information Activity and Media of Public Information." *Bulletin* No. 4. Belgrade: Federation of Yugoslav Journalists (December 1970): 2-10.

Sparkes, Vernone. "Community Cable Casting in the United States and Canada: Different Approaches to a Common Objective," *Journal of Broadcasting* (Fall, 1976).

Sterling, Claire. "Tito's New Balancing Act." *The Atlantic Monthly,* CCXXXI:VI (June 1973), 43-50.

Stojanović, Svetozar. "Contemporary Yugoslavian Philosophy." *Ethics* LXXVI:IV (July 1966): 297-281.

Stoković, Živorad. "Broj i prosečan tiraž jugoslovenskih listova i časopisa." *Novinar i novinarstvo* (Beograd) VI:III-IV (Fall 1970): 189-195.

———. "Tiraž jugoslovenskih dnevnih i većih nedeljnih listova u 1970 godini." *Novinar i novinarstvo* (Beograd) VII:I-II (1971): 179-181.

"Studentenzeitschrift in Belgrad verabschiedat sich unter Protest." *Die Welt,* Nr. 288:11 (Dec. 1969.)

Supek, Rudi. "Power Structure of Statist and Self-Governing Socialism." Paper presented at the Joint Conference of the Center for Comparative and European Studies and the Bureau of Applied Social Research, Yale University, New Haven, Conn., May 16, 1970.

"Tanjug Editor Quits after Attack on Soviet." *New York Times,* June 24, 1970.

Thayer, Lee. "On the Mass Media and Mass Communication: Notes toward a Theory." Unpublished paper, Department of Communication Studies, Simon Fraser University, Burnaby, B.C., 1974.

———. "On Theory Building in Communication: I. Some Conceptual Problems." *Journal of Communication* XIII (1963): 217-235.

Timotijevich, Dushan. "The Training of Journalists in Yugoslavia." *Training of Journalists* (Quarterly Review of the International Center for Higher Education in Journalism, University of Strasbourg) XVI (March 1963): 57-69.

Tito, Josip Broz. "Štampa treba da prati mere i da pruža pomoć." *Naša štampa* (Beograd), XX:180, (Nov. 1970), 1.

———. "Tito Claims Dissidents Crushed as Long Purge Ends." *Montreal Star,* May 27, 1974, p. 4.

Todorović, Mijalko. *Report on the Final Draft of the Constitution of the Socialist Federal Republic of Yugoslavia* (Ljubljana: Kopisna Delavska Univerza, 1974).

Tozi, Djordje, and D. Petrović. "Political Relations and Composition of Assemblies and Socio-Political Communities." *Socialism* XII:3 (1969): 1591.

Trayes, Edward J. "A Survey of Salaries of AP-Served Dailies." *Journalism Quarterly* XLVI:IV (Winter 1969): 825-828.

Tuchman, Gaye. "Objectivity as Strategic Ritual: An Examination of Newspapermen's Notion of Objectivity." *American Journal of Sociology* CXXVII:IV (Jan. 1972): 660-679.

Varis, Tapio. "Global Traffic in Television." *Journal of Communication* XXIV:1 (Winter 1974): 102-109.

Vidmar, Neil, and Milton Rokeach. "Archie Bunker's Bigotry: A Study in Selective Perception and Exposure."*Journal of Communication* XXIV:I (Winter 1974): 36-47.

"Vjesnik Was on the Way to Becoming the Voice for the Croatian 'Mass Movement.' "
Vjesnik XII (March 12, 1972): 3-4.

Vreg, France. "Adekvatno naučno, a ne pragmatističko obrazovanje novinara." *Naša štampa* (Beograd) XX:182 (May 1971): 5.

————. "Open and Closed Communication Systems." Paper presented at the Association Internationale des Etudes et Recherches sur L'information (A.I.E.R.I.) Conference, Constanz, Germany, Aug., 1970.

————. "Socialist Democracy and Opinion Pluralism." *Teorija in praksa* (Ljubljana) VI:I (1969): 209-218.

Vuković, Zdrsvko. "Televizija Beograd — drugi program i kolor 1.1. 1972." *Naša štampa* XX:182 (Jan. 1971): 1.

Ward, Benjamin. "Political Power and Economic Change in Yugoslavia." *American Economic Review* CVIII:II (1968): 568-579.

Westley, Bruce, and Malcolm S. MacLean. "A Conceptual Model for Communication Research." *Journalism Quarterly* XXXIV:I (Winter 1957): 31-38.

White, David Manning. "The 'Gate Keeper': A Case Study in the Selection of News." *Journalism Quarterly* XXVII (Summer 1950): 383-390.

Wilenski, Harold. "The Professionalization of Everyone?" *American Journal of Sociology* LXXX:II (Sept. 1964): 137-158.

Yu, Frederick, and John Luter. "The Foreign Correspondent and His Work." *Columbia Journalism Review* III (1964): 5-12.

Yugoslav Embassy, Washington. "On the Ideological and Moral Fitness of Professors and Teaching Staff at Belgrade University." *Telos* XVIII (Winter 1973/74): 156-158.

Žlender, Danilo. "The Training of Journalists in Yugoslavia." *Gazette* XII (Spring 1966): 35-43.

Zrimšek, Pavle. "Otvorenost komunikacijskog prostora kao drustvena norma." Unpublished paper, Ljubljana University, Ljubljana, Oct. 1972.

Zvan, Antun. "Ecstacy and Hangover of a Revolution." *Praxis* (Zagreb) VIII:3/4 (Fall/Winter 1971): 475-486.

Index